Pillsbury favorite casseroles

Pillsbury favorite casseroles

PUBLISHED BY

Taste of Home Books
Reiman Media Group, Inc.
5400 S. 60th St., Greendale WI 53129
www.reimanpub.com

This edition published by arrangement with Wiley Publishing, Inc.

Printed in U.S.A.

International Standard Book Number (10): 0-89821-594-3
International Standard Book Number (13): 978-0-89821-594-6
Library of Congress Number: 2007926632

CREDITS

General Mills, Inc.

PUBLISHER, COOKBOOKS: Maggie Gilbert/Lynn Vettel
EDITOR: Sharon Secor
RECIPE DEVELOPMENT AND TESTING: Pillsbury Test Kitchens
PHOTOGRAPHY AND FOOD STYLING: General Mills Photo Studios

Reiman Media Group, Inc.

PRESIDENT: Barbara Newton
EDITOR IN CHIEF: Catherine Cassidy
VICE PRESIDENT, EXECUTIVE EDITOR/BOOKS: Heidi Reuter Lloyd
CREATIVE DIRECTOR: Ardyth Cope
SENIOR BOOK EDITOR: Mark Hagen
ART DIRECTOR: Gretchen Trautman
LAYOUT DESIGNERS: Catherine Fletcher, Kathy Crawford, Julie Stone
PROOFREADERS: Linne Bruskewitz, Jean Steiner
INDEXER: Jean Steiner
FOUNDER: Roy Reiman

For more great recipes, visit Pillsbury.com.

FRONT COVER PHOTOGRAPH:
Chicken Pot Pie Bubble Bake, p. 55

TITLE PAGE PHOTOGRAPH:
Ranch Potato-Topped Chicken Bake, p. 17

BACK COVER PHOTOGRAPHS:
Make-Ahead Cheeseburger Lasagna, p. 226; Sloppy Joe Shepherd's Pie, p. 54; Orange-Cumin Chicken and Vegetables, p. 162; Cheddary Vegetable Gratin, p. 136; Chicago Deep-Dish Sausage Pizza, p. 67

contents

Meat and
Potato Casserole
page 194

Italian Zucchini
Crescent Pie
page 153

Cheesy
Tortilla Lasagna
page 114

Discover a New Favorite Tonight!

Few foods can top the homemade appeal and hearty satisfaction of a bubbling casserole. Piping hot from the oven and brimming with comfort, casseroles are all-time staples when it comes to cozy family dinners.

With *Pillsbury Favorite Casseroles*, it's easier than ever to bring those time-honored classics to your table. Each of the 313 casseroles, slow-cooked dishes, skillet suppers and other meal-in-one specialties earned a stamp of approval from Pillsbury, so you know it's teeming with the flavor you expect from America's most-loved Test Kitchen.

You'll even find winning recipes from Pillsbury Bake-Off® Contests. Try Chicken and White Bean Bruschetta Bake from Shannon Kohn. Her prize-worthy recipe appears on page 25. Or turn to page 81 for Barbara Lee's Chicken Cheese Enchiladas. Not only did these one-dish greats win over Bake-Off® judges, but they're tried-and-true favorites from family cooks just like you.

Flip through the pages and you'll notice that step-by-step instructions and gorgeous color photos make this cookbook an absolute delight for novice cooks and experienced chefs alike. In addition, "Prep Times" and/or "Ready In" guidelines accompany all of the recipes, helping you set a meal-in-one supper on the table, no matter how busy your schedule becomes.

And because we understand the importance nutrition plays in meal planning, we've included Nutritional Information with every recipe. Plus, Dietary Exchanges are featured with most of the items, helping anyone who is counting carbohydrates.

Between the mouth-watering dishes, easy instructions and handy tips, you're sure to reach for this savory collection time and again. In fact, with *Pillsbury Favorite Casseroles* at your side, a new dinner staple is always on the horizon. Dig into the goodness of a casserole tonight and discover your new family favorite.

Chapters Loaded with Taste

Divided into 13 taste-tempting chapters, *Pillsbury Favorite Casseroles* keeps the perfect recipe at your fingertips. You'll never have to search for a weeknight main course, potluck contribution or dinner-party entree again. Just take a look at the assortment of dishes you'll find in each section:

classics with a twist

You'll see some of your all-time favorites in a new light with the savory selections found in this chapter. For instance, we captured the flavor of chicken cordon bleu in a heartwarming casserole the whole family will love. In addition, you'll find exciting variations of lasagna, chicken Alfredo and more.

easy-prep oven meals

Simple assembly is the key to this chapter's assortment of mouth-watering sensations. An easy solution to workweek dinners and the perfect contribution to bring-a-dish events, these 20 entrees come together in a pinch and bake to perfection without much effort on your part.

one-dish dinners

There's nothing like a meal-in-one to make supper planning a snap. Simply add a green salad and dinner is ready. Southern Turkey-Stuffing Bake, Linguine with Creamy Chicken Primavera and Sweet 'n Sour Pork Skillet are just a sampling of the recipes included.

savory meat pies

Here's a chapter that you'll truly come to depend on because it features 35 classic entrees. Discover the unbeatable flavor of Deep-Dish Ground Beef Pot Pies or Quick Beef Stew in Bread Bowls. In addition, this section features several pizzas perfect for casual get-togethers on cozy movie nights at home.

southwestern & italian favorites

Liven up dinnertime routines with a south-of-the-border dish such as Fiesta Enchilada Bake. Or, perhaps you're in the mood for an Italian specialty like Spinach Pesto Manicotti. Regardless of which direction your taste buds lead you, these full-flavored casseroles always hit the spot!

fish & seafood

Creamy hot bakes, cheesy pasta tosses and the other delights found in this section prove just how comforting seafood can be. Dig into classics like bubbling tuna casserole or discover a new standby such as Salsa Cod with White Beans. Either way, you're sure to create a memorable meal for everyone at your table.

meatless entrees

Whether meatless items are a nightly feature in your home or you turn to veggie main courses only on occasion, you'll enjoy these piping-hot casseroles. Garden Vegetable Lasagna and Portobello-Broccoli Stir Fry are only two of the change-of-pace dishes waiting for you.

side dish casseroles

Versatile is the ideal way to describe this collection of dinner accompaniments. Looking for a lip-smacking item to serve alongside supper tonight? Try Orange Glazed Carrots and Sugar Snap Peas. Need to bring a dish to a backyard barbecue? Whip up a batch of No-Fuss Party Potatoes.

breakfast & brunch

Start the day off right with this collection of egg bakes and other eye-openers. Some recipes offer make-ahead convenience while others rely on easy prep work for hurried mornings. Regardless of which dish you choose, these golden casseroles promise to have sleepyheads racing to the breakfast table.

skillet & stovetop suppers

When time is at a premium, turn to this fantastic assortment of 40 in-a-snap dinners...each prepared on the stovetop. Here you'll find everything from chicken sautés and sausage stir fries to colorful pasta creations and pork stews—many of which are ready in only half an hour.

tasty meals for two

Just because you're cooking for two doesn't mean you have to forgo the comfort of a succulent casserole. These recipes pare down serving sizes without skimping on flavor so you can enjoy cozy classics without dealing with leftovers.

slow-cooked favorites

You may want to set a bookmark at the beginning of this chapter because it offers 42 slow-cooked specialties! Loaded with dinner-in-one convenience and stick-to-your-ribs comfort, each recipe simmers to perfection during the day. Try one this week and come home to an aromatic delight that can't be beat.

make-ahead casseroles

One of the benefits of serving a casserole is the fact that you can often prepare it a day in advance. With a little extra planning, you can surprise your family with Overnight Meatball and Pasta Casserole, Artichoke and Bacon Potato Bake or Make-Ahead Turkey Tetrazzini even on your busiest night.

classics with a twist

Bubbling pot pies, golden potato gratins and indulgent pasta bakes...these are some of the hallmarks of comfort food. When recipe fatigue invades, however, revise those standbys with a simple ingredient or two. From a lasagna featuring Mediterranean flavors to a savory stew topped with crescent rolls, the following classics rely on basic items for mouth-watering revamps you're sure to cherish.

Cheesy Chicken
Cordon Bleu
page 12

Zesty Italian
Crescent
Casserole
page 19

Ranch
Potato-Topped
Chicken Bake
page 17

crescent-topped hunters'-style chicken
page 13

italian crescent braid

PREP TIME: 25 MINUTES
READY IN: 55 MINUTES
SERVINGS: 4

1   cup chopped cooked ham

1/3 cup pepperoni slices

2   Italian plum tomatoes, chopped

1   cup shredded mozzarella cheese (4 oz.)

1   (2-1/4 oz.) can sliced ripe olives, drained

1/3 cup tomato pasta sauce

1   (8 oz.) can Pillsbury® Refrigerated Crescent Dinner Rolls

1   to 2 tablespoons grated Parmesan cheese

1 Heat oven to 375°F. Spray cookie sheet with nonstick cooking spray. In large bowl, combine all ingredients except crescent rolls and Parmesan cheese; mix well.

2 Unroll dough onto sprayed cookie sheet. Press to form 13x7-inch rectangle, pressing perforations to seal.

3 Spoon ham mixture in 3-inch-wide strip lengthwise down center of dough. With scissors or sharp knife, make cuts about 1-1/2 inches apart on long sides of dough to within 1/2 inch of filling. Alternately cross strips over filling. Tuck ends under; press to seal. Sprinkle dough with Parmesan cheese.

4 Bake at 375°F for 23 to 30 minutes or until deep golden brown. Cool 5 minutes. Cut crosswise into slices to serve.

NUTRITIONAL INFORMATION PER SERVING: Calories 430 • Total Fat 25g • Saturated Fat 9g • Cholesterol 40mg • Sodium 1,550mg • Total Carbohydrate 28g • Dietary Fiber 2g • Sugars 6g • Protein 22g. DIETARY EXCHANGES: 2 Starch • 2 Other Carbohydrate • 2-1/2 Lean Meat • 3 Fat.

SIMPLE SUBSTITUTION: To give this braid a no-fuss pizza flavor, use your favorite pizza sauce—homemade or from a jar—in place of the pasta sauce.

chicken and vegetable biscuits alfredo

READY IN: 25 MINUTES
SERVINGS: 4

4   Pillsbury® Oven Baked Frozen Buttermilk Biscuits (from 25 oz. bag)

2   cups cubed cooked chicken

2   cups Green Giant® Frozen Mixed Vegetables (from 1 lb. bag)

1/4 teaspoon pepper

1   (16 oz.) jar Alfredo pasta sauce

1   (4 oz.) can Green Giant® Mushroom Pieces and Stems, drained

1 Heat oven to 375°F. Place biscuits on ungreased cookie sheet; bake 14 to 18 minutes or until golden brown.

2 Meanwhile, in 3-quart saucepan, mix remaining ingredients. Cook over medium heat 6 to 8 minutes, stirring occasionally, until vegetables are tender and mixture is thoroughly heated.

3 Split warm biscuits; place bottom halves of biscuits on plates. Top each with 1 cup chicken mixture and the top half of the biscuit.

HIGH ALTITUDE (3500-6500 FT): Thaw vegetables before using.

NUTRITIONAL INFORMATION PER SERVING: Calories 760 • Total Fat 50g • Saturated Fat 25g • Trans Fat 6g • Cholesterol 170mg • Sodium 1,230mg • Total Carbohydrate 42g • Dietary Fiber 5g • Sugars 8g • Protein 36g. DIETARY EXCHANGES: 2-1/2 Starch • 1/2 Other Carbohydrate • 4 Lean Meat • 7 Fat.

oven pork and cannellini bean stew

PREP TIME: 15 MINUTES
READY IN: 2 HOURS 30 MINUTES
SERVINGS: 4

1 lb. boneless pork shoulder, cut into 3/4-inch pieces

1/2 cup chopped onion (1 medium)

2 garlic cloves, minced

1/2 teaspoon seasoned salt

4 small new red potatoes (about 2 inches in diameter), unpeeled, quartered

1 (19 oz.) can cannellini beans, drained

1 (15 oz.) can tomato sauce with Italian seasonings

1 (14 oz.) can chicken broth

2 cups Green Giant® Frozen Cut Green Beans

1 Heat oven to 325°F. Spray Dutch oven with nonstick cooking spray. Heat over medium-high heat until hot. Add pork, onion and garlic; sprinkle with seasoned salt. Cook 4 to 6 minutes or until pork is browned, stirring occasionally.

2 Add all remaining ingredients except green beans; mix well. Cover.

3 Bake covered at 325°F for 1 hour 30 minutes.

4 Uncover Dutch oven; stir in green beans. Cover; bake an additional 30 to 45 minutes or until the pork and vegetables are tender.

HIGH ALTITUDE (3500-6500 FT):
Bake covered at 350°F for 1 hour 30 minutes. Continue as directed.

NUTRITIONAL INFORMATION PER SERVING:
Calories 525 • Total Fat 15g • Saturated Fat 5g • Cholesterol 75mg • Sodium 1,640mg • Total Carbohydrate 68g • Dietary Fiber 14g • Sugars 9g • Protein 43g.
DIETARY EXCHANGES: 3 Starch • 1 Vegetable • 4-1/2 Lean Meat • 1/2 Fat.

german potato and sausage casserole

PREP TIME: 15 MINUTES
READY IN: 1 HOUR 5 MINUTES
SERVINGS: 6

1 (28 oz.) package frozen seasoned chunky-style hash-brown potatoes, thawed

1 (14 oz.) can sauerkraut, drained, rinsed

1 (10-3/4 oz.) can condensed cream of potato soup

1-1/3 cups half-and-half

Paprika

1 lb. cooked kielbasa or Polish sausage, cut into 6 pieces

1 Heat oven to 375°F. Spray 13x9-inch (3-quart) glass baking dish with nonstick cooking spray. In large bowl, combine potatoes and sauerkraut; toss to mix.

2 In medium bowl, combine soup and half-and-half; blend well. Add soup mixture to potato mixture; mix well. Pour potato mixture into sprayed baking dish. Sprinkle with paprika. Arrange sausage pieces over potato mixture, pressing lightly into mixture.

3 Bake at 375°F for 45 to 50 minutes or until bubbly and potatoes are tender.

NUTRITIONAL INFORMATION PER SERVING:
Calories 520 • Total Fat 34g • Saturated Fat 13g • Cholesterol 75mg • Sodium 2,040mg • Total Carbohydrate 38g • Dietary Fiber 5g • Sugars 4g • Protein 16g.
DIETARY EXCHANGES: 2-1/2 Starch • 2-1/2 Other Carbohydrate • 1 High-Fat Meat • 5 Fat.

creamy tomato, meatballs and rice bake

beef pepper steak casserole

creamy tomato, meatballs and rice bake

PREP TIME: 30 MINUTES
READY IN: 2 HOURS
SERVINGS: 4

1 lb. extra-lean ground beef
1/4 cup finely chopped onion
1/2 teaspoon salt
1/4 teaspoon pepper
3/4 cup uncooked converted long-grain rice
1 cup half-and-half
1 (10-3/4 oz.) can condensed tomato soup with roasted garlic and herbs
1 (14.5 oz.) can diced tomatoes with roasted garlic, undrained
2 tablespoons chopped fresh parsley

1 Heat oven to 350°F. Spray 8-inch square (2-quart) glass baking dish with nonstick cooking spray. In medium bowl, combine ground beef, onion, salt and pepper; mix well. Shape mixture into 12 meatballs; place in sprayed baking dish.

2 In medium bowl, combine all remaining ingredients except parsley; mix well. Pour over meatballs. Cover tightly with foil.

3 Bake at 350°F for 1-1/2 hours or until rice is tender. Let stand 10 minutes before serving. Sprinkle with parsley.

NUTRITIONAL INFORMATION PER SERVING:
Calories 520 • Total Fat 21g • Saturated Fat 10g • Cholesterol 95mg • Sodium 970mg • Total Carbohydrate 54g • Dietary Fiber 3g • Sugars 16g • Protein 28g.
DIETARY EXCHANGES: 2-1/2 Starch • 1 Fruit • 3-1/2 Other Carbohydrate • 1 Vegetable • 2-1/2 Lean Meat • 1 Fat.

HEALTHY HINT:
To reduce the fat in each serving of this casserole by about 6 grams and the calories by about 60, use 1 cup of nonfat milk or water in place of the half-and-half.

beef pepper steak casserole

PREP TIME: 25 MINUTES
READY IN: 45 MINUTES
SERVINGS: 6

2 tablespoons oil
1 medium green bell pepper, cut into bite-sized strips
1 medium red bell pepper, cut into bite-sized strips
1 medium onion, cut into thin wedges
1 lb. beef strips for stir frying
1 (12 oz.) jar beef gravy
1 (10 oz.) can diced tomatoes and green chiles, undrained
1 egg
1 tablespoon water
1 (7 oz.) can Pillsbury® Refrigerated Breadsticks (6 breadsticks)

1 Heat oven to 375°F. Heat oil in 12-inch skillet over medium-high heat until hot. Add bell peppers and onion; cook and stir 3 minutes. Add beef strips; cook and stir 3 to 5 minutes or until the beef is lightly browned and the vegetables are softened.

2 Add gravy and tomatoes; mix well. Cook until mixture is hot and bubbly, stirring occasionally. Remove from heat. Pour mixture into ungreased 8-inch square (2-quart) glass baking dish.

3 In small bowl, beat egg and water until well blended. Separate dough into 6 breadsticks. Tie each into loose knot. Arrange knots on top of hot beef mixture. Brush knots with egg mixture. Discard any remaining egg mixture.

4 Bake at 375°F for 15 to 20 minutes or until breadsticks are deep golden brown.

NUTRIONAL INFORMATION PER SERVING:
Calories 290 • Total Fat 12g • Saturated Fat 3g • Cholesterol 75mg • Sodium 700mg • Total Carbohydrate 25g • Dietary Fiber 2g • Sugars 5g • Protein 20g.
DIETARY EXCHANGES: 1-1/2 Starch • 1-1/2 Other Carbohydrate • 2 Lean Meat • 1 Fat.

cheesy chicken cordon bleu

PREP TIME: 20 MINUTES
READY IN: 1 HOUR
SERVINGS: 4

4 boneless skinless chicken breast halves

2 (1 oz.) slices 97% fat-free ham, cut in half

1/4 cup fat-free cream cheese (from 8 oz. tub)

1/4 cup shredded Swiss cheese (1 oz.)

1 egg white

1/2 cup Progresso® Italian Style Bread Crumbs

Nonstick cooking spray

Paprika

1 Heat oven to 350°F. Spray 15x10x1-inch baking pan with nonstick cooking spray.

2 Place 1 chicken breast half, boned side up, between 2 pieces of plastic wrap or waxed paper. Working from center, gently pound chicken with flat side of meat mallet or rolling pin until about 1/4 inch thick; remove wrap. Repeat with remaining chicken breast halves.

3 Place 1 half slice ham on each chicken breast half. Spread each with 1 tablespoon cream cheese; sprinkle each with 1 tablespoon Swiss cheese. Starting at short end, roll up. Secure with wooden toothpicks; press edges to seal.

4 Place egg white in small shallow bowl; beat slightly. Place breads crumbs in another shallow bowl. Carefully dip chicken rolls in egg white; coat with bread crumbs. Place chicken rolls, seam side down, in sprayed pan. Spray tops of each roll with cooking spray.

5 Bake at 350°F for 35 to 40 minutes or until chicken is fork-tender and juices run clear. Remove toothpicks before serving. Sprinkle with paprika.

NUTRITIONAL INFORMATION PER SERVING: Calories 260 • Total Fat 8g • Saturated Fat 2g • Cholesterol 90mg • Sodium 540mg • Total Carbohydrate 12g • Dietary Fiber 1g • Sugars 2g • Protein 36g. **DIETARY EXCHANGES:** 1 Starch • 1 Other Carbohydrate • 4-1/2 Very Lean Meat • 1/2 Fat.

honey-mustard roasted chicken with sweet potatoes

PREP TIME: 15 MINUTES
READY IN: 1 HOUR 15 MINUTES
SERVINGS: 4

4 bone-in chicken leg quarters (thigh and leg), skin removed if desired

2 medium dark-orange sweet potatoes (about 12 oz.), peeled, cut into 1-inch pieces (about 3 cups)

4 Green Giant® Nibblers® Frozen Corn-on-the-Cob

3/4 cup purchased honey-mustard salad dressing

1/2 teaspoon dried rosemary leaves

1/2 teaspoon salt

2 cups Green Giant Select® Frozen Whole Green Beans

1 Heat oven to 425°F. Spray shallow roasting pan with nonstick cooking spray. Arrange the chicken, skin side down, sweet potatoes and corn in sprayed pan.

2 In small bowl, combine salad dressing, rosemary and salt; mix well. Brush half of mixture over the chicken and vegetables.

3 Bake at 425°F for 30 minutes.

4 Remove pan from oven. Turn chicken over and stir vegetables. Add green beans to pan. Drizzle remaining salad dressing mixture over chicken and vegetables.

5 Return to oven; bake an additional 25 to 30 minutes or until chicken is fork-tender and juices run clear, and vegetables are tender.

NUTRITIONAL INFORMATION PER SERVING: Calories 555 • Total Fat 31g • Saturated Fat 7g • Cholesterol 105mg • Sodium 700mg • Total Carbohydrate 40g • Dietary Fiber 5g • Sugars 17g • Protein 34g. **DIETARY EXCHANGES:** 2 Starch • 4 Medium-Fat Meat • 2 Fat.

crescent-topped hunters'-style chicken

PREP TIME: 25 MINUTES
READY IN: 55 MINUTES
SERVINGS: 8

1 tablespoon oil

1 cup fresh baby carrots, quartered lengthwise

1 medium onion, halved, thinly sliced

1 lb. chicken breast strips for stir frying

2 cups Green Giant® Frozen Cut Green Beans, thawed

1 (14.5 oz.) can diced tomatoes, undrained

1 (4.5 oz.) jar Green Giant® Sliced Mushrooms, drained

1 (12 oz.) jar brown mushroom gravy

1/4 cup Pillsbury BEST® All-Purpose Flour

1/4 teaspoon salt

1 (8 oz.) can Pillsbury® Refrigerated Crescent Dinner Rolls

1 tablespoon sesame seed

1 Heat oven to 375°F. Spray 13x9-inch (3-quart) glass baking dish or 3-quart oval casserole with nonstick cooking spray. Heat oil in large nonstick skillet over medium-high heat until hot. Add carrots and onion; cook and stir 3 minutes. Add chicken; cook 4 to 5 minutes or until chicken is no longer pink in center and the vegetables are tender, stirring frequently.

2 Add green beans, tomatoes and mushrooms; mix well. In small bowl, combine gravy, flour and salt; blend well. Add to chicken mixture; cook and stir until mixture is bubbly. Remove from heat. Pour into sprayed baking dish.

3 Separate dough into 8 triangles. Starting from shortest side of each triangle, roll up halfway; arrange over hot chicken mixture so pointed ends are toward center. Spray rolls with cooking spray; sprinkle with sesame seed.

4 Bake at 375°F for 18 to 23 minutes or until crescent rolls are deep golden brown.

NUTRITIONAL INFORMATION PER SERVING: Calories 270 • Total Fat 11g • Saturated Fat 2g • Cholesterol 35mg • Sodium 720mg • Total Carbohydrate 25g • Dietary Fiber 3g • Sugars 6g • Protein 17g.
DIETARY EXCHANGES: 1-1/2 Starch • 1-1/2 Other Carbohydrate • 1 Vegetable • 1-1/2 Very Lean Meat • 1-1/2 Fat.

TIP: Store refrigerated dough products in the body of the refrigerator, not in the door panel.

presto nuggets and noodles

READY IN: 20 MINUTES
SERVINGS: 4

1 Cook chicken nuggets as directed on package. Carefully cut each nugget in half or cut strips into 4 pieces.

2 Meanwhile, cook noodles to desired doneness as directed on package, adding sugar snap peas during last 3 to 4 minutes of cooking time. Drain; return to saucepan.

1 (11 oz.) package frozen breaded chicken nuggets or strips

6 oz. uncooked medium egg noodles (3 cups)

1-1/2 cups Green Giant Select® Frozen Sugar Snap Peas

1/2 cup purchased stir fry sauce

2 tablespoons honey

1/2 teaspoon lemon-pepper seasoning

1/4 cup chopped honey-roasted peanuts

3 Add stir fry sauce, honey and lemon-pepper seasoning, toss to coat. Add chicken; toss gently. Sprinkle with peanuts.

NUTRITIONAL INFORMATION PER SERVING:
Calories 550 • Total Fat 22g • Saturated Fat 5g • Cholesterol 85mg • Sodium 2,220mg • Total Carbohydrate 60g • Dietary Fiber 3g • Sugars 16g • Protein 28g.
DIETARY EXCHANGES: 4 Starch • 4 Other Carbohydrate • 2-1/2 Medium-Fat Meat • 2 Fat.

TIP: Sugar snap peas are a cross between English and snow peas. They are sweet like English peas and entirely edible like snow peas. Look for fresh sugar snap peas during spring and summer; the rest of the year, use the frozen variety.

spicy southwestern potatoes and ham

PREP TIME: 15 MINUTES
READY IN: 1 HOUR 15 MINUTES
SERVINGS: 6

1/2 cup gourmet spreadable cheese with garlic and herbs (from 4 to 6.5 oz. pkg.)

1 cup half-and-half

1 tablespoon finely chopped chipotle chiles in adobo sauce, if desired

1 (1 lb. 4 oz.) package refrigerated sliced home fries potatoes

1 (1 lb.) package Green Giant® Frozen Broccoli Cuts, thawed

1 cup cooked ham strips (2x1/4x1/4-inch)

1 cup shredded Cheddar cheese (4 oz.)

1 Heat oven to 350°F. Spray 13x9-inch (3-quart) glass baking dish with nonstick cooking spray. Place spreadable cheese in medium bowl. Gradually stir in half-and-half and chiles; blend well. Set aside.

2 In sprayed baking dish, layer potatoes, broccoli and ham. Pour spreadable cheese mixture over top; sprinkle with Cheddar cheese. Cover with foil.

3 Bake at 350°F for 45 minutes. Uncover; bake an additional 15 minutes or until bubbly around edges.

NUTRITIONAL INFORMATION PER SERVING:
Calories 310 • Total Fat 20g • Saturated Fat 12g • Cholesterol 65mg • Sodium 760mg • Total Carbohydrate 18g • Dietary Fiber 2g • Sugars 4g • Protein 14g.
DIETARY EXCHANGES: 1 Starch • 1 Other Carbohydrate • 1-1/2 High-Fat Meat • 1-1/2 Fat.

hamburger stroganoff casserole

PREP TIME: 25 MINUTES
READY IN: 1 HOUR 5 MINUTES
SERVINGS: 6

8 oz. uncooked medium egg noodles (4 cups)

1 lb. lean ground beef

12 oz. small fresh whole mushrooms, halved (3-1/2 cups)

2 garlic cloves, minced

2 (1.0 to 1.3 oz.) packages beef or pork gravy mix

1/4 teaspoon pepper

2-1/2 cups water

1 (8 oz.) container sour cream

1/2 teaspoon nutmeg

1/4 cup chopped fresh parsley

1 Heat oven to 375°F. Spray 3-quart casserole with nonstick cooking spray. Cook egg noodles as directed on package. Drain; cover to keep warm.

2 Meanwhile, in 12-inch nonstick skillet, cook ground beef, mushrooms and garlic over medium-high heat for 5 to 7 minutes or until beef is thoroughly cooked, stirring frequently. Drain; remove beef mixture from skillet.

3 In same skillet, combine gravy mix, pepper and water; mix well. Cook over medium-high heat for 3 to 5 minutes or until bubbly and thickened, stirring constantly. Remove from heat. Stir in sour cream and nutmeg.

4 Add cooked noodles and beef mixture to gravy; stir to combine. Spoon mixture into sprayed casserole; cover.

5 Bake at 375°F for 30 to 40 minutes or until bubbly and thoroughly heated. Sprinkle with parsley.

NUTRITIONAL INFORMATION PER SERVING:
Calories 360 • Total Fat 20g • Saturated Fat 9g • Cholesterol 85mg • Sodium 840mg • Total Carbohydrate 24g • Dietary Fiber 1g • Sugars 3g • Protein 21g.
DIETARY EXCHANGES: 1-1/2 Starch • 1-1/2 Other Carbohydrate • 2-1/2 Medium-Fat Meat • 1-1/2 Fat.

roasted sausage, apples and peppers

READY IN: 30 MINUTES
SERVINGS: 4

1 (16 oz.) ring cooked Polish sausage or kielbasa

2 medium any color bell peppers, cut into 2-inch pieces

1/4 cup apple jelly

1 tablespoon Dijon mustard

2 medium unpeeled apples, quartered

1 Heat oven to 425°F. Spray 13x9-inch (3-quart) glass baking dish with nonstick cooking spray. Place sausage and bell peppers in sprayed baking dish. Pierce sausage several times with fork.

2 In small saucepan, combine jelly and mustard. Heat over low heat until melted, stirring frequently. Brush half of jelly mixture over sausage and bell peppers.

3 Bake at 425°F for 10 minutes.

4 Remove baking dish from oven. Add apples to baking dish. Brush remaining jelly mixture over sausage, bell peppers and apples.

5 Return to oven; bake an additional 10 minutes or until thoroughly heated. Cut sausage before serving.

HIGH ALTITUDE (3500-6500 FT): Increase second bake time to 15 minutes.

NUTRITIONAL INFORMATION PER SERVING:
Calories 465 • Total Fat 32g • Saturated Fat 12g • Cholesterol 65mg • Sodium 1,250mg • Total Carbohydrate 30g • Dietary Fiber 3g • Sugars 22g • Protein 14g.
DIETARY EXCHANGES: 1/2 Starch • 1/2 Fruit • 1 Other Carbohydrate • 1-1/2 High-Fat Meat • 4 Fat.

chicken cordon bleu casserole

PREP TIME: 15 MINUTES
READY IN: 1 HOUR 5 MINUTES
SERVINGS: 4

1/2 cup chicken broth

1/2 cup sour cream

1 (12 oz.) jar chicken gravy

5 oz. uncooked dumpling egg noodles (3 cups)

1 cup Green Giant® Frozen Sweet Peas

1/2 cup diced cooked ham

1 teaspoon paprika

1/4 teaspoon pepper

4 (4 oz.) boneless skinless chicken breast halves

1/2 teaspoon seasoned salt

4 (1 oz.) slices Swiss cheese, halved

1 Heat oven to 375°F. In large bowl, combine broth, sour cream and gravy; mix well with wire whisk. Stir in uncooked noodles, peas, ham, paprika and 1/8 teaspoon of the pepper. Spoon into ungreased shallow 2-quart casserole.

2 Place chicken over noodle mixture; sprinkle with seasoned salt and remaining 1/8 teaspoon pepper. Cover with foil.

3 Bake covered at 375°F for 30 minutes.

4 Uncover casserole; bake 20 minutes or until chicken is fork-tender and juices run clear, and noodles are tender and thoroughly heated.

5 Place 2 cheese slice halves over each chicken breast half. Bake an additional 5 minutes or until cheese is melted.

HIGH ALTITUDE (3500-6500 FT): Increase chicken broth to 3/4 cup; thaw peas by rinsing with warm water. Bake covered at 400°F for 40 minutes. Continue as directed.

NUTRITIONAL INFORMATION PER SERVING: Calories 550 • Total Fat 25g • Saturated Fat 12g • Cholesterol 155mg • Sodium 1,220mg • Total Carbohydrate 35g • Dietary Fiber 3g • Sugars 4g • Protein 46g.
DIETARY EXCHANGES: 2 Starch • 5-1/2 Lean Meat • 1-1/2 Fat.

ranch potato-topped chicken bake

PREP TIME: 20 MINUTES
READY IN: 50 MINUTES
SERVINGS: 6

FILLING

- 2 cups cubed cooked chicken or turkey
- 2 cups Green Giant® Frozen Mixed Vegetables, thawed
- 2 (10-3/4 oz.) cans condensed 98% fat-free cream of chicken soup with 30% less sodium
- 1/2 cup chicken broth

POTATOES

- 1-3/4 cups water
- 1 cup milk
- 2-1/4 cups plain mashed potato mix (dry)
- 1 (1 oz.) package dry ranch dip mix
- 1 egg, slightly beaten

1 Heat oven to 375°F. In large saucepan, combine all filling ingredients; mix well. Cook over medium heat until mixture is bubbly and thoroughly heated, stirring occasionally. Spoon into ungreased 13x9-inch (3-quart) glass baking dish.

2 In medium saucepan, bring water to a boil. Remove from heat. Add milk. Stir in plain mashed potato mix and ranch dip mix with fork until moistened. Let stand 1 minute. Add egg; blend well. Cool 5 minutes. Spoon or pipe potato mixture around edge of hot chicken mixture.

3 Bake at 375°F for 25 to 30 minutes or until potatoes are set and light golden brown.

NUTRITIONAL INFORMATION PER SERVING:
Calories 320 • Total Fat 8g • Saturated Fat 3g • Cholesterol 85mg • Sodium 1,160mg • Total Carbohydrate 41g • Dietary Fiber 3g • Sugars 4g • Protein 21g.
DIABETIC EXCHANGES: 2-1/2 Starch • 2-1/2 Other Carbohydrate • 2 Lean Meat.

teriyaki chicken and rice

PREP TIME: 10 MINUTES
READY IN: 1 HOUR 15 MINUTES
SERVINGS: 4

2 cups fresh baby carrots, halved lengthwise

1 cup uncooked regular long-grain white rice

1 (14 oz.) can baby corn nuggets, drained

1 (14 oz.) can chicken broth

5 tablespoons teriyaki sauce

3 to 3-1/2 lb. cut-up frying chicken, skin removed if desired

1/4 cup orange marmalade

1/2 teaspoon ginger

3/4 cup cashew halves and pieces

1 Heat oven to 375°F. Spray 13x9-inch (3-quart) glass baking dish with nonstick cooking spray. In sprayed baking dish, combine carrots, rice, corn nuggets, broth and 2 tablespoons of the teriyaki sauce; mix well.

2 Arrange chicken pieces over rice mixture. In small bowl, combine remaining 3 tablespoons teriyaki sauce, orange marmalade and ginger; blend well. Spoon mixture over chicken and rice mixture. Cover with foil.

3 Bake covered at 375°F for 45 minutes.

4 Uncover baking dish; bake an additional 15 to 30 minutes or until chicken is fork-tender and juices run clear. Sprinkle with cashews.

HIGH ALTITUDE (3500-6500 FT): Add 1/4 cup water to carrot and rice mixture. Bake covered at 400°F for 45 minutes. Uncover baking dish; bake an additional 25 to 40 minutes.

NUTRITIONAL INFORMATION PER SERVING: Calories 860 • Total Fat 34g • Saturated Fat 8g • Cholesterol 130mg • Sodium 1,830mg • Total Carbohydrate 90g • Dietary Fiber 5g • Sugars 20g • Protein 54g.
DIETARY EXCHANGES: 4-1/2 Starch • 1 Other Carbohydrate • 5-1/2 Medium-Fat Meat • 1 Fat.

zesty italian crescent casserole

PREP TIME: 20 MINUTES
READY IN: 45 MINUTES
SERVINGS: 6

- 1 lb. lean ground beef
- 1/4 cup chopped onion
- 1 cup tomato pasta sauce
- 1-1/2 cups shredded mozzarella or Monterey Jack cheese (6 oz.)
- 1/2 cup sour cream
- 1 (8 oz.) can Pillsbury® Refrigerated Crescent Dinner Rolls
- 1/3 cup grated Parmesan cheese
- 2 tablespoons margarine or butter, melted

1 Heat oven to 375°F. In large skillet, cook ground beef and onion over medium heat for 8 to 10 minutes or until beef is thoroughly cooked, stirring frequently. Drain. Stir in the pasta sauce; cook until thoroughly heated.

2 Meanwhile, in medium bowl, combine mozzarella cheese and sour cream; mix well.

3 Pour hot beef mixture into ungreased 9-1/2 or 10-inch glass deep-dish pie pan or 11x7-inch (2-quart) glass baking dish. Spoon cheese mixture over beef mixture.

4 Unroll dough over cheese mixture. (If using pie pan, separate dough into 8 triangles; arrange points toward center over cheese mixture, crimping outside edges if necessary.) In a small bowl, mix Parmesan cheese and margarine. Spread evenly over dough.

5 Bake at 375°F for 18 to 25 minutes or until deep golden brown.

HIGH ALTITUDE (3500-6500 FT):
Bake at 375°F for 22 to 25 minutes.

NUTRITIONAL INFORMATION PER SERVING:
Calories 510 • Total Fat 32g • Saturated Fat 13g • Cholesterol 75mg • Sodium 1,000mg • Total Carbohydrate 28g • Dietary Fiber 1g • Sugars 10g • Protein 28g.
DIETARY EXCHANGES: 2 Starch • 3 Medium-Fat Meat • 3 Fat.

southwestern potato nugget hot dish

PREP TIME: 20 MINUTES
READY IN: 50 MINUTES
SERVINGS: 6

- 1 lb. lean ground beef
- 1 tablespoon Old El Paso® Taco Seasoning Mix (from 1.25 oz. pkg.)
- 2/3 cup water
- 1/2 cup sour cream
- 1 (10-3/4 oz.) can condensed cream of onion soup
- 1 (1 lb.) pkg. Green Giant® Frozen Mixed Vegetables
- 1 cup shredded taco-flavored cheese (4 oz.)
- 1 (1 lb.) package frozen miniature potato nuggets

1 Heat oven to 450°F. Spray 2-quart casserole with nonstick cooking spray. Cook ground beef in large skillet over medium-high heat until thoroughly cooked, stirring frequently. Drain. Stir in taco seasoning mix and water. Cook and stir 2 minutes.

2 Stir in sour cream, soup, frozen vegetables and cheese. Cook until bubbly, stirring occasionally. Spoon mixture into sprayed casserole. Top with potato nuggets.

3 Bake at 450°F for 25 to 30 minutes or until mixture is bubbly and potato nuggets are golden brown.

NUTRITIONAL INFORMATION PER SERVING:
Calories 540 • Total Fat 31g • Saturated Fat 15g • Cholesterol 80mg • Sodium 1,320mg • Total Carbohydrate 41g • Dietary Fiber 5g • Sugars 3g • Protein 24g.
DIETARY EXCHANGES: 2 Starch • 1/2 Fruit • 2-1/2 Other Carbohydrate • 1 Vegetable • 2-1/2 Medium-Fat Meat • 2-1/2 Fat.

harvest pork chop bake

PREP TIME: 15 MINUTES
READY IN: 55 MINUTES
SERVINGS: 4

2 tablespoons olive oil

1/2 teaspoon dried sage leaves

1/2 teaspoon dried marjoram leaves

1/2 teaspoon garlic-pepper blend

1/2 teaspoon seasoned salt

4 (6 to 8 oz.) bone-in pork loin chops (3/4 inch thick)

1 small butternut squash (about 2 lb.), peeled, seeded and cut into 1/2 to 1-inch pieces (about 3 cups)

1 medium green bell pepper, cut into 1/2-inch pieces

1 medium red onion, cut into 1/2-inch wedges

1 Heat oven to 425°F. Spray 15x10-inch baking pan with sides with nonstick cooking spray. In large bowl, combine oil, sage, marjoram, garlic-pepper blend and seasoned salt; mix well. Brush some of mixture over both sides of pork chops. Place the pork chops in corners of sprayed pan.

2 Add squash, bell pepper and onion to remaining mixture in bowl; toss to coat. Arrange vegetables in pan with the pork chops.

3 Bake at 425°F for 35 to 40 minutes or until pork chops are no longer pink in center and squash is tender, turning chops and stirring vegetables once.

NUTRITIONAL INFORMATION PER SERVING: Calories 360 • Total Fat 16g • Saturated Fat 4g • Cholesterol 75mg • Sodium 230mg • Total Carbohydrate 25g • Dietary Fiber 3g • Sugars 9g • Protein 29g. DIETARY EXCHANGES: 1-1/2 Starch • 3-1/2 Lean Meat • 1 Fat.

overnight mediterranean lasagna

PREP TIME: 15 MINUTES
READY IN: 13 HOURS 25 MINUTES
SERVINGS: 8

1 (26 to 28 oz.) jar basil and tomato-flavored tomato pasta sauce

1 (2-1/4 oz.) can sliced ripe olives, drained

1 cup water

1 (15 oz.) container ricotta cheese

2 tablespoons lemon juice

2 teaspoons dried oregano leaves

8 uncooked lasagna noodles

4 cups shredded mozzarella cheese (16 oz.)

1 (4 oz.) package basil and tomato feta cheese, crumbled

1 (9 oz.) package Green Giant® Frozen Spinach, thawed, well drained

1 In medium bowl, combine pasta sauce, olives and water; blend well. In another medium bowl, combine ricotta cheese, lemon juice and oregano; mix well.

2 In ungreased 13x9-inch (3-quart) glass baking dish or lasagna pan, spread 1 cup of pasta sauce mixture. Top with 4 uncooked noodles, half of the ricotta cheese mixture, half of the mozzarella cheese, half of the feta cheese and all of the spinach.

3 Repeat layering with 1/2 cup sauce mixture, remaining 4 noodles, 1 cup of the remaining mozzarella cheese, remaining ricotta mixture, remaining feta cheese and remaining sauce mixture. Cover tightly with

plastic wrap; refrigerate at least 12 hours or overnight.

4 Heat oven to 350°F. Uncover baking dish; bake 35 minutes. Sprinkle with remaining 1 cup mozzarella cheese. Bake, uncovered, an additional 15 to 20 minutes or until casserole is bubbly, noodles are tender, and the cheese is melted. Let stand 15 minutes before serving.

NUTRIONAL INFORMATION PER SERVING: Calories 420 • Total Fat 20g • Saturated Fat 11g • Cholesterol 55mg • Sodium 1,000mg • Total Carbohydrate 30g • Dietary Fiber 3g • Sugars 2g • Protein 29g. DIETARY EXCHANGES: 1/2 Starch • 1-1/2 Fruit • 2 Other Carbohydrate • 4 Medium-Fat Meat.

greek seasoned turkey tenderloins

PREP TIME: 10 MINUTES
READY IN: 1 HOUR
SERVINGS: 4

2 (1/2 lb.) turkey breast tenderloins

2 large russet potatoes (about 1 lb.), unpeeled, cut into 1-inch pieces

1 (9 oz.) package frozen artichoke hearts, thawed, drained

1/2 cup purchased Greek vinaigrette salad dressing

1 (3 oz.) portobello mushroom cap, cut into 1/2-inch-thick slices

2 Italian plum tomatoes, quartered

2 green onions, cut into 1/2-inch pieces

1 Heat oven to 425°F. Spray 15x10x1-inch pan with nonstick cooking spray. Arrange turkey tenderloins, potatoes and artichoke hearts in sprayed pan. Brush with about half of the salad dressing.

2 Bake at 425°F for 30 minutes.

3 Remove pan from oven. Turn turkey over and stir vegetables. Add mushroom slices, tomatoes and onions to pan; brush turkey and vegetables with remaining salad dressing.

4 Return to oven; bake an additional 15 to 20 minutes or until turkey is fork-tender and juices run clear. To serve, cut turkey crosswise into slices. Serve any pan juices with turkey and vegetables. If desired, season to taste with salt and pepper.

NUTRITIONAL INFORMATION PER SERVING: Calories 375 • Total Fat 14g • Saturated Fat 1g • Cholesterol 80mg • Sodium 520mg • Total Carbohydrate 36g • Dietary Fiber 6g • Sugars 6g • Protein 32g. DIETARY EXCHANGES: 1-1/2 Starch • 1 Vegetable • 3-1/2 Very Lean Meat • 2-1/2 Fat.

easy-prep oven meals

A memorable dinner takes only moments to assemble with these supper-time lifesavers. Ideal for weeknight dining, potluck contributions and casual get-togethers, the home-style, oven-baked specialties in this chapter are sure to take top standing on your recipe list. Low on preparation, but big on taste, these dishes keep time in the kitchen to a minimum so you can create more memories at the table.

Chili Dog
Casserole
page 31

Oven-Braised
Beef Short
Ribs
page 31

Ham and
Vegetables
au Gratin
page 26

chicken and white bean bruschetta bake
page 25

ginger-orange glazed pork chops and vegetables

READY IN: 30 MINUTES
SERVINGS: 4

- 1 (9 oz.) package Green Giant® Harvest Fresh® Frozen Baby Cut Carrots
- 1/3 cup orange marmalade
- 1/4 cup hoisin sauce
- 1-1/2 teaspoons grated gingerroot
- 4 (4 oz.) boneless center-cut pork loin chops
- 1/4 teaspoon salt
- 1/8 teaspoon pepper
- 1 (9 oz.) package Green Giant® Harvest Fresh® Frozen Sugar Snap Peas
- 1 (8 oz.) can sliced water chestnuts, drained

1 Heat oven to 450°F. Spray 15x10x1-inch baking pan with nonstick cooking spray. To thaw carrots, cut small slit in center of pouch; place on microwave-safe plate. Microwave on High for 5 minutes. Set aside.

2 In small bowl, combine marmalade, hoisin sauce and gingerroot; mix well. Reserve 2 tablespoons sauce; set aside.

3 Sprinkle pork chops with salt and pepper. Place pork in corners of sprayed pan. Place thawed carrots in center of pan. Drizzle some of sauce over carrots; brush pork with sauce.

4 Bake at 450°F for 5 minutes. Remove pan from oven. Brush pork and carrots with sauce. Add sugar snap peas and water chestnuts to carrots; toss gently.

5 Return to oven; bake an additional 8 to 10 minutes or until pork is no longer pink in center and vegetables are tender, spooning pan juices over vegetables halfway through baking. Place pork chops and vegetables on large serving platter. Drizzle chops with reserved 2 tablespoons sauce.

NUTRITIONAL INFORMATION PER SERVING: Calories 350 • Total Fat 8g • Saturated Fat 3g • Cholesterol 60mg • Sodium 610mg • Total Carbohydrate 46g • Dietary Fiber 5g • Sugars 29g • Protein 24g.
DIETARY EXCHANGES: 1-1/2 Starch • 1 Fruit • 2-1/2 Other Carbohydrate • 1 Vegetable • 2-1/2 Lean Meat.

crispy-topped meatballs and baked beans

PREP TIME: 10 MINUTES
READY IN: 1 HOUR 5 MINUTES
SERVINGS: 6

- 1 (16 oz.) can baked beans, undrained
- 1 (15 oz.) can kidney beans, drained
- 1-1/2 cups Green Giant® Frozen Cut Green Beans
- 1/2 cup frozen chopped onion
- 1/4 cup barbecue sauce
- 12 frozen cooked Italian meatballs (about 5 oz.)
- 1 (3/4 oz.) can shoestring potatoes (about 1 cup)

1 Heat oven to 375°F. Spray shallow 2-quart casserole with nonstick cooking spray. In sprayed casserole, combine all ingredients except shoestring potatoes; mix well. Cover.

2 Bake covered at 375°F for 30 minutes.

3 Uncover casserole; sprinkle evenly with shoestring potatoes, pressing lightly. Bake uncovered an additional 20 to 25 minutes or until bubbly and thoroughly heated.

NUTRITIONAL INFORMATION PER SERVING: Calories 355 • Total Fat 13g • Saturated Fat 5g • Cholesterol 65mg • Sodium 950mg • Total Carbohydrate 47g • Dietary Fiber 9g • Sugars 10g • Protein 22g.
DIETARY EXCHANGES: 2-1/2 Starch • 2 Medium-Fat Meat • 1/2 Fat.

chicken and white bean bruschetta bake

PREP TIME: 15 MINUTES
READY IN: 45 MINUTES
SERVINGS: 4

Shannon Kohn
Simpsonville, SC

- 1 (19 oz.) can Progresso® Cannellini (white kidney) Beans, drained, rinsed
- 1 (14.5 oz.) can diced tomatoes with Italian herbs, drained
- 1 (6 oz.) package refrigerated cooked Italian-style chicken breast strips, cut into 1-inch pieces
- 1 tablespoon balsamic vinegar
- 1/2 teaspoon salt
- 1 (11 oz.) can Pillsbury® Refrigerated Original Breadsticks
- 2 cups shredded 6-cheese Italian cheese blend (8 oz.)
- 1/2 teaspoon dried basil leaves, crushed
- 1 tablespoon chopped fresh parsley, if desired

1 Heat oven to 375°F. Spray 13x9-inch (3-quart) glass baking dish with nonstick cooking spray. In large bowl, mix beans, tomatoes, chicken, vinegar and salt.

2 Unroll dough; separate into 12 breadsticks. Cut each breadstick into 4 equal pieces. Stir 1/4 of breadstick pieces at a time into bean mixture. Stir in 1 cup of the cheese. Spoon into baking dish, gently smoothing top. Top evenly with remaining 1 cup cheese; sprinkle with basil.

3 Bake 25 to 30 minutes or until bubbly and top is golden brown. To serve, spoon into individual shallow soup bowls; sprinkle with parsley.

NUTRITIONAL INFORMATION PER SERVING:
Calories 630 • Total Fat 20g • Saturated Fat 10g • Trans Fat 1g • Cholesterol 80mg • Sodium 1,880mg • Total Carbohydrate 73g • Dietary Fiber 8g • Sugars 10g • Protein 40g.
DIETARY EXCHANGES: 3-1/2 Starch • 1 Other Carbohydrate • 1 Vegetable • 4 Very Lean Meat • 3 Fat.

honey-mustard roasted chicken and squash

PREP TIME: 15 MINUTES
READY IN: 1 HOUR
SERVINGS: 4

- 4 bone-in chicken breasts, skin removed
- 1 medium butternut squash (2 lb.), peeled, cut into 1-inch cubes (4 cups)
- 1 medium red onion, cut into 8 wedges
- 3/4 cup reduced-fat honey-mustard dressing
- 1/2 teaspoon salt
- 1/2 teaspoon dried rosemary leaves, crushed
- 1/4 teaspoon garlic powder
- 2 cups Green Giant Select® Frozen Sugar Snap Peas (from 1 lb. bag)

1 Heat oven to 425°F. Spray shallow roasting pan with nonstick cooking spray. Place chicken in pan; arrange squash and onion around chicken.

2 In small bowl, mix dressing, salt, rosemary and garlic powder. Brush chicken and vegetables with about half of the dressing mixture.

3 Bake uncovered 20 minutes. Remove from oven. Stir vegetables; add sugar snap peas to pan. Brush chicken and vegetables with remaining dressing mixture.

4 Return to oven; bake 20 to 25 minutes longer or until thermometer inserted in center of thickest part of breasts reads 170°F, and vegetables are tender. If desired, garnish with fresh herb sprigs.

NUTRITIONAL INFORMATION PER SERVING:
Calories 340 • Total Fat 7g • Saturated Fat 1g • Trans Fat 0g • Cholesterol 75mg • Sodium 770mg • Total Carbohydrate 38g • Dietary Fiber 4g • Sugars 23g • Protein 30g.
DIETARY EXCHANGES: 1 Starch • 1 Other Carbohydrate • 1 Vegetable • 3-1/2 Very Lean Meat • 1 Fat.

italian meatball and biscuit bake

PREP TIME: 20 MINUTES
READY IN: 1 HOUR 10 MINUTES
SERVINGS: 12

1 (16 oz.) bag frozen cooked Italian-style meatballs

1 (16.3 oz.) can Pillsbury® Grands!® Homestyle Refrigerated Buttermilk Biscuits

1 (14 oz.) jar tomato pasta sauce

1-1/2 cups shredded mozzarella cheese (6 oz.)

1 Heat oven to 375°F. Spray 13x9-inch (3-quart) glass baking dish with nonstick cooking spray. In large microwavable bowl, microwave meatballs on Medium 3 to 5 minutes or until thawed.

2 Separate dough into 8 biscuits. Cut each biscuit into 8 pieces; place in large bowl with meatballs. Gently stir in pasta sauce to coat. Spoon and spread mixture in baking dish.

3 Bake 30 to 40 minutes or until edges are deep golden brown and biscuit pieces are no longer doughy on bottom. Sprinkle with cheese; bake 2 to 5 minutes longer or until cheese is melted. Cool 10 minutes before serving.

NUTRITIONAL INFORMATION PER SERVING: Calories 300 • Total Fat 15g • Saturated Fat 6g • Trans Fat 2.5g • Cholesterol 45mg • Sodium 870mg • Total Carbohydrate 27g • Dietary Fiber 0g • Sugars 6g • Protein 14g. DIETARY EXCHANGES: 2 Starch • 1 High-Fat Meat • 1 Fat.

SIMPLE SUBSTITUTION: Try shredded fresh Parmesan cheese or an Italian blend of shredded cheese for the mozzarella in this recipe.

ham and vegetables au gratin

PREP TIME: 30 MINUTES
READY IN: 1 HOUR
SERVINGS: 6

1 (1 lb.) bag Green Giant Select® Frozen Broccoli, Carrots & Cauliflower

2 cups cubed (1/2-inch) cooked ham

1/4 cup butter or margarine

1/4 cup all-purpose flour

1/2 teaspoon salt

1/4 teaspoon pepper

2 cups milk

1-1/2 cups shredded Swiss cheese (6 oz.)

1 Heat oven to 375°F. In ungreased 2-quart casserole, cook frozen vegetables in microwave as directed on bag; drain. Stir in ham.

2 In 2-quart saucepan, melt butter over medium heat. Add flour, salt and pepper; cook, stirring constantly with wire whisk, until bubbly and smooth. Remove from heat. Stir in milk and 1/2 cup of the cheese. Heat to boiling, stirring constantly. Boil and stir 1 minute. Pour over vegetables and ham; stir gently to mix. Sprinkle remaining 1 cup cheese over top.

3 Bake uncovered 25 to 30 minutes or until bubbly around edges.

NUTRITIONAL INFORMATION PER SERVING: Calories 330 • Total Fat 21g • Saturated Fat 11g • Trans Fat 0.5g • Cholesterol 80mg • Sodium 1,040mg • Total Carbohydrate 13g • Dietary Fiber 2g • Sugars 5g • Protein 23g. DIETARY EXCHANGES: 1/2 Starch • 1 Vegetable • 3 Lean Meat • 2-1/2 Fat.

cheesy beef and tomato bake

PREP TIME: 20 MINUTES
READY IN: 55 MINUTES
SERVINGS: 4

1   lb. lean ground beef

1   (1 oz.) package onion soup mix

2   medium tomatoes, chopped

1-1/2   cups uncooked instant rice

1-1/2   cups water

1   medium tomato, sliced

1   cup shredded colby-Monterey Jack cheese blend (4 oz.)

1 Heat oven to 400°F. Spray 8-inch square (2-quart) glass baking dish or 2-quart casserole with nonstick cooking spray.

2 Cook ground beef in large skillet over medium-high heat until thoroughly cooked, stirring frequently. Drain. Stir in soup mix, chopped tomatoes, rice and water. Bring to a boil. Pour into sprayed baking dish. Cover tightly with foil.

3 Bake at 400°F for 20 to 25 minutes or until liquid is absorbed and rice is tender. Uncover; top with tomato slices. Sprinkle with cheese. Bake uncovered an additional 10 minutes or until the cheese is melted.

NUTRITIONAL INFORMATION PER SERVING:
Calories 500 • Total Fat 25g • Saturated Fat 12g • Cholesterol 95mg • Sodium 870mg • Total Carbohydrate 38g • Dietary Fiber 2g • Sugars 5g • Protein 31g.
DIETARY EXCHANGES: 2-1/2 Starch • 2 1/2 Other Carbohydrate • 3-1/2 Medium-Fat Meat • 1 Fat.

corn-crisped chicken and potato dinner

PREP TIME: 20 MINUTES
READY IN: 1 HOUR
SERVINGS: 4

1/3   cup buttermilk

1   teaspoon salt

1/4   teaspoon ground red pepper (cayenne)

2/3   cup corn flake crumbs

4   bone-in skinless chicken breast halves

4   medium russet or Idaho baking potatoes, unpeeled, cut into 1-inch cubes

1   red or green bell pepper, seeded, cut into 1x1/2-inch pieces

1   medium onion, cut into 8 wedges

2   tablespoons grated Parmesan cheese

1/2   teaspoon garlic powder

1/2   teaspoon paprika

2   tablespoons margarine or butter, melted

1 Heat oven to 400°F. Spray 15x10x1-inch baking pan with nonstick cooking spray.

2 In shallow bowl, combine buttermilk, salt and ground red pepper; mix well. Place corn flake crumbs in another shallow bowl. Dip chicken in buttermilk mixture; coat with crumbs. Place crumb-coated chicken breast halves in corners of sprayed pan.

3 In large bowl, combine potatoes, bell pepper and onion. Sprinkle with cheese, garlic powder and paprika; toss to coat evenly. Place in center of baking pan. Drizzle margarine over chicken and vegetables.

4 Bake at 400°F for 30 to 40 minutes or until chicken is fork-tender, juices run clear and potatoes are tender, stirring the vegetables once halfway through baking.

NUTRITIONAL INFORMATION PER SERVING:
Calories 410 • Total Fat 13g • Saturated Fat 3g • Cholesterol 75mg • Sodium 840mg • Total Carbohydrate 41g • Dietary Fiber 4g • Sugars 5g • Protein 32g.
DIETARY EXCHANGES: 2-1/2 Starch • 2-1/2 Other Carbohydrate • 3-1/2 Very Lean Meat • 2 Fat.

hawaiian sausage and rice bake

PREP TIME: 20 MINUTES
READY IN: 1 HOUR 5 MINUTES
SERVINGS: 4

1-1/4 cups water

2 tablespoons butter

1 (6.2 oz.) package fast-cooking long-grain and wild rice mix (with seasoning packet)

1/2 cup pineapple preserves

1 lb. cooked kielbasa, halved lengthwise, cut into 1-inch slices

1 medium onion, finely chopped

1 medium green bell pepper, cut into 3/4-inch pieces

1 medium red bell pepper, cut into 3/4-inch pieces

1 (8 oz.) can pineapple chunks in unsweetened juice, undrained

1 Heat oven to 375°F. In small saucepan, bring water and butter to a boil.

2 In ungreased 2-1/2-quart casserole, combine all ingredients including contents of seasoning packet and boiling water; mix well. Cover.

3 Bake at 375°F for 40 to 45 minutes or until rice is tender. Let stand 10 minutes before serving.

NUTRITIONAL INFORMATION PER SERVING: Calories 720 • Total Fat 37g • Saturated Fat 15g • Cholesterol 90mg • Sodium 1,780mg • Total Carbohydrate 76g • Dietary Fiber 3g • Sugars 32g • Protein 21g.
DIETARY EXCHANGES: 3 Starch • 2 Fruit • 5 Other Carbohydrate • 1-1/2 High-Fat Meat • 4-1/2 Fat.

HEALTHY HINT: To reduce the fat in each serving of this casserole by about 25 grams, use turkey kielbasa or smoked turkey sausage in place of kielbasa.

cheddar potatoes with ham and beans

PREP TIME: 15 MINUTES
READY IN: 1 HOUR 30 MINUTES
SERVINGS: 4

1 (1 lb. 4 oz.) package refrigerated potato wedges

1 cup cooked ham strips (2x1/4x1/4-inch)

1 (14.5 oz.) can Green Giant® French Style Green Beans, drained

1 (10-3/4 oz.) can condensed fiesta nacho cheese soup or cheesy broccoli soup

1/2 cup milk

1 cup shredded Cheddar cheese (4 oz.)

1 tablespoon butter, melted

1/2 cup Progresso® Plain Bread Crumbs

1 Heat oven to 350°F. Spray 12x8-inch (2-quart) glass baking dish with nonstick cooking spray. Place potatoes, ham and green beans in sprayed baking dish.

2 In small bowl, combine soup, milk and 1/2 cup of the cheese; mix well. Pour over mixture in baking dish; stir gently to mix. Sprinkle with remaining 1/2 cup cheese.

3 In small bowl, combine butter and bread crumbs; mix well. Sprinkle over top.

4 Bake at 350°F for 1 hour 10 minutes to 1 hour 15 minutes or until mixture is bubbly.

NUTRITIONAL INFORMATION PER SERVING: Calories 430 • Total Fat 20g • Saturated Fat 11g • Cholesterol 65mg • Sodium 1,610mg • Total Carbohydrate 39g • Dietary Fiber 6g • Sugars 9g • Protein 24g.
DIETARY EXCHANGES: 2-1/2 Starch • 2-1/2 Other Carbohydrate • 2-1/2 Lean Meat • 2 Fat.

hawaiian sausage
and rice bake

cheddar potatoes with ham and beans

meatball stroganoff biscuit casserole

PREP TIME: 15 MINUTES
READY IN: 45 MINUTES
SERVINGS: 4

1 (12 oz.) package frozen cooked Swedish-style meatballs, thawed

1 (12 oz.) jar beef gravy

1 (4.5 oz.) jar Green Giant® Sliced Mushrooms, drained

1/2 cup frozen pearl onions, thawed

1/2 cup sour cream

2 teaspoons Worcestershire sauce

4 Pillsbury® Oven Baked Frozen Buttermilk Biscuits (from 25 oz. bag)

1 tablespoon chopped fresh parsley, if desired

1 Heat oven to 375°F. Spray 8-inch square (2-quart) glass baking dish with nonstick cooking spray. In medium microwavable bowl, microwave meatballs on Medium 2 to 4 minutes or until thawed.

2 In 8-inch saucepan, mix thawed meatballs and remaining ingredients except biscuits and parsley. Cook over medium-high heat 5 to 8 minutes, stirring frequently, until mixture is bubbly and thoroughly heated.

3 Pour mixture into baking dish. Arrange frozen biscuits over top.

4 Bake 25 to 30 minutes or until biscuits are deep golden brown and filling is bubbly. Sprinkle individual servings with parsley.

HIGH ALTITUDE (3500-6500 FT): Bake at 375°F 30 to 35 minutes.

NUTRITIONAL INFORMATION PER SERVING: Calories 510 • Total Fat 28g • Saturated Fat 11g • Trans Fat 5g • Cholesterol 110mg • Sodium 1,390mg • Total Carbohydrate 40g • Dietary Fiber 2g • Sugars 7g • Protein 26g.
DIETARY EXCHANGES: 2 Starch • 1/2 Other Carbohydrate • 3 Lean Meat • 3-1/2 Fat.

oven-braised beef short ribs

PREP TIME: 20 MINUTES
READY IN: 2 HOURS 50 MINUTES
SERVINGS: 6

3-1/2 to 4 lb. beef short ribs, trimmed of fat

1 (14.5 oz.) can diced tomatoes, undrained

1/2 cup beef broth

1/2 cup Zinfandel wine or cranberry juice

1/4 cup Pillsbury BEST® All-Purpose Flour

1/4 cup chili sauce

1/2 teaspoon dried thyme leaves

1/2 teaspoon dried marjoram leaves

1/2 teaspoon salt

1/2 teaspoon garlic-pepper blend

2 cups fresh baby carrots

1 medium onion, halved, thinly sliced

1 Heat oven to 325°F. Spray 12-inch nonstick skillet with nonstick cooking spray. Heat over medium-high heat until hot. Add short ribs; cook 6 to 8 minutes or until browned on all sides.

2 In ungreased 13x9-inch (3-quart) glass baking dish, combine tomatoes, broth, wine, flour, chili sauce, thyme, marjoram, salt and garlic-pepper blend; mix well. Add browned ribs, carrots and onion; stir gently to mix. (Baking dish will be full.) Cover with foil.

3 Bake covered at 325°F for 2 hours.

4 Uncover baking dish; bake an additional 20 to 30 minutes or until ribs are tender and liquid is slightly thickened.

HIGH ALTITUDE (3500-6500 FT): Bake covered at 350°F for 2 hours. Uncover baking dish; bake an additional 30 to 40 minutes.

NUTRITIONAL INFORMATION PER SERVING: Calories 285 • Total Fat 15g • Saturated Fat 6g • Cholesterol 60mg • Sodium 580mg • Total Carbohydrate 16g • Dietary Fiber 2g • Sugars 8g • Protein 22g.
DIETARY EXCHANGES: 1 Starch • 1 Vegetable • 2-1/2 Medium-Fat Meat • 1/2 Fat.

chili dog casserole

PREP TIME: 20 MINUTES
READY IN: 45 MINUTES
SERVINGS: 8

CASSEROLE

2 (15 oz.) cans chili without beans

1 (16 oz.) package miniature hot dogs

8 oz. pasteurized prepared cheese product, cut up

1 cup Old El Paso® Thick 'n Chunky Salsa

TOPPING

1 (11.5 oz.) can Pillsbury® Refrigerated Cornbread Twists

1/2 teaspoon chili powder

1 Heat oven to 350°F. Spray 13x9-inch (3-quart) glass baking dish with nonstick cooking spray. In Dutch oven or large saucepan, combine all casserole ingredients. Cook over medium heat until cheese is melted and mixture is bubbly, stirring frequently. Spoon into sprayed baking dish.

2 Separate dough into 16 strips. Gently twist each strip; arrange over hot chili mixture. Sprinkle twists with chili powder.

3 Bake at 375°F for 20 to 25 minutes or until cornbread twists are deep golden brown.

NUTRITIONAL INFORMATION PER SERVING: Calories 510 • Total Fat 32g • Saturated Fat 12g • Cholesterol 60mg • Sodium 2,010mg • Total Carbohydrate 33g • Dietary Fiber 2g • Sugars 10g • Protein 22g.
DIETARY EXCHANGES: 1-1/2 Starch • 1/2 Fruit • 2 Other Carbohydrate • 2-1/2 High-Fat Meat • 2 Fat.

grilled chicken and tortellini with red pepper cream

READY IN: 30 MINUTES
SERVINGS: 4

- 1 (9 oz.) package refrigerated cheese-filled tortellini
- 2 cups Green Giant Select® Frozen Broccoli Florets, large pieces cut up
- 1/3 cup drained roasted red bell peppers (from a jar)
- 1 (10 oz.) container refrigerated Alfredo sauce
- 1 (6 oz.) package refrigerated grilled chicken breast strips
- 2 tablespoons diced roasted red bell peppers (from a jar)
- 2 tablespoons butter, melted
- 1/4 cup Progresso® Italian Style Bread Crumbs

1 Cook tortellini and broccoli as directed on tortellini package. Drain; return tortellini and broccoli to saucepan.

2 Meanwhile, puree 1/3 cup roasted peppers in blender. Add the Alfredo sauce; blend until mixed.

3 Add Alfredo sauce mixture, chicken and 2 tablespoons roasted peppers to tortellini and broccoli in saucepan; mix well. Cook and stir over medium heat for 2 to 3 minutes or until thoroughly heated, stirring occasionally. Spoon into ungreased shallow 1- to 1-1/2-quart casserole. In small bowl, combine butter and bread crumbs; mix well. Sprinkle over top.

4 Broil 4 to 6 inches from heat for 1 to 2 minutes or until topping is golden brown.

NUTRITIONAL INFORMATION PER SERVING:
Calories 490 • Total Fat 23g • Saturated Fat 14g • Cholesterol 115mg • Sodium 990mg • Total Carbohydrate 46g • Dietary Fiber 3g • Sugars 5g • Protein 25g.
DIETARY EXCHANGES: 2-1/2 Starch • 2-1/2 Other Carbohydrate • 1 Vegetable • 2 Very Lean Meat • 4 Fat.

TIP: You can use a food processor with a metal blade to puree the red peppers; combine them with the Alfredo sauce.

tater nugget hot dish

PREP TIME: 20 MINUTES
READY IN: 1 HOUR 10 MINUTES
SERVINGS: 6

- 1 lb. lean (at least 80%) ground beef
- 3/4 cup chopped onions (1 medium)
- 1/2 cup chopped celery (1 medium stalk)
- 1 (10-3/4 oz.) can condensed cream of mushroom soup
- 1 (10-3/4 oz.) can condensed cream of chicken soup
- 1 cup Green Giant® Frozen Cut Green Beans (from 1 lb. bag), thawed
- 1/8 teaspoon garlic powder
- 1/8 teaspoon pepper
- 1 (16 oz.) bag frozen potato nuggets (4 cups)

1 Heat oven to 375°F. In 10-inch nonstick skillet, cook ground beef, onion and celery over medium heat, stirring frequently, until beef is thoroughly cooked; drain.

2 Stir in both soups, the green beans, garlic powder and pepper; spoon into ungreased 2-quart casserole. Top with potato nuggets.

3 Bake 40 to 50 minutes or until the mixture is bubbly and the potato nuggets are golden brown.

HIGH ALTITUDE (3500-6500 FT):
After stirring in both soups, the green beans, garlic powder and pepper, cook until thoroughly heated before spooning into baking dish.

NUTRITIONAL INFORMATION PER SERVING:
Calories 425 • Total Fat 23g • Saturated Fat 9g • Cholesterol 50mg • Sodium 1,330mg • Total Carbohydrate 35g • Dietary Fiber 3g • Sugars 4g • Protein 20g.
DIETARY EXCHANGES: 2 Starch • 2 Medium-Fat Meat • 2-1/2 Fat.

oven-barbecue swiss steak

PREP TIME: 10 MINUTES
READY IN: 1 HOUR 40 MINUTES
SERVINGS: 6

1 (14.5 oz.) can diced tomatoes, undrained

1 (12 oz.) jar beef gravy

1/2 cup barbecue sauce

1 cup Green Giant® Niblets® Frozen Corn

1 medium onion, cut into thin wedges

1-1/2 lb. boneless beef round steak, cut into serving-sized pieces

2 tablespoons chopped fresh parsley

6 cups hot mashed potatoes

1 Heat oven to 325°F. In ungreased 13x9-inch (3-quart) glass baking dish, combine tomatoes, gravy and barbecue sauce; blend well. Add corn and onion; mix well. Place beef pieces in mixture; spoon mixture over beef. Cover mixture with foil.

2 Bake covered at 325°F for 1 hour 30 minutes or until beef is fork-tender. Sprinkle with parsley. To serve, spoon mashed potatoes into individual shallow bowls. Top each with beef and vegetable mixture.

HIGH ALTITUDE (3500-6500 FT): Use thinly cut boneless beef round steak. Bake at 350°F for 2 hours 45 minutes.

NUTRITIONAL INFORMATION PER SERVING: Calories 470 • Total Fat 16g • Saturated Fat 4g • Cholesterol 65mg • Sodium 1,100mg • Total Carbohydrate 56g • Dietary Fiber 5g • Sugars 12g • Protein 30g. **DIETARY EXCHANGES:** 3-1/2 Starch • 3 Lean Meat • 1 Fat.

ratatouille-stuffed shells

PREP TIME: 40 MINUTES
READY IN: 1 HOUR 20 MINUTES
SERVINGS: 4

12 uncooked jumbo pasta shells

1 tablespoon olive oil

1-1/2 cups frozen bell pepper and onion stir fry

2 garlic cloves, minced

1-1/2 cups diced eggplant

1 small zucchini, diced

1/2 cup sliced oil and herb-packed sun-dried tomatoes with 1 tablespoon of the oil

1 (2.25 oz.) can sliced ripe olives, drained

1 (14 or 15 oz.) jar tomato pasta sauce

1 cup shredded 6-cheese Italian cheese blend (4 oz.)

1 Heat oven to 350°F. Spray 11x7-inch (2-quart) glass baking dish with nonstick cooking spray. Cook pasta shells to desired doneness as directed on package. Drain; cover shells to keep warm.

2 Meanwhile, heat olive oil in large skillet over medium heat until hot. Add bell pepper and onion stir fry and garlic; cook and stir 2 to 3 minutes or until crisp-tender. Add eggplant and zucchini; cook and stir 3 minutes.

3 Stir in tomatoes with tomato oil, olives and 1/4 cup of the pasta sauce. Cook until thoroughly heated, stirring frequently. Stir in 1/2 cup of the cheese.

4 Fill each cooked pasta shell with about 1/4 cup vegetable mixture. Place in sprayed baking dish. Spoon remaining pasta sauce over shells. Cover with foil.

5 Bake at 350°F for 30 minutes. Uncover baking dish; sprinkle with remaining cheese. Bake uncovered an additional 5 to 10 minutes or until bubbly and the cheese is melted.

NUTRITIONAL INFORMATION PER SERVING:
Calories 435 • Total Fat 22g • Saturated Fat 6g • Cholesterol 25mg • Sodium 890mg • Total Carbohydrate 51g • Dietary Fiber 5g • Sugars 13g • Protein 13g.
DIETARY EXCHANGES: 3 Starch • 3 Other Carbohydrate • 1 Vegetable • 1/2 High-Fat Meat • 3-1/2 Fat.

overnight cheesy chicken casserole

PREP TIME: 15 MINUTES
READY IN: 9 HOURS 25 MINUTES
SERVINGS: 4

6 oz. uncooked mini lasagna noodles (3 cups)

1-1/4 cups water

1 cup Green Giant® Niblets® Frozen Corn

1/2 cup sliced green onions

1 Italian plum tomato, chopped (1/2 cup)

1/4 cup chopped fresh cilantro

1/4 cup sliced ripe olives

1 (16 oz.) jar double Cheddar cheese pasta sauce

1 (6 oz.) package refrigerated grilled chicken strips (1-1/2 cups)

1 cup shredded colby-Monterey Jack cheese blend (4 oz.)

1 Spray 12x8-inch (2-quart) glass baking dish with nonstick cooking spray. In large bowl, combine all ingredients except cheese; mix well to coat all uncooked noodles with sauce. Spoon into sprayed baking dish. Cover tightly with foil. Refrigerate at least 8 hours or overnight.

2 Heat oven to 350°F. Bake covered 1 hour. Uncover; sprinkle with cheese. Bake uncovered an additional 5 to 10 minutes or until cheese is melted and casserole is bubbly.

NUTRITIONAL INFORMATION PER SERVING:
Calories 430 • Total Fat 14g • Saturated Fat 6g • Cholesterol 50mg • Sodium 830mg • Total Carbohydrate 50g • Dietary Fiber 5g • Sugars 5g • Protein 25g.
DIETARY EXCHANGES: 3-1/2 Starch • 3-1/2 Other Carbohydrate • 2 Very Lean Meat • 2 Fat.

wild rice and beef casserole

PREP TIME: 15 MINUTES
READY IN: 55 MINUTES
SERVINGS: 4

1 (6.2 oz.) package fast-cooking long-grain and wild rice mix (with seasoning packet)

1 lb. lean ground beef

1 (10-3/4 oz.) can condensed tomato soup

1/4 cup milk

1/4 teaspoon pepper

1 cup shredded Cheddar cheese (4 oz.)

1 Heat oven to 350°F. Spray 2-quart casserole with nonstick cooking spray. Prepare rice mix as directed on package, omitting margarine.

2 Meanwhile, brown ground beef in medium skillet over medium-high heat until thoroughly cooked, stirring frequently. Drain. Add soup, milk, pepper and cooked rice mixture; mix well. Spoon into sprayed casserole. Cover.

3 Bake at 350°F for 30 minutes. Uncover; sprinkle with cheese. Bake uncovered an additional 5 to 10 minutes or until cheese is melted.

NUTRITIONAL INFORMATION PER SERVING:
Calories 540 • Total Fat 26g • Saturated Fat 12g • Cholesterol 100mg • Sodium 1,150mg • Total Carbohydrate 43g • Dietary Fiber 1g • Sugars 6g • Protein 33g.
DIETARY EXCHANGES: 3 Starch • 3 Other Carbohydrate • 3-1/2 Medium-Fat Meat • 1 Fat.

quick california casserole

PREP TIME: 35 MINUTES
READY IN: 1 HOUR
SERVINGS: 8

CASSEROLE

1 (10-3/4 oz.) condensed cream of onion soup

2 cups water

1 (15 oz.) jar small onions, undrained

1/3 cup Pillsbury BEST® All-Purpose Flour

1/2 teaspoon seasoned pepper blend

2 lb. beef strips for stir frying

3 tablespoons butter

DUMPLINGS

2 tablespoons butter, melted

1/2 cup Progresso® Plain Bread Crumbs

1 (12 oz.) can Pillsbury® Golden Layers® Refrigerated Biscuits

SAUCE

1/4 cup half-and-half

1/4 cup cream cheese spread with herbs (from 8 oz. container)

1 Heat oven to 375°F. Spray 13x9-inch (3-quart) glass baking dish or 3-quart casserole with nonstick cooking spray. In medium bowl, combine soup and water; blend well. Stir in onions. Set aside.

2 In large bowl or plastic bag, combine flour and seasoned pepper blend; mix well. Add beef strips; shake to coat well with flour mixture.

3 Melt 3 tablespoons butter in large wok or 12-inch skillet over medium-high heat. Add beef; cook and stir until browned. Add soup mixture; bring to a boil. Spoon beef mixture into sprayed baking dish.

4 In small bowl, combine 2 tablespoons butter and bread crumbs; mix well. Separate dough into 10 biscuits; cut each in half. Gently roll each biscuit piece in crumb mixture, rolling to coat well. Arrange biscuit pieces over hot beef mixture.

5 Bake at 375°F for 19 to 23 minutes or until biscuits are deep golden brown.

6 Meanwhile, in small saucepan, combine sauce ingredients; blend well. Cook over medium heat until bubbly and slightly thickened, stirring frequently. Serve sauce with casserole. Sprinkle casserole with chopped chives, if desired.

NUTRITIONAL INFORMATION PER SERVING:
Calories 450 • Total Fat 23g • Saturated Fat 10g • Cholesterol 95mg • Sodium 1,160mg • Total Carbohydrate 33g • Dietary Fiber 2g • Sugars 4g • Protein 27g.
DIETARY EXCHANGES: 2 Starch • 2 Other Carbohydrate • 3 Lean Meat • 2-1/2 Fat.

one-dish dinners

Whether baked to perfection in the oven or quickly sauteed on the stovetop, meal-in-one favorites take center stage in every busy cook's recipe book. Mix up your supper-time routine by trying one tonight. Pairing tender meats with colorful vegetables, filling pasta, versatile rice or flaky biscuit toppings, the must-try sensations found here take the guesswork out of dinner planning each and every time.

Mediterranean
Meatball Supper
Skillet
page 46

Oven-Roasted
Pork Chops and
Vegetables
page 44

Southern
Turkey-Stuffing
Bake
page 40

southwestern
turkey-tater casserole
page 50

bow-thai chicken

READY IN: 25 MINUTES
SERVINGS: 4

Pillsbury
Bake-Off

Mille Meehan
Richmond, VA

3 cups uncooked bow tie
   pasta (7-1/2 oz.)

1/8 teaspoon curry powder

2 teaspoons soy sauce

1/2 to 3/4 lb. chicken breast
   strips for stir frying, cut in
   half crosswise

1 tablespoon oil

1 (1 lb. 5 oz.) package
   Green Giant® Create A
   Meal!® Frozen Szechuan
   Stir Fry Meal Starter

2 teaspoons lime juice

1 teaspoon peanut butter

3/4 cup purchased Alfredo
   sauce

3 tablespoons coconut

3 green onions, sliced

   Lime wedges

1 Cook pasta in large saucepan to desired doneness as directed on package. Drain; return to saucepan. Cover to keep warm.

2 Meanwhile, in medium bowl, combine curry powder and soy sauce. Add chicken strips; toss to coat. Heat oil in large skillet or wok over medium-high heat until hot. Add chicken; cook and stir 4 to 5 minutes or until no longer pink in center.

3 Add frozen sauce and vegetables from meal starter. Bring to a boil. Reduce heat; cover and cook 6 to 9 minutes or until vegetables are crisp-tender, stirring frequently. Stir in lime juice and peanut butter.

4 Add Alfredo sauce to cooked pasta; toss to coat. Spoon vegetable mixture over pasta mixture; stir well. Spoon onto individual serving plates. Sprinkle with coconut, onions and peanuts from packet. Garnish each serving with a lime wedge.

NUTRITIONAL INFORMATION PER SERVING:
Calories 560 • Total Fat 19g • Saturated Fat 8g • Cholesterol 75mg • Sodium 1,540mg • Total Carbohydrate 64g • Dietary Fiber 5g • Sugars 14g • Protein 33g.
DIETARY EXCHANGES: 3 Starch • 1 Fruit • 4 Other Carbohydrate • 1 Vegetable • 3 Very Lean Meat • 3 Fat.

harvest pork, sweet potatoes and rice

PREP TIME: 20 MINUTES
READY IN: 1 HOUR 20 MINUTES
SERVINGS: 6

1 lb. boneless pork loin, cut into 1/2- to 1-inch pieces

1 medium red onion, cut into thin wedges (1 cup)

2 sweet potatoes, peeled, cubed (3 cups)

1-1/2 cups Green Giant® Frozen Cut Green Beans (from 1 lb. bag)

1 cup uncooked regular long-grain white rice

3 teaspoons curry powder

1/2 teaspoon salt

1/4 teaspoon ground ginger

2 cups apple juice

2 tablespoons real maple syrup

1 Heat oven to 350°F. Spray 13x9-inch (3-quart) glass baking dish with nonstick cooking spray.

2 In 10-inch nonstick skillet, cook pork and onion over medium-high heat 5 minutes, stirring occasionally, until pork is no longer pink in center.

3 In baking dish, mix pork mixture and all remaining ingredients. Cover with foil.

4 Bake 1 hour or until the rice is tender.

NUTRITIONAL INFORMATION PER SERVING:
Calories 375 • Total Fat 7g • Saturated Fat 2g • Cholesterol 50mg • Sodium 240mg • Total Carbohydrate 57g • Dietary Fiber 3g • Sugars 21g • Protein 21g.
DIETARY EXCHANGES: 2 Starch • 2 Other Carbohydrate • 2 Lean Meat.

chicken, spinach and rice supper

READY IN: 40 MINUTES
SERVINGS: 4

1 tablespoon olive oil

4 medium green onions, chopped (1/4 cup)

1 cup uncooked regular long-grain white rice

1 (14.5 oz.) can diced tomatoes with Italian-style herbs, undrained

1 (14 oz.) can chicken broth

1/4 teaspoon pepper

2 cups cut-up deli rotisserie chicken (from 2- to 2-1/2 lb. chicken)

2-1/2 cups Green Giant® Frozen Cut Leaf Spinach (half of 1 lb. bag)

1 In 12-inch skillet, heat oil over medium heat. Add onions; cook 1 to 2 minutes, stirring frequently, until tender.

2 Stir in rice, tomatoes, broth and pepper. Heat to boiling over high heat. Reduce heat to low; cover and simmer 15 minutes, stirring occasionally, until most of liquid is absorbed.

3 Stir in chicken and spinach. Cook uncovered 6 to 8 minutes longer or until thoroughly heated, stirring frequently to prevent sticking.

HIGH ALTITUDE (3500-6500 FT):
In Step 2, add 1/2 cup water to rice mixture; simmer 25 minutes. In Step 3, cook over medium heat.

NUTRITIONAL INFORMATION PER SERVING:
Calories 410 • Total Fat 10g • Saturated Fat 2g • Trans Fat 0g • Cholesterol 60mg • Sodium 960mg • Total Carbohydrate 53g • Dietary Fiber 3g • Sugars 6g • Protein 28g.
DIETARY EXCHANGES: 3 Starch • 1 Vegetable • 2-1/2 Lean Meat • 1/2 Fat.

southern turkey-stuffing bake

PREP TIME: 15 MINUTES
READY IN: 1 HOUR 30 MINUTES
SERVINGS: 6

1	cup chopped onions (2 medium)
4	slices bacon, cut into small pieces
4	cups seasoned cornbread stuffing mix
1-1/2	cups water
2	cups Green Giant® Frozen Cut Broccoli
1/2	teaspoon dried thyme leaves
1/2	teaspoon seasoned salt
1/2	teaspoon garlic powder
1/8	teaspoon ground red pepper (cayenne)
2	(3/4 lb.) turkey breast tenderloins

1 Heat oven to 350°F. Spray 11x7-inch (2-quart) glass baking dish with nonstick cooking spray. In Dutch oven, cook onions and bacon over medium-high heat for 4 to 5 minutes or until bacon is browned and onions are tender, stirring occasionally. Remove from heat.

2 Add cornbread mix and water; mix well. Stir in broccoli. Spread in sprayed baking dish.

3 In small bowl, combine thyme, seasoned salt, garlic powder and ground red pepper; mix well. Rub on turkey tenderloins. Arrange over stuffing mixture; press into stuffing slightly. Cover with foil.

4 Bake covered at 350°F for 1 hour.

5 Uncover baking dish; bake an additional 10 to 15 minutes or until turkey is no longer pink in center. To serve, cut turkey into crosswise slices.

HIGH ALTITUDE (3500-6500 FT):
Bake covered at 350°F for 1 hour 15 minutes. Uncover baking dish; bake an additional 15 minutes.

NUTRITIONAL INFORMATION PER SERVING:
Calories 355 • Total Fat 5g • Saturated Fat 1g • Cholesterol 80mg • Sodium 1,000mg • Total Carbohydrate 42g • Dietary Fiber 3g • Sugars 4g • Protein 35g.
DIETARY EXCHANGES: 3 Starch • 3-1/2 Very Lean Meat • 1/2 Fat.

chicken with pineapple and brown rice

PREP TIME: 10 MINUTES
READY IN: 1 HOUR 35 MINUTES
SERVINGS: 4

- 1 cup uncooked regular brown rice
- 1 (14-1/2 oz.) can ready-to-serve chicken broth
- 1 (8 oz.) can pineapple tidbits in unsweetened juice, undrained
- 1/2 cup chopped green bell pepper
- 1/2 cup chopped carrot
- 1/4 cup chopped cashews
- 1/2 teaspoon ginger
- 4 boneless skinless chicken breast halves
- 2 tablespoons purchased teriyaki baste and glaze

1 Heat oven to 375°F. Spray 12x8-inch (2-quart) glass baking dish with nonstick cooking spray. In sprayed baking dish, combine rice and broth; mix well. Cover with foil. Bake at 375°F for 45 minutes.

2 Remove rice from oven; uncover. Add pineapple with liquid, bell pepper, carrot, cashews and ginger; mix well. Place chicken over rice mixture; press slightly into rice. Brush the chicken with teriyaki baste and glaze.

3 Return to oven; bake uncovered an additional 30 to 40 minutes or until chicken is fork-tender, its juices run clear and rice is tender.

NUTRITIONAL INFORMATION PER SERVING:
Calories 450 • Total Fat 10g • Saturated Fat 2g • Cholesterol 75mg • Sodium 670mg • Total Carbohydrate 54g • Dietary Fiber 3g • Sugars 12g • Protein 35g.
DIETARY EXCHANGES: 2-1/2 Starch • 1 Fruit • 3-1/2 Other Carbohydrate • 4 Very Lean Meat • 1 Fat.

tuscan-style pork 'n pasta

READY IN: 30 MINUTES
SERVINGS: 4

- 3/4 lb. pork tenderloin, cut into 1/2-inch pieces
- 1 (1 lb.) package Green Giant® Pasta Accents® Garlic Frozen Vegetables with Pasta
- 1/4 to 1/2 teaspoon crushed red pepper flakes
- 1 (15.5 oz.) can great northern beans, undrained
- 3 Italian plum tomatoes, seeded, chopped
- 1/4 cup grated fresh Parmesan cheese (1 oz.)
- 2 tablespoons chopped fresh basil or parsley

1 Spray large nonstick skillet with nonstick cooking spray. Heat over medium-high heat until hot. Add pork; cook 10 to 12 minutes or until browned, stirring frequently.

2 Add frozen vegetables with pasta and pepper flakes; mix well. Bring to a boil. Reduce heat to medium; cover and cook 7 to 8 minutes or until pork is no longer pink in center and vegetables are crisp-tender, stirring occasionally.

3 Add beans and tomatoes; cover and cook 1 minute or until thoroughly heated. Sprinkle with cheese and basil. Garnish with fresh sprig of basil, if desired.

NUTRITIONAL INFORMATION PER SERVING:
Calories 430 • Total Fat 12g • Saturated Fat 6g • Cholesterol 70mg • Sodium 580mg • Total Carbohydrate 52g • Dietary Fiber 9g • Sugars 5g • Protein 38g.
DIETARY EXCHANGES: 3 Starch • 3 Other Carbohydrate • 1 Vegetable • 4 Lean Meat.

pork diane skillet supper

PREP TIME: 35 MINUTES
READY IN: 50 MINUTES
SERVINGS: 4

2 tablespoons butter or margarine

1 lb. pork tenderloins, cut crosswise into 1/4-inch slices

1 (14 oz.) can chicken broth

2 teaspoons Worcestershire sauce

1/4 teaspoon salt

1/8 teaspoon pepper

8 small red potatoes, quartered

1/2 cup sliced green onions

1 cup sliced fresh mushrooms

2 tablespoons Pillsbury BEST® All-Purpose Flour

1 Melt butter in 12-inch skillet or Dutch oven over medium-high heat. Add pork slices; cook 3 to 5 minutes or until browned on both sides. Remove pork from skillet; set aside.

2 Reserve 1/4 cup of the broth in 1-cup measuring cup or small bowl. Add remaining broth, Worcestershire sauce, salt, pepper and potatoes to skillet. Bring to a boil. Reduce heat; cover and simmer 13 to 17 minutes or until potatoes are tender.

3 Reserve 2 tablespoons of the onions for the garnish. Stir the remaining onions, mushrooms and pork slices into the potatoes. Cover and simmer an additional 5 minutes or until the pork is no longer pink in center.

4 Add flour to reserved broth in measuring cup; blend until smooth. Gradually stir into pork mixture. Cook over medium-high heat for 2 to 3 minutes or until mixture is bubbly and thickened, stirring constantly. Sprinkle with reserved onions.

HIGH ALTITUDE (3500-6500 FT): Increase cook time of pork slices to 7 to 9 minutes. Add 1/4 cup water when adding broth, Worcestershire sauce, salt, pepper and potatoes to skillet; increase simmer time covered to 19 to 22 minutes.

NUTRITIONAL INFORMATION PER SERVING: Calories 425 • Total Fat 11g • Saturated Fat 5g • Cholesterol 85mg • Sodium 730mg • Total Carbohydrate 49g • Dietary Fiber 4g • Sugars 3g • Protein 33g.
DIETARY EXCHANGES: 3 Starch • 3-1/2 Very Lean Meat • 1-1/2 Fat.

mexican meatball stew

PREP TIME: 10 MINUTES
READY IN: 1 HOUR 25 MINUTES
SERVINGS: 6

1 cup frozen pearl onions (from 16 oz. bag), thawed

1 (16 oz.) bag frozen cooked meatballs (about 32 meatballs), thawed

1 (15 oz.) can black beans, drained, rinsed

1 (11 oz.) can Green Giant® Mexicorn® Whole Kernel Corn, Red and Green Peppers, drained

2 (14.5 oz.) cans diced tomatoes with mild green chiles, undrained

1 (12 oz.) can vegetable juice

1 (1.25 oz.) envelope Old El Paso® Taco Seasoning Mix

1 cup shredded Mexican cheese blend (4 oz.)

1/2 cup sour cream

1/2 cup guacamole

1 Heat oven to 375°F. In 3-quart Dutch oven or casserole, mix onions, meatballs, beans, corn, tomatoes, vegetable juice and the taco seasoning mix; cover.

2 Bake 1 hour 5 minutes to 1 hour 15 minutes or until mixture is hot, bubbly and thickened. Sprinkle individual servings with cheese; top each with sour cream and guacamole.

NUTRITIONAL INFORMATION PER SERVING: Calories 545 • Total Fat 27g • Saturated Fat 12g • Cholesterol 110mg • Sodium 1,570mg • Total Carbohydrate 55g • Dietary Fiber 9g • Sugars 15g • Protein 30g.
DIETARY EXCHANGES: 2-1/2 Starch • 1 Vegetable • 3 Medium-Fat Meat • 2 Fat.

TIP: For an easy supper accompaniment, serve warm flour tortillas or golden corn bread twists with the meatball stew. Glasses of cold lemonade lend a refreshing touch.

pork diane skillet supper

oven-roasted pork chops and vegetables

PREP TIME: 15 MINUTES
READY IN: 1 HOUR 10 MINUTES
SERVINGS: 4

2 tablespoons frozen apple juice concentrate

1 tablespoon olive or vegetable oil

1 tablespoon Dijon mustard

1/2 teaspoon seasoned salt

1/2 teaspoon dried marjoram leaves

1/2 teaspoon garlic-pepper blend

4 bone-in center-cut pork chops (1/2 inch thick), trimmed of fat

1-1/2 cups fresh baby carrots

1 medium red onion, cut into 8 wedges

2 cups Green Giant Select® Frozen Whole Green Beans

1 Heat oven to 425°F. Spray 15x10x1-inch baking pan with nonstick cooking spray. In large bowl, combine apple juice concentrate, oil, mustard, seasoned salt, marjoram and garlic-pepper blend; mix well.

2 Brush pork chops with about half of oil mixture; set pork aside. Add carrots and onion to remaining oil mixture; toss to coat. Arrange vegetables in sprayed pan. Bake at 425°F for 15 minutes.

3 Remove vegetables from oven. Add green beans; stir gently to combine. Arrange pork chops on vegetable mixture.

4 Return to oven; bake an additional 30 to 40 minutes or until pork chops are no longer pink in center and vegetables are fork-tender. Serve pork and vegetables with pan drippings.

NUTRITIONAL INFORMATION PER SERVING:
Calories 240 • Total Fat 11g • Saturated Fat 3g • Cholesterol 60mg • Sodium 400mg • Total Carbohydrate 13g • Dietary Fiber 3g • Sugars 8g • Protein 22g.
DIETARY EXCHANGES: 1/2 Fruit • 1/2 Other Carbohydrate • 1 Vegetable • 3 Lean Meat • 1/2 Fat.

easy chicken-macaroni with fire-roasted tomato sauce

PREP TIME: 15 MINUTES
READY IN: 50 MINUTES
SERVINGS: 5

2 (14.5 oz.) cans crushed fire-roasted tomatoes, undrained

3/4 cup water

2 cups uncooked elbow macaroni (6 oz.)

1/2 cup roasted red bell peppers (from a jar), chopped

1/2 cup sliced green onions (8 medium)

1/4 cup sliced ripe olives

1 (9 oz.) package refrigerated grilled chicken strips, cut into small pieces

1-1/2 cups shredded mozzarella cheese (6 oz.)

1 Heat oven to 350°F. Spray 13x9-inch (3-quart) glass baking dish with nonstick cooking spray. In large bowl, mix tomatoes, water and uncooked macaroni. Stir in all remaining ingredients except cheese; spoon into baking dish. Cover tightly with foil.

2 Bake 20 to 25 minutes or until noodles are tender and mixture is hot and bubbly. Uncover; sprinkle with cheese. Bake uncovered 5 to 10 minutes longer or until cheese is melted.

HIGH ALTITUDE (3500-6000 FT):
Heat oven to 375°F. Increase water to 1-1/4 cups. Bake 35 to 40 minutes. Continue as directed above.

NUTRITIONAL INFORMATION PER SERVING:
Calories 360 • Total Fat 10g • Saturated 5g • Cholesterol 60mg • Sodium 690mg • Total Carbohydrate 37g • Dietary Fiber 3g • Sugars 6g • Protein 31g.
DIETARY EXCHANGES: 2 Starch • 1 Vegetable • 3 Lean Meat.

linguine with creamy chicken primavera

READY IN: 30 MINUTES
SERVINGS: 6

6 oz. uncooked linguine or fettuccine

1 lb. chicken breast strips for stir frying

1 cup sliced fresh mushrooms

1 cup fresh baby carrots, quartered lengthwise

1/2 medium red bell pepper, cut into thin bite-sized strips

1 (9 oz.) package Green Giant® Frozen Sugar Snap Peas

1/2 cup water

1 (16 oz.) jar Alfredo pasta sauce

1/4 cup dry white wine or milk

3 tablespoons chopped fresh basil

1 Cook linguine as directed on package. Drain; cover to keep warm.

2 Meanwhile, spray 12-inch nonstick skillet with nonstick cooking spray. Heat over medium-high heat until hot. Add chicken; cook 4 to 6 minutes or until chicken is lightly browned and no longer pink in center, stirring frequently.

3 Add mushrooms, carrots, bell pepper, sugar snap peas and water to skillet. Bring to a boil. Reduce heat; cover and simmer 6 to 8 minutes or until vegetables are crisp-tender. Drain; return chicken and vegetables to skillet.

4 Stir in Alfredo sauce, wine and basil. Cook 2 to 4 minutes or until mixture is thoroughly heated, stirring occasionally. Serve chicken mixture over linguine. If desired, sprinkle with shredded fresh Parmesan cheese.

NUTRITIONAL INFORMATION PER SERVING:
Calories 490 • Total Fat 27g • Saturated Fat 16g • Cholesterol 120mg • Sodium 490mg • Total Carbohydrate 34g • Dietary Fiber 3g • Sugars 5g • Protein 28g.
DIETARY EXCHANGES: 2 Starch • 1 Vegetable • 2-1/2 Very Lean Meat • 5 Fat.

mediterranean meatball
supper skillet

sweet 'n sour
pork skillet

mediterranean meatball supper skillet

READY IN: 45 MINUTES
SERVINGS: 4

2 teaspoons olive oil

1 small onion, cut into thin wedges

3/4 cup uncooked regular long-grain white rice

1 medium green bell pepper, cut into 1/2-inch pieces

20 frozen cooked Italian meatballs (about 10 oz.)

1 (2-1/4 oz.) can sliced ripe olives, drained

1-1/2 cups water

1 medium zucchini, halved lengthwise, sliced

1 (14.5 oz.) can diced tomatoes with Italian herbs, undrained

1/2 cup crumbled feta cheese (2 oz.)

1 Heat oil in large skillet over medium-high heat until hot. Add onion; cook 3 to 4 minutes or until crisp-tender, stirring frequently.

2 Add rice, bell pepper, meatballs, olives and water. Bring to a boil. Reduce heat; cover and simmer 20 minutes, stirring once halfway through cooking.

3 Stir in zucchini and tomatoes. Cover; cook an additional 8 to 10 minutes or until zucchini is tender and liquid is absorbed, stirring occasionally. Sprinkle with cheese.

HIGH ALTITUDE (3500-6500 FT): Increase water to 2-1/2 cups. Increase simmer time covered to 30 minutes. After stirring in zucchini and tomatoes, cover and increase cook time to 17 to 19 minutes.

NUTRITIONAL INFORMATION PER SERVING: Calories 460 • Total Fat 20g • Saturated Fat 8g • Cholesterol 90mg • Sodium 870mg • Total Carbohydrate 49g • Dietary Fiber 3g • Sugars 6g • Protein 21g.
DIETARY EXCHANGES: 3 Starch • 1 Vegetable • 1-1/2 Medium-Fat Meat • 2-1/2 Fat.

TIP: Look for frozen meatballs in the grocery store's freezer case; use plain or Italian-seasoned meatballs in this recipe. Cut large meatballs in half or in quarters before use.

sweet 'n sour pork skillet

READY IN: 30 MINUTES
SERVINGS: 4

- 4 oz. uncooked dumpling egg noodles (2-1/2 cups)
- 3 boneless pork loin chops (about 1 lb.), cut into 1/4-inch-thick strips
- 1/2 teaspoon salt
- 1/4 teaspoon pepper
- 2 green onions, cut diagonally into 1/2-inch slices
- 1 (1 lb. 5 oz.) package Green Giant® Create a Meal!® Frozen Sweet & Sour Stir Fry Meal Starter
- 1 cup chow mein noodles

1 Cook noodles in Dutch oven or large saucepan as directed on package. Drain; return to Dutch oven and cover to keep warm.

2 Meanwhile, spray 12-inch nonstick skillet with nonstick cooking spray. Heat over medium-high heat until hot. Sprinkle pork strips with salt and pepper. Add pork and onions to skillet; cook 5 to 7 minutes or until pork is browned, stirring frequently.

3 Add frozen vegetables, contents of pineapple pouch and frozen sauce from packet; mix well. Cover; cook an additional 7 to 10 minutes or until vegetables are crisp-tender, stirring frequently.

4 Add cooked noodles; toss gently to coat. Cook and stir 2 to 3 minutes or until thoroughly heated. Serve topped with chow mein noodles.

HIGH ALTITUDE (3500-6500 FT):
Thaw frozen meal starter before use.

NUTRITIONAL INFORMATION PER SERVING:
Calories 470 • Total Fat 13g • Saturated Fat 4g • Cholesterol 95mg • Sodium 930mg • Total Carbohydrate 58g • Dietary Fiber 3g • Sugars 24g • Protein 30g.
DIETARY EXCHANGES: 3-1/2 Starch • 1 Vegetable • 2-1/2 Lean Meat • 1 Fat.

cheesy broccoli and chicken casserole

PREP TIME: 15 MINUTES
READY IN: 1 HOUR 5 MINUTES
SERVINGS: 4

- 1-1/2 cups shredded reduced-fat Cheddar cheese (6 oz.)
- 1/2 cup chopped red bell pepper (1/2 medium)
- 1/2 cup light mayonnaise
- 1 (10-3/4 oz.) can condensed 98% fat-free cream of celery soup with 30% less sodium
- 1 (8 oz.) can sliced water chestnuts, drained
- 1 (14 oz.) bag Green Giant Select® Frozen Broccoli Florets, thawed, larger pieces cut up
- 2 cups diced cooked chicken

1 Heat oven to 375°F. Spray 13x9-inch (3-quart) glass baking dish with nonstick cooking spray. In large bowl, mix cheese, bell pepper, mayonnaise, soup and water chestnuts. Stir in the broccoli and the chicken; pour into baking dish.

2 Bake 45 to 50 minutes or until hot and bubbly.

NUTRITIONAL INFORMATION PER SERVING:
Calories 405 • Total Fat 19g • Saturated Fat 5g • Cholesterol 80mg • Sodium 970mg • Total Carbohydrate 25g • Dietary Fiber 4g • Sugars 8g • Protein 34g.
DIETARY EXCHANGES: 1-1/2 Starch • 1 Vegetable • 4 Lean Meat • 1 Fat.

dumpling-topped chicken stew

READY IN: 45 MINUTES
SERVINGS: 6

- 2 tablespoons margarine or butter
- 1 lb. boneless skinless chicken breast halves, cubed
- 1 (7.5 oz.) can Pillsbury® Refrigerated Buttermilk Biscuits
- 1 (12 oz.) can PET® Evaporated Skim Milk
- 1 (10-3/4 oz.) can condensed 98% fat-free cream of chicken soup
- 1 (1 lb.) package Green Giant® Frozen Mixed Vegetables
- 1 teaspoon poultry seasoning
- 1/4 teaspoon paprika

1 Melt margarine in Dutch oven over medium-high heat. Add chicken; cook 5 to 8 minutes or until chicken is no longer pink, stirring occasionally.

2 Meanwhile, separate dough into 10 biscuits; cut each biscuit in half. Set biscuits aside.

3 Add milk, soup, vegetables and poultry seasoning to Dutch oven; mix well. Bring to a boil, stirring frequently.

4 Quickly place biscuits in single layer over stew. Sprinkle top of biscuits with paprika. Cover tightly. Reduce heat; simmer 15 to 20 minutes or until the biscuits are light and fluffy.

NUTRITIONAL INFORMATION PER SERVING:
Calories 320 • Total Fat 8g • Saturated Fat 2g • Cholesterol 50mg • Sodium 700mg • Total Carbohydrate 37g • Dietary Fiber 3g • Sugars 10g • Protein 26g.
DIETARY EXCHANGES: 2 Starch • 2 Other Carbohydrate • 1 Vegetable • 2-1/2 Very Lean Meat • 1 Fat.

light tater nugget hot dish

PREP TIME: 20 MINUTES
READY IN: 1 HOUR 5 MINUTES
SERVINGS: 6

- 1 lb. lean ground turkey
- 3/4 cup chopped onions
- 1/2 cup chopped celery
- 1/2 teaspoon garlic powder
- 1/8 teaspoon pepper
- 1 (10-3/4 oz.) can condensed 98% fat-free cream of mushroom soup with 30% less sodium
- 1/3 cup skim milk
- 1 teaspoon chicken-flavor instant bouillon
- 1 (1 lb.) package Green Giant® Frozen Cut Green Beans, thawed
- 2 cups frozen potato nuggets (from 16 oz. pkg.)

1 Heat oven to 375°F. Spray 12x8-inch (2-quart) glass baking dish with nonstick cooking spray.

2 In large skillet, combine ground turkey, onions, celery, garlic powder and pepper. Cook over medium-high heat until turkey is thoroughly cooked. Drain well.

3 Stir in soup, milk, bouillon and green beans. Spoon into sprayed baking dish. Top evenly with potato nuggets.

4 Bake at 375°F for 35 to 45 minutes or until casserole is bubbly and potato nuggets are golden brown.

NUTRITIONAL INFORMATION PER SERVING:
Calories 290 • Total Fat 13g • Saturated Fat 4g • Cholesterol 60mg • Sodium 750mg • Total Carbohydrate 25g • Dietary Fiber 4g • Sugars 6g • Protein 19g.
DIETARY EXCHANGES: 1-1/2 Starch • 1-1/2 Other Carbohydrate • 1 Vegetable • 2 Very Lean Meat • 2 Fat.

spicy pork chops caribbean

PREP TIME: 15 MINUTES
READY IN: 35 MINUTES
SERVINGS: 4

Susan Carroll
Rochester, NY

- 1 (8 oz.) package uncooked yellow rice
- 2-1/2 cups water
- 4 (1/2-inch thick) boneless pork chops
- 1 (3 oz.) package seasoned coating mix for pork
- 1-1/4 cups Green Giant Select® LeSueur® Frozen Baby Sweet Peas
- 2 tablespoons oil
- 1-1/4 cups frozen chopped onions
- 1 cup fresh cilantro leaves
- 2 firm ripe bananas, peeled, thinly sliced
- 2 (4.5 oz.) cans Old El Paso® Chopped Green Chiles
- 1 (7 oz.) jar roasted red bell peppers, drained, coarsely chopped
- 1/2 teaspoon curry powder
- 1/2 teaspoon pumpkin pie spice
- 1/4 to 1 teaspoon crushed red pepper flakes
- 1/4 teaspoon dried shredded orange peel
- 1/3 cup orange juice
  Avocado slices
  Fresh cilantro leaves

1 Heat oven to 425°F. Line 15x10x1-inch baking pan with foil. Cook rice in water as directed on package. Cover to keep warm.

2 Meanwhile, coat pork chops with coating mix as directed on package. Place in foil-lined pan. Bake at 425°F for 15 to 20 minutes or until pork is no longer pink in center.

3 Cook peas as directed on package. Drain; stir into the rice.

4 Heat oil in large skillet over medium heat until hot. Add onions, cilantro and bananas; cook 3 minutes or until bananas are just tender, stirring frequently. Add all remaining ingredients; mix well. Bring to a boil. Reduce heat to low; cook 5 minutes or until thickened, stirring occasionally.

5 Spoon rice mixture onto individual serving plates. Top each with pork chop and banana mixture. If desired, garnish with avocado and additional cilantro.

NUTRITIONAL INFORMATION PER SERVING: Calories 750 • Total Fat 21g • Saturated Fat 6g • Cholesterol 105mg • Sodium 1,000mg • Total Carbohydrate 93g • Dietary Fiber 8g • Sugars 16g • Protein 47g. DIETARY EXCHANGES: 5 Starch • 1 Fruit • 6 Other Carbohydrate • 1 Vegetable • 4-1/2 Very Lean Meat • 2-1/2 Fat.

pork chops with cheesy pasta

READY IN: 35 MINUTES
SERVINGS: 4

4 (4 oz.) boneless pork loin chops

1/2 teaspoon seasoned salt

1 (1.8 oz.) package white sauce mix

2-1/2 cups skim milk

1 (7 oz.) package uncooked elbow macaroni

1-1/2 cups Green Giant® Frozen Cut Green Beans

1/2 cup shredded Cheddar & American cheese blend (2 oz.)

1 Sprinkle pork chops with seasoned salt. Spray 12-inch nonstick skillet with nonstick cooking spray. Heat over medium-high heat until hot. Add pork chops; cook until browned on both sides. Remove from skillet.

2 Add white sauce mix and milk to skillet; mix well. Cook over medium-high heat until mixture boils, stirring constantly. Stir in uncooked macaroni, green beans and cheese; mix well. Place pork chops over mixture.

3 Reduce heat to low; cover and simmer 15 to 20 minutes or until macaroni is tender and pork is no longer pink in center, stirring occasionally.

NUTRITIONAL INFORMATION PER SERVING: Calories 520 • Total Fat 15g • Saturated Fat 6g • Cholesterol 85mg • Sodium 900mg • Total Carbohydrate 54g • Dietary Fiber 3g • Sugars 9g • Protein 42g.
DIETARY EXCHANGES: 3 Starch • 3-1/2 Other Carbohydrate • 1/2 Low-Fat Milk • 4 Lean Meat.

southwestern turkey-tater casserole

PREP TIME: 25 MINUTES
READY IN: 1 HOUR 15 MINUTES
SERVINGS: 6

1 lb. lean ground turkey

2 teaspoons chili powder

1 teaspoon ground cumin

2 cups Green Giant® Frozen Cut Green Beans (from 1 lb. bag)

1 (18 oz.) can Progresso® Vegetable Classics Creamy Mushroom Soup

1 (14.5 oz.) can diced tomatoes, drained

1 (11 oz.) can Green Giant® Mexicorn® Whole Kernel Corn with Red and Green Peppers

3 cups frozen potato nuggets (from 32 oz. bag)

1 Heat oven to 350°F. In 12-inch skillet, cook ground turkey over medium heat, stirring frequently, until no longer pink; drain. Stir in chili powder and cumin. Spoon into ungreased 13x9-inch (3-quart) glass baking dish.

2 Gently stir in green beans, soup, tomatoes and corn. Top with potato nuggets in single layer.

3 Bake uncovered 45 to 50 minutes or until bubbly around edges and potatoes are golden brown.

NUTRITIONAL INFORMATION PER SERVING: Calories 420 • Total Fat 20g • Saturated Fat 8g • Trans Fat 2.5g • Cholesterol 60mg • Sodium 980mg • Total Carbohydrate 38g • Dietary Fiber 5g • Sugars 6g • Protein 21g.
DIETARY EXCHANGES: 2 Starch • 1 Vegetable • 2 Medium-Fat Meat • 2 Fat.

chicken and black bean bake

PREP TIME: 15 MINUTES
READY IN: 55 MINUTES
SERVINGS: 8

Janet Mercer
Winter Park, FL

1 (12 oz.) package bulk hot pork sausage

3/4 cup Pillsbury BEST® Self Rising Flour

3 cups shredded Cheddar cheese (12 oz.)

3 cups diced cooked chicken or turkey

1-1/2 cups Old El Paso® Thick 'n Chunky Salsa

1 (15 oz.) can Progresso® Black Beans, drained, rinsed

2 eggs

2 (4.5 oz.) cans Old El Paso® Chopped Green Chiles

Old El Paso® Thick 'n Chunky Salsa

Sour cream

Fresh cilantro leaves

1 Heat oven to 350°F. Cook sausage in medium skillet over medium-high heat until thoroughly cooked, stirring frequently. Drain.

2 Lightly spoon flour into measuring cup; level off. In large bowl, combine flour, sausage and 1 cup of the cheese; mix well. Spread into ungreased 13x9-inch (3-quart) glass baking dish. Sprinkle with chicken. Top with 1-1/2 cups salsa and beans.

3 In medium bowl, combine eggs and chiles; beat well. Stir in 1 cup of the cheese. Pour over mixture in baking dish. Sprinkle with remaining 1 cup of the cheese.

4 Bake at 350°F for 25 to 35 minutes or until set and edges are golden brown. Cool 5 minutes. Spoon onto individual serving plates. Garnish each serving with additional salsa, sour cream and cilantro.

NUTRITIONAL INFORMATION PER SERVING:
Calories 510 • Total Fat 29g • Saturated Fat 15g • Cholesterol 170mg • Sodium 1,280mg • Total Carbohydrate 24g • Dietary Fiber 5g • Sugars 5g • Protein 37g.
DIETARY EXCHANGES: 1-1/2 Starch • 1-1/2 Other Carbohydrate • 4-1/2 Medium-Fat Meat • 1 Fat.

creole chicken and orzo

READY IN: 35 MINUTES
SERVINGS: 5

1 tablespoon olive or vegetable oil

1 lb. chicken breast strips for stir frying

7 oz. uncooked orzo or rosamarina (1 cup)

2 (14.5 oz.) cans stewed tomatoes, undrained, cut up

1 (9 oz.) package frozen baby lima beans, thawed

1 teaspoon garlic salt

1 teaspoon dried basil leaves

1/2 teaspoon hot pepper sauce

1 Heat oil in 12-inch skillet over medium-high heat until hot. Add chicken; cook 3 minutes, stirring frequently.

2 Stir in all remaining ingredients. Bring to a boil. Reduce heat; cover and simmer 20 to 25 minutes or until liquid is absorbed and orzo is tender, stirring occasionally.

HIGH ALTITUDE (3500-6500 FT): Add 1/2 cup water when adding all remaining ingredients to chicken. Increase simmer time covered to 25 to 30 minutes.

NUTRITIONAL INFORMATION PER SERVING:
Calories 370 • Total Fat 7g • Saturated Fat 1g • Cholesterol 55mg • Sodium 740mg • Total Carbohydrate 53g • Dietary Fiber 6g • Sugars 13g • Protein 30g.
DIETARY EXCHANGES: 3 Fruit • 1 Vegetable • 2-1/2 Very Lean Meat • 1 Fat.

savory meat pies

Guaranteed to warm spirits when cool winds blow, pip-ing-hot meat pies provide the sort of satisfaction that is sure to send autumn chills on their way. In addition, flaky pot pies, oven-baked sandwiches and piled-high pizzas make workweek dinners a success no matter what time of year it may be. Most important, these traditional tastes turn get-togethers into comfy affairs to remember.

Quick Beef Stew
in Bread Bowls
page 70

Crescent-
Topped Pot
Roast Pie
page 59

Spanish
Chicken Pizza
page 59

sloppy joe shepherd's pie
page 54

mojo black bean-chicken pizza

PREP TIME: 20 MINUTES
READY IN: 30 MINUTES
SERVINGS: 8

Ginny Solomon
Brooksville, FL

1/4 cup chopped fresh cilantro or parsley

1/4 cup mojo criollo marinade (Spanish marinating sauce) or zesty Italian dressing

1/2 small red onion, cut into very thin strips

1/4 teaspoon kosher (coarse) salt

1/8 teaspoon cracked black pepper

1 (15 oz.) can Progresso® Black Beans, drained, rinsed

1 (6 oz.) package refrigerated grilled chicken strips

1 (13.8 oz.) can Pillsbury® Refrigerated Pizza Crust

3/4 cup shredded Monterey Jack cheese (3 oz.)

3/4 cup shredded mozzarella cheese (3 oz.)

1 Heat oven to 400°F. In medium bowl, mix cilantro, marinade, onion, salt, pepper, beans and chicken. Let stand 10 to 15 minutes to marinate.

2 Meanwhile, lightly spray large cookie sheet with cooking spray. Unroll dough on cookie sheet; starting in center, press into 15x11-inch rectangle. Bake 8 to 12 minutes or until light golden brown.

3 Spread chicken mixture over partially baked crust to within 1/2 inch of edges. Sprinkle both cheeses over top. Bake 8 minutes longer or until cheese is melted and crust is golden brown around edges. Cut into 8 rectangles.

NUTRITIONAL INFORMATION PER SERVING:
Calories 290 • Total Fat 8g • Saturated Fat 4g • Cholesterol 30mg • Sodium 870mg • Total Carbohydrate 37g • Dietary Fiber 3g • Sugars 5g • Protein 18g.
DIETARY EXCHANGES: 2 Starch • 1/2 Other Carbohydrate • 1-1/2 Medium-Fat Meat.

SIMPLE SUBSTITUTION: One boneless skinless chicken breast, cooked on the grill and cut into thin strips, can be used in place of purchased chicken strips.

---

sloppy joe shepherd's pie

PREP TIME: 25 MINUTES
READY IN: 55 MINUTES
SERVINGS: 4

1 lb. lean ground beef

1/2 cup chopped onion (1 medium)

1-1/2 cups Green Giant® Frozen Mixed Vegetables

1 (15.5 oz.) can sloppy Joe sandwich sauce

1 pouch roasted garlic mashed potatoes (from 7.2 oz. pkg.)

1-1/4 cups hot water

1/2 cup milk

2 tablespoons margarine or butter

Paprika

1 Heat oven to 350°F. In large nonstick skillet, cook ground beef and onion over medium-high heat for 5 to 7 minutes or until beef is thoroughly cooked, stirring frequently. Drain.

2 Add mixed vegetables and sandwich sauce; mix well. Bring to a boil. Reduce heat; simmer 5 minutes or until vegetables are tender, stirring occasionally. Spoon into ungreased 8-inch square (2-quart) glass baking dish.

3 Meanwhile, cook mashed potatoes as directed on

package, using hot water, milk and margarine. Let stand 5 minutes. Spoon or pipe potatoes around edges of hot beef mixture. Sprinkle paprika over the potatoes.

4 Bake at 350°F for 25 to 30 minutes or until bubbly and thoroughly heated.

NUTRITIONAL INFORMATION PER SERVING:
Calories 630 • Total Fat 36g • Saturated Fat 13g • Cholesterol 120mg • Sodium 900mg • Total Carbohydrate 41g • Dietary Fiber 5g • Sugars 11g • Protein 41g.
DIETARY EXCHANGES: 2-1/2 Starch • 4-1/2 Medium-Fat Meat • 2-1/2 Fat.

biscuit cheeseburger casserole

PREP TIME: 15 MINUTES
READY IN: 35 MINUTES
SERVINGS: 5

- 1 lb. lean (at least 80%) ground beef
- 1/4 cup chopped onion (1/2 medium)
- 1/4 cup chopped green bell pepper
- 1 (8 oz.) can tomato sauce
- 1/4 cup ketchup
- 1/8 teaspoon pepper
- 8 (3/4 oz.) slices American cheese or American pasteurized prepared cheese product
- 1 (7.5 oz.) can Pillsbury® Country® Refrigerated Biscuits (from 4-can pack)

1 Heat oven to 400°F. In 12-inch nonstick skillet, cook ground beef, onion and bell pepper over medium-high heat until beef is thoroughly cooked, stirring frequently. Drain.

2 Stir in tomato sauce, ketchup and pepper; simmer 5 minutes, stirring occasionally.

3 Spoon 1/3 of beef mixture into ungreased 2-quart casserole. Top with 4 slices of the cheese. Repeat layers. Top with remaining beef mixture, spreading to edge of casserole.

4 Separate dough into 10 biscuits. Arrange biscuits in single layer around edge of hot mixture in casserole.

5 Bake at 400°F for 13 to 17 minutes or until biscuits are golden brown.

HIGH ALTITUDE (3500-6500 FT):
Bake at 400°F for 17 to 19 minutes.

NUTRITIONAL INFORMATION PER SERVING:
Calories 470 • Total Fat 27g • Saturated Fat 12g • Cholesterol 85mg • Sodium 1,460mg • Total Carbohydrate 28g • Dietary Fiber 1g • Sugars 12g • Protein 29g.
DIETARY EXCHANGES: 2 Starch • 3 Medium-Fat Meat • 2 Fat.

chicken pot pie bubble bake

PREP TIME: 25 MINUTES
READY IN: 1 HOUR 10 MINUTES
SERVINGS: 6

- 1 (10-3/4 oz.) can condensed cream of chicken soup
- 1-1/3 cups milk
- 1 teaspoon Italian seasoning
- 2 cups refrigerated new potato wedges (from 20 oz. bag), each cut in half crosswise
- 3 cups cubed deli rotisserie chicken (without skin)
- 1 (1 lb.) bag Green Giant® Frozen Mixed Vegetables, thawed
- 1 (12 oz.) can Pillsbury® Golden Homestyle® Refrigerated Buttermilk Biscuits
- 1/2 cup shredded Cheddar cheese (2 oz.)

1 Heat oven to 375°F. Spray 13x9-inch (3-quart) glass baking dish with nonstick cooking spray. In large bowl, mix soup, milk and Italian seasoning. Stir in potatoes, chicken and thawed vegetables.

2 Separate dough into 10 biscuits. Cut each into quarters; add to potato mixture. Stir gently to mix well; spoon into baking dish.

3 Bake uncovered 35 to 40 minutes or until top is deep golden brown and biscuits are no longer doughy inside. Sprinkle with cheese. Bake 4 to 6 minutes longer or until cheese is melted.

NUTRITIONAL INFORMATION PER SERVING:
Calories 510 • Total Fat 22g • Saturated Fat 7g • Cholesterol 75mg • Sodium 1,100mg • Total Carbohydrate 48g • Dietary Fiber 5g • Sugars 9g • Protein 30g.
DIETARY EXCHANGES: 2 Starch • 1 Other Carbohydrate • 1 Vegetable • 3 Lean Meat • 2-1/2 Fat.

chili pot pie

beef and mushroom stroganoff pie

PREP TIME: 35 MINUTES
READY IN: 1 HOUR 25 MINUTES
SERVINGS: 6

1 (15 oz.) package Pillsbury® Refrigerated Pie Crusts, softened as directed on package

1 lb. lean ground beef

1 cup sliced fresh mushrooms

1/2 cup chopped onion

2 garlic cloves, minced

1 (2.3 oz.) package beefy mushroom soup mix

1/8 teaspoon pepper

1/2 cup water

1 (3 oz.) package cream cheese, softened

1/2 cup sour cream

1 Prepare pie crust as directed on package for two-crust pie using 9-inch glass pie pan.

2 Heat oven to 375°F. In large skillet, cook ground beef, mushrooms, onion and garlic over medium heat until beef is thoroughly cooked, stirring frequently. Drain.

3 Stir in soup mix, pepper and water. Add cream cheese; cook and stir until cream cheese is melted and mixture is hot. Remove from heat. Stir in sour cream. Pour into crust-lined pan. Top with second crust; seal edges and flute. Cut slits in several places in top crust.

4 Bake at 375°F for 45 to 50 minutes or until crust is deep golden brown. Let stand 10 minutes before serving. Cut into wedges to serve.

NUTRITIONAL INFORMATION PER SERVING: Calories 590 • Total Fat 37g • Saturated Fat 17g • Cholesterol 90mg • Sodium 1,010mg • Total Carbohydrate 45g • Dietary Fiber 1g • Sugars 5g • Protein 18g. DIETARY EXCHANGES: 3 Starch • 3 Other Carbohydrate • 1-1/2 Medium-Fat Meat • 5-1/2 Fat.

chili pot pie

PREP TIME: 15 MINUTES
READY IN: 35 MINUTES
SERVINGS: 5

1 lb. lean (at least 80%) ground beef

1 cup chopped onions (2 medium)

1 cup chopped green bell pepper (1 medium)

1 cup sliced fresh mushrooms

2 teaspoons chili powder

1 (15 oz.) can black beans, drained, rinsed

1 (15 oz.) can pizza sauce

1 (10-3/4 oz.) can condensed Cheddar cheese soup

1 (10.2 oz.) can Pillsbury® Grands!® Flaky Layers Refrigerated Original or Buttermilk Biscuits (5 biscuits)

1/2 cup shredded Cheddar cheese (2 oz.)

1 Heat oven to 375°F. In 12-inch nonstick skillet, cook ground beef and onion over medium-high heat until beef is thoroughly cooked, stirring frequently. Drain.

2 Stir in bell pepper, mushrooms, chili powder, beans, pizza sauce and soup. Cook about 5 minutes or until mixture comes to a simmer, stirring occasionally. Spoon hot mixture into ungreased 2-1/2-quart casserole.

3 Separate dough into 5 biscuits. Cut each in half crosswise; place, cut side down, around edge of hot mixture. Sprinkle with cheese.

4 Bake at 375°F for 15 to 20 minutes or until biscuits are golden brown and no longer doughy on bottom.

HIGH ALTITUDE (3500-6500 FT): After stirring in bell pepper, mushrooms, chili powder, beans, pizza sauce and soup, cook about 6 minutes, stirring occasionally. Bake pie at 375°F for 20 to 25 minutes.

NUTRITIONAL INFORMATION PER SERVING: Calories 660 • Total Fat 31g • Saturated Fat 11g • Cholesterol 75mg • Sodium 2,060mg • Total Carbohydrate 67g • Dietary Fiber 9g • Sugars 16g • Protein 37g. DIETARY EXCHANGES: 3 Starch • 1 Other Carbohydrate • 4 Lean Meat • 3-1/2 Fat.

chicken and blue cheese bundles

PREP TIME: 35 MINUTES
READY IN: 50 MINUTES
SERVINGS: 4

1 tablespoon butter or margarine

1 medium onion, chopped (1/2 cup)

1 cup chopped fresh mushrooms

1/4 cup dry white wine or chicken broth

1/2 teaspoon dried rosemary leaves, crushed

1/4 teaspoon dried thyme leaves

1-3/4 cups chopped deli rotisserie chicken (without skin)

1/4 cup crumbled blue cheese (1 oz.)

1 (8 oz.) can Pillsbury® Refrigerated Crescent Dinner Rolls

1 Heat oven to 375°F. In 10-inch nonstick skillet, melt butter over medium heat. Add onion; cook 5 minutes, stirring occasionally. Add mushrooms; cook, stirring occasionally, until onions and mushrooms are tender.

2 Reduce heat to medium-low. Add wine, rosemary and thyme; cook 4 to 5 minutes, stirring occasionally, until liquid has evaporated. Remove from heat. Stir in the chicken and blue cheese.

3 Separate dough into 4 rectangles; press or roll each into 5-inch square, firmly pressing perforations to seal. Spoon about 1/2 cup chicken mixture onto center of each dough square. Bring all 4 corners of dough up over chicken mixture; pinch seams to seal. Place on ungreased cookie sheet.

4 Bake 11 to 14 minutes or until crust is golden brown.

HIGH ALTITUDE (3500-6500 FT): In Step 4, bake 13 to 16 minutes.

NUTRITIONAL INFORMATION PER SERVING: Calories 390 • Total Fat 21g • Saturated Fat 8g • Trans Fat 3.5g • Cholesterol 65mg • Sodium 610mg • Total Carbohydrate 25g • Dietary Fiber 1g • Sugars 5g • Protein 23g. DIETARY EXCHANGES: 1-1/2 Starch • 1/2 Other Carbohydrate • 2-1/2 Lean Meat • 2-1/2 Fat.

flaky chicken and bean wedges

READY IN: 25 MINUTES
SERVINGS: 8

1 Pillsbury® Refrigerated Pie Crust (from 15 oz. box), softened as directed on box

1 cup chopped deli rotisserie chicken (from 2 to 2-1/2 lb. chicken)

1 can (15 oz.) Progresso® Red Kidney Beans, drained, rinsed

1 teaspoon ground cumin

2 tablespoons chopped fresh cilantro

1/2 cup whipped cream cheese (from 8 oz. container), softened

1 cup shredded taco-seasoned cheese (4 oz.)

1 cup Old El Paso® Thick 'n Chunky Salsa

1 Heat oven to 425°F. Remove pie crust from pouch; unroll on ungreased cookie sheet. Generously prick crust with fork. Bake 6 to 8 minutes or until light golden brown.

2 Meanwhile, in 10-inch skillet, cook chicken, beans and cumin over medium heat about 2 minutes, stirring frequently, until thoroughly heated. Stir in cilantro if desired.

3 Spread cream cheese over partially baked crust. Top with chicken mixture; sprinkle with cheese.

4 Bake 2 to 3 minutes longer or until cheese is melted and crust is golden brown. Cut into wedges; serve warm with salsa.

NUTRITIONAL INFORMATION PER SERVING: Calories 320 • Total Fat 17g • Saturated Fat 8g • Trans Fat 0g • Cholesterol 45mg • Sodium 520mg • Total Carbohydrate 28g • Dietary Fiber 3g • Sugars 3g • Protein 14g. DIETARY EXCHANGES: 2 Starch • 1 Lean Meat • 2-1/2 Fat.

crescent-topped pot roast pie

PREP TIME: 45 MINUTES
READY IN: 1 HOUR 10 MINUTES
SERVINGS: 4

- 1 tablespoon oil
- 1 lb. boneless beef top sirloin steak (1-inch thick), cut into thin bite-sized strips
- 2 cups matchstick-cut (2x1/8x1/8-inch) carrots (from 10 oz. bag)
- 2 cups thinly sliced celery (3 to 4 medium stalks)
- 1 medium onion, halved, thinly sliced
- 1 (12 oz.) jar beef gravy
- 1 tablespoon Dijon mustard
- 1 (6 oz.) jar Green Giant® Sliced Mushrooms, drained
- 1 (8 oz.) can Pillsbury® Refrigerated Crescent Dinner Rolls
- 1 tablespoon sesame seed

1 Heat oven to 375°F. Spray 11x7-inch (2-quart) glass baking dish with nonstick cooking spray. In 10-inch nonstick skillet, heat oil over medium-high heat. Add beef strips; cook 5 to 7 minutes, stirring frequently, until browned. Remove beef from skillet; place on plate.

2 In same skillet, cook carrots, celery and onion 10 minutes, stirring occasionally, until crisp-tender.

3 Return beef to skillet and stir in gravy, mustard and mushrooms. Cook about 2 minutes or until hot and bubbly. Pour into baking dish.

4 Separate dough into 8 triangles. Arrange triangles over filling, overlapping about 1/4 inch to create a braided appearance. Spray triangles with nonstick cooking spray; sprinkle with sesame seed.

5 Bake 22 to 24 minutes or until the crust is deep golden brown.

HIGH ALTITUDE (3500-6500 FT):
Bake at 375°F for 24 to 26 minutes.

NUTRITIONAL INFORMATION PER SERVING:
Calories 460 • Total Fat 19g • Saturated Fat 5g • Cholesterol 65mg • Sodium 1,550mg • Total Carbohydrate 44g • Dietary Fiber 5g • Sugars 14g • Protein 33g.
DIETARY EXCHANGES: 1-1/2 Starch • 1 Other Carbohydrate • 1 Vegetable • 3-1/2 Lean Meat • 1-1/2 Fat.

spanish chicken pizza

PREP TIME: 15 MINUTES
READY IN: 30 MINUTES
SERVINGS: 4

- 1 (10 oz.) package prebaked thin Italian pizza crust (12 inch)
- 1 cup diced cooked chicken breast
- 1 cup shredded mozzarella cheese (4 oz.)
- 3 medium Italian plum tomatoes, sliced
- 1/2 cup quartered artichoke hearts (from 14 oz. can), drained, coarsely chopped
- 3 medium pimiento-stuffed green olives, sliced

1 Heat oven to 450°F. On ungreased cookie sheet, place pizza crust; sprinkle chicken evenly over crust. Sprinkle with 2/3 cup of the cheese.

2 Arrange tomato slices over cheese. Top with artichokes and olives; sprinkle with remaining 1/3 cup cheese.

3 Bake 10 to 12 minutes or until cheese is melted and pizza is thoroughly heated.

NUTRITIONAL INFORMATION PER SERVING:
Calories 350 • Total Fat 11g • Saturated Fat 6g • Cholesterol 50mg • Sodium 680mg • Total Carbohydrate 36g • Dietary Fiber 3g • Sugars 2g • Protein 27g.
DIETARY EXCHANGES: 2-1/2 Starch • 3 Lean Meat.

poppin' fresh barbecups

PREP TIME: 20 MINUTES
READY IN: 35 MINUTES
SERVINGS: 10

1   lb. ground beef

1/2 cup barbecue sauce

1   tablespoon instant minced onion or 1/4 cup chopped onion

1   to 2 tablespoons brown sugar

1   (12 oz.) can Hungry Jack® Refrigerated Flaky Biscuits

1/2 cup shredded Cheddar or American cheese (2 oz.)

1 Heat oven to 400°F. Grease 10 muffin cups. In large skillet, brown ground beef until thoroughly cooked. Drain. Stir in barbecue sauce, onion and brown sugar. Cook 1 minute to blend flavors, stirring constantly.

2 Separate dough into 10 biscuits. Place 1 biscuit in each greased muffin cup; firmly press in bottom and up sides, forming 1/4-inch rim. Spoon about 1/4 cup beef mixture into each biscuit-lined cup. Sprinkle each with cheese.

3 Bake at 400°F for 10 to 12 minutes or until edges of biscuits are golden brown. Cool 1 minute; remove from pan.

NUTRITIONAL INFORMATION PER SERVING: Calories 240 • Total Fat 13g • Saturated Fat 5g • Cholesterol 35mg • Sodium 520mg • Total Carbohydrate 19g • Dietary Fiber 1g • Sugars 5g • Protein 11g. DIETARY EXCHANGES: 1 Starch • 1/2 Fruit • 1-1/2 Other Carbohydrate • 1 Medium-Fat Meat • 1-1/2 Fat.

savory beef and mushroom pie

PREP TIME: 35 MINUTES
READY IN: 1 HOUR 20 MINUTES
SERVINGS: 6

- 1 (15 oz.) package Pillsbury® Refrigerated Pie Crusts, softened as directed on package
- 1 lb. lean ground beef
- 1-1/2 cups sliced fresh mushrooms
- 3/4 cup chopped onions
- 3 tablespoons Pillsbury BEST® All-Purpose Flour
- 1 envelope savory herb with garlic soup mix (from 2.4 oz. pkg.)
- 1/2 cup half-and-half
- 1 (3 oz.) package cream cheese, softened
- 1/2 cup shredded Swiss cheese (2 oz.)

1 Prepare pie crusts as directed on package for two-crust pie using 9-inch pie pan.

2 Heat oven to 375°F. In 12-inch nonstick skillet, cook ground beef, mushrooms, onions and flour over medium heat for 10 to 12 minutes or until beef is thoroughly cooked and liquid from mushrooms has evaporated, stirring frequently.

3 Stir in soup mix and half-and-half. Add cream cheese; cook until cream cheese has melted and mixture is hot, stirring constantly. Remove from heat. Stir in Swiss cheese.

4 Pour beef mixture into crust-lined pan. Top with second crust; seal edges and flute. Cut slits in several places in top crust.

5 Bake at 375°F for 35 to 45 minutes or until crust is golden brown. Let stand 10 minutes before serving. Cut into wedges to serve.

HIGH ALTITUDE (3500-6500 FT): Cook ground beef mixture over medium-high heat. After baking pie for 20 minutes, cover edge of crust with strips of foil to prevent excessive browning.

NUTRITIONAL INFORMATION PER SERVING: Calories 620 • Total Fat 39g • Saturated Fat 19g • Cholesterol 90mg • Sodium 890mg • Total Carbohydrate 45g • Dietary Fiber 1g • Sugars 7g • Protein 22g. DIETARY EXCHANGES: 3 Starch • 3 Other Carbohydrate • 2 Medium-Fat Meat • 5-1/2 Fat.

spicy mexican pizza

PREP TIME: 25 MINUTES
READY IN: 40 MINUTES
SERVINGS: 8

Tamara Strange
Winder, GA

- 1 (13.8 oz.) can Pillsbury® Refrigerated Pizza Crust
- 1/2 lb. chorizo sausage (not smoked)
- 1 (8 oz.) can tomato sauce
- 1/2 to 1 chipotle chile in adobo sauce (from 7 or 11 oz. can)
- 1/4 cup chopped fresh cilantro
- 1 (2.25 oz.) can sliced ripe olives, drained
- 2 cups shredded Colby-Monterey Jack cheese blend (8 oz.)

1 Heat oven to 400°F. Grease 15x10x1-inch pan with shortening or spray with cooking spray. Unroll dough; place in greased pan. Starting at center, press out dough to edge of pan. Prick dough 15 to 20 times evenly with fork.

2 Bake at 400°F for 8 to 10 minutes or until crust is very light brown. Meanwhile, remove sausage from casings; place in 10-inch skillet. Cook over medium-high heat, stirring frequently and breaking up sausage, until no longer pink. Remove sausage from skillet; drain well on paper towels. In blender, puree tomato sauce and chipotle chile until smooth.

3 Remove partially baked crust from oven. Spread tomato sauce mixture evenly over crust. Sprinkle cooked sausage, cilantro, olives and cheese over sauce.

4 Return to oven; bake an additional 12 to 15 minutes or until cheese is melted and crust is crisp and lightly browned. Cut into squares. Serve warm.

NUTRITIONAL INFORMATION PER SERVING: Calories 380 • Total Fat 22g • Saturated Fat 10g • Cholesterol 50mg • Sodium 1,140mg • Total Carbohydrate 27g • Dietary Fiber 1g • Sugars 5g • Protein 18g.

country beef pot pie

PREP TIME: 35 MINUTES
READY IN: 1 HOUR 20 MINUTES
SERVINGS: 6

1 (15 oz.) package Pillsbury® Refrigerated Pie Crusts, softened as directed on package

1 tablespoon oil

3/4 lb. boneless beef sirloin steak, cut into 1/2-inch cubes

1 medium onion, chopped (1/2 cup)

1 (12 oz.) jar beef gravy

1 tablespoon cornstarch

2 teaspoons sugar

1/8 teaspoon pepper

2 cups Green Giant® Frozen Mixed Vegetables

2 cups frozen southern-style hash-brown potatoes (from 32 oz. pkg.)

Sesame seed

1 Heat oven to 400°F. Prepare pie crusts as directed on package for two-crust pie using 9-inch glass pie pan.

2 Heat oil in large skillet over medium-high heat until hot. Add beef and onion; cook and stir until beef is browned. Drain.

3 In small bowl, combine gravy, cornstarch, sugar and pepper; mix well. Add to beef in skillet. Stir in vegetables and potatoes. Cook about 5 minutes or until vegetables are thawed, stirring occasionally.

4 Spoon mixture into pie crust-lined pan. Top with second crust; seal edges and flute. Cut slits in several places in top crust; sprinkle with sesame seed if desired.

5 Bake at 400°F for 35 to 45 minutes or until golden brown. Let stand 10 minutes before serving.

NUTRITIONAL INFORMATION PER SERVING: Calories 545 • Total Fat 24g • Saturated Fat 10g • Cholesterol 45mg • Sodium 670mg • Total Carbohydrate 63g • Dietary Fiber 4g • Sugars 8g • Protein 19g.
DIETARY EXCHANGES: 4 Starch • 1 Lean Meat • 4 Fat.

chicken cordon bleu pizza

PREP TIME: 15 MINUTES
READY IN: 33-37 MINUTES
SERVINGS: 4

Merrill Degroot
Belgrade, MT

1 (13.8 oz.) can Pillsbury® Refrigerated Pizza Crust

1/3 cup purchased garlic ranch salad dressing

1 cup shredded smoked Provolone cheese (4 oz.)

4 oz. refrigerated roasted chicken breast strips

2 oz. sliced Canadian bacon, halved

2 tablespoons cooked real bacon pieces

4 green onions, sliced

1/4 cup chopped tomato

1 cup shredded mozzarella cheese (4 oz.)

1 Heat oven to 425°F. Grease 12-inch pizza pan. Unroll dough; place in greased pan. Starting at center, press out dough to edge of pan. Spread salad dressing over dough. Sprinkle with the Provolone cheese. Top with all remaining ingredients. Bake at 425°F for 18 to 22 minutes or until crust is deep golden brown.

NUTRITIONAL INFORMATION PER SERVING: Calories 605 • Total Fat 28g • Total Carbohydrate 51g.

layered italian beef pie

PREP TIME: 30 MINUTES
READY IN: 1 HOUR 10 MINUTES
SERVINGS: 8

Ruth Boudreaux
Broussard, LA

1 Pillsbury® Refrigerated Pie Crust (from 15 oz. pkg.), softened as directed on package

1 lb. lean ground beef

1 cup tomato pasta sauce with mushrooms and onions

2 eggs

1/4 cup grated Parmesan cheese

1 (9 oz.) package Green Giant® Frozen Spinach, thawed, squeezed to drain

2 cups shredded mozzarella cheese (8 oz.)

1/2 cup sliced ripe olives

1 Heat oven to 450°F. Prepare pie crust as directed on package for one-crust baked shell using 9-inch glass pie pan. Bake at 450°F for 9 to 11 minutes or until light golden brown. Reduce oven temperature to 350°F.

2 Meanwhile, brown ground beef in large skillet over medium-high heat until thoroughly cooked, stirring frequently. Drain well. Add pasta sauce; mix well. Bring to a boil. Reduce heat; simmer 10 minutes or until thoroughly heated.

3 Beat eggs in medium bowl until well blended. Add Parmesan cheese and spinach; mix well. Spoon half of beef mixture into baked shell. Sprinkle with 1 cup of the mozzarella cheese and 1/4 cup of the olives. Spoon spinach mixture evenly over cheese. Top with remaining beef mixture.

4 Bake at 350°F for 25 to 35 minutes or until filling is thoroughly heated. If necessary, cover edge of crust with strips of foil after 15 to 20 minutes of baking to prevent excessive browning.

5 Sprinkle pie with remaining 1 cup mozzarella cheese and 1/4 cup olives. Bake an additional 4 to 5 minutes or until cheese is melted. Let stand 5 minutes before serving.

HIGH ALTITUDE (3500-6500 FT):
Bake pie as directed, covering edge of crust with foil after 15 to 20 minutes of baking. After topping pie with cheese and olives, bake an additional 5 to 7 minutes.

NUTRITIONAL INFORMATION PER SERVING:
Calories 395 • Total Fat 24g • Saturated Fat 11g • Cholesterol 110mg • Sodium 610mg • Total Carbohydrate 22g • Dietary Fiber 1g • Sugars 4g • Protein 23g.
DIETARY EXCHANGES: 1-1/2 Starch • 2-1/2 Medium-Fat Meat • 2 Fat.

main dish crescent reubens

PREP TIME: 20 MINUTES
READY IN: 55 MINUTES
SERVINGS: 6

1 (8 oz.) can Pillsbury® Refrigerated Crescent Dinner Rolls

3 (7x4-inch) slices Swiss or mozzarella cheese

1 (12 oz.) can corned beef, chopped

1 (14 oz.) can sauerkraut, well drained

3 eggs, slightly beaten

3/4 cup milk

1 tablespoon instant minced onion or 1/4 cup chopped onion

1 teaspoon dried parsley flakes

1/4 teaspoon salt

1 Heat oven to 425°F. Unroll dough into 2 long rectangles. Place in ungreased 13x9-inch pan; press over bottom and 1/2 inch up sides to form crust. Press perforations to seal.

2 Arrange cheese slices over dough. Spoon corned beef and sauerkraut over cheese. In medium bowl, combine all remaining ingredients; mix well. Pour over sauerkraut.

3 Bake at 425°F for 25 to 35 minutes or until filling is set and crust is deep golden brown. Cool 5 minutes. Cut into squares.

HIGH ALTITUDE (3500-6500 FT):
Bake 28 to 35 minutes.

NUTRITIONAL INFORMATION PER SERVING:
Calories 395 • Total Fat 21g • Saturated Fat 9g • Cholesterol 170mg • Sodium 1,640mg • Total Carbohydrate 24g • Dietary Fiber 2g • Sugars 8g • Protein 27g.
DIETARY EXCHANGES: 1-1/2 Starch • 1-1/2 Other Carbohydrate • 3-1/2 Medium-Fat Meat • 1/2 Fat.

swiss ham ring-around

PREP TIME: 20 MINUTES
READY IN: 50 MINUTES
SERVINGS: 8

Mrs. Lyman Francis
Cheshire, CT

1 tablespoon butter, softened

1/4 cup chopped fresh parsley or 2 tablespoons dried parsley flakes

2 tablespoons finely chopped onion or 1-1/2 teaspoons instant minced onion

2 tablespoons prepared mustard

1 teaspoon lemon juice

1-1/2 cups shredded Swiss cheese (6 oz.)

1 cup chopped fresh broccoli or Green Giant® Frozen Chopped Broccoli, cooked, drained

1 cup diced cooked ham (6 oz.)

1 (8 oz.) can Pillsbury® Refrigerated Crescent Dinner Rolls

1 Heat oven to 350°F. Grease large cookie sheet. In large bowl, combine butter, parsley, onion, mustard and lemon juice; blend well. Add cheese, cooked broccoli and ham; mix lightly. Set aside.

2 Unroll dough into 8 triangles. Arrange triangles on greased cookie sheet with shortest sides toward center, overlapping in wreath shape and leaving a 3-inch round opening in center.

3 Spoon ham filling on widest part of dough. Pull end points of triangles over filling and tuck under dough to form a ring.

4 Bake at 350°F for 25 to 30 minutes or until ring is golden brown.

NUTRITIONAL INFORMATION PER SERVING: Calories 230 • Total Fat 14g • Saturated Fat 7g • Cholesterol 35mg • Sodium 640mg • Total Carbohydrate 13g • Dietary Fiber 1g • Sugars 2g • Protein 12g. DIETARY EXCHANGES: 1 Starch • 1 Other Carbohydrate • 1-1/2 Medium-Fat Meat • 1 Fat.

tiny ham and pineapple pot pies

PREP TIME: 40 MINUTES
READY IN: 1 HOUR
SERVINGS: 16 APPETIZERS

1/2 cup finely chopped cooked ham (about 3 oz.)

1/2 cup finely shredded Swiss cheese (2 oz.)

1/2 cup well-drained canned crushed pineapple

1 tablespoon finely chopped green onion (1 medium)

1/2 teaspoon ground mustard

1 (15 oz.) box Pillsbury® Refrigerated Pie Crusts, softened as directed on box

1 egg, beaten

1 teaspoon sesame seed

1 Heat oven to 450°F (425°F for dark pans). In small bowl, mix ham, cheese, pineapple, onion and mustard.

2 Remove pie crusts from pouches; unroll on work surface. From each crust, cut 8 (3-inch) rounds and 8 (2-inch) rounds, rerolling crusts if necessary. Press 3-inch rounds in bottoms and up sides of 16 ungreased mini muffin cups so edges of crusts extend slightly over sides of cups.

3 Spoon about 1 rounded tablespoon ham mixture into each crust-lined cup. Brush edges of crust lightly with beaten egg.

4 With tip of knife, cut small vent in each 2-inch pie-crust round. Place 1 round over filling in each cup; press edges together, pushing toward cup so crust does not extend over sides. Brush top crusts with beaten egg; sprinkle with sesame seed if desired.

5 Bake 10 to 14 minutes or until top crusts are deep golden brown. Remove from muffin cups; cool 5 minutes.

NUTRITIONAL INFORMATION PER SERVING: Calories 150 • Total Fat 9g • Saturated Fat 3.5g • Trans Fat 0g • Cholesterol 25mg • Sodium 200mg • Total Carbohydrate 14g • Dietary Fiber 0g • Sugars 1g • Protein 3g. DIETARY EXCHANGES: 1 Starch • 1-1/2 Fat.

wild west pizza

PREP TIME: 20 MINUTES
READY IN: 35 MINUTES
SERVINGS: 6

- 1 (13.8 oz.) can Pillsbury® Refrigerated Pizza Crust
- 1/2 lb. lean (at least 80%) ground beef
- 1/4 teaspoon salt
- 1/8 teaspoon pepper
- 1 (16 oz.) can Old El Paso® Refried Beans
- 1 cup Old El Paso® Taco Sauce or Thick 'n Chunky Salsa
- 1 (11 oz.) can Green Giant® Mexicorn® Whole Kernel Corn with Red and Green Peppers, well drained
- 1 cup shredded Cheddar cheese (4 oz.)
- 2 cups shredded lettuce
- 1 medium tomato, chopped (3/4 cup)
- 1/2 cup sliced green onions (8 medium)

1 Heat oven to 400°F. Spray large cookie sheet or 14-inch pizza pan with nonstick cooking spray. Unroll dough; place on cookie sheet or in pan. Starting at center, press out dough into 14x12-inch rectangle or to edge of pizza pan. Bake 8 to 10 minutes or until edges of crust begin to brown.

2 Meanwhile, in 8-inch skillet, cook ground beef sprinkled with salt and pepper over medium-high heat, stirring frequently, until thoroughly cooked; drain.

3 Remove partially baked crust from oven. Spread refried beans evenly over crust. Spread 1/2 cup of the taco sauce over beans. Top with ground beef mixture, corn and cheese.

4 Return to oven; bake 10 to 14 minutes longer or until cheese is melted and crust is golden brown. Top with lettuce, tomato and onions. Cut into wedges or squares; serve with remaining 1/2 cup taco sauce.

NUTRITIONAL INFORMATION PER SERVING: Calories 420 • Total Fat 13g • Saturated Fat 6g • Trans Fat 0.5g • Cholesterol 45mg • Sodium 1,290mg • Total Carbohydrate 55g • Dietary Fiber 6g • Sugars 7g • Protein 22g.
DIETARY EXCHANGES: 3 Starch • 1/2 Other Carbohydrate • 2 Medium-Fat Meat.

fiesta chicken empanada

PREP TIME: 15 MINUTES
READY IN: 40 MINUTES
SERVINGS: 6

- 1 (15 oz.) box Pillsbury® Refrigerated Pie Crusts, softened as directed on box
- 1 tablespoon olive oil
- 1 medium onion, sliced
- 1/2 medium red bell pepper, cut into 2x1/4-inch strips
- 1/2 medium green bell pepper, cut into 2x1/4-inch strips
- 1/2 medium yellow bell pepper, cut into 2x1/4-inch strips
- 1 (10 oz.) can chunk white chicken breast in water, drained
- 4 teaspoons dried fajita seasoning
- 1/2 cup Old El Paso® Cheese 'n Salsa Dip (from 15 oz. jar)
- 1 egg, beaten
- Sour cream
- Old El Paso® Cheese 'n Salsa Dip

1 Heat oven to 425°F. Remove 1 pie crust from pouch; unroll crust onto ungreased 14-inch pizza pan or cookie sheet.

2 In 10-inch skillet, heat oil over medium-high heat. Add onion and bell peppers; cook 5 minutes, stirring occasionally, until tender. Stir in chicken and fajita seasoning.

3 Spoon chicken mixture evenly onto crust in pan to within 1 inch of edge. Spread 1/2 cup dip over chicken mixture. Brush edge of crust with water. Remove second crust from pouch. Unroll crust; place over filling, pressing edge firmly to seal. Brush top with beaten egg.

4 Bake 20 to 25 minutes or until deep golden brown, covering crust edge with strips of foil after 10 to 15 minutes of baking to prevent excessive browning. Cut into wedges; garnish with sour cream and additional dip if desired.

HIGH ALTITUDE (3500-6500 FT): Bake at 425°F for 25 to 30 minutes.

NUTRITIONAL INFORMATION PER SERVING: Calories 420 • Total Fat 24g • Saturated Fat 8g • Cholesterol 65mg • Sodium 1,000mg • Total Carbohydrate 41g • Dietary Fiber 1g • Sugars 5g • Protein 10g. DIETARY EXCHANGES: 2-1/2 Starch • 1/2 Vegetable • 4-1/2 Fat.

cheeseburger pot pie

PREP TIME: 25 MINUTES
READY IN: 45 MINUTES
SERVINGS: 6

- 1-1/2 lb. lean ground beef
- 1/4 cup chopped onion
- 3/4 cup ketchup
- 2 tablespoons chopped pickle
- 1/8 teaspoon pepper
- 1 cup shredded sharp Cheddar cheese (4 oz.)
- 1 Pillsbury® Refrigerated Pie Crust (from 15 oz. pkg.), softened as directed on package

1 Heat oven to 450°F. Brown ground beef in large skillet over medium-high heat until thoroughly cooked, stirring frequently. Drain.

2 Reduce heat to medium. Add onion; cook 5 to 8 minutes or until onion is tender, stirring occasionally. Add ketchup, pickle and pepper; mix well. Cook 2 to 3 minutes or until thoroughly heated.

3 Spoon beef mixture into ungreased 9-inch pie pan. Sprinkle with cheese. Unroll pie crust. Place crust over hot beef mixture. Flute edges; cut slits in several places in crust.

4 Bake at 450°F for 13 to 20 minutes or until crust is golden brown and filling is bubbly. Cover edge of crust with strips of foil during last 10 minutes of baking to prevent excessive browning.

NUTRITIONAL INFORMATION PER SERVING: Calories 480 • Total Fat 30g • Saturated Fat 14g • Cholesterol 100mg • Sodium 710mg • Total Carbohydrate 27g • Dietary Fiber 1g • Sugars 5g • Protein 26g. DIETARY EXCHANGES: 2 Starch • 2 Other Carbohydrate • 3 Medium-Fat Meat • 2-1/2 Fat.

mushroom-garlic cream tartlets

PREP TIME: 15 MINUTES
READY IN: 35 MINUTES
SERVINGS: 24 APPETIZERS

2 tablespoons butter or margarine

1 (8 oz.) package fresh mushrooms, finely chopped

1 tablespoon Pillsbury BEST® All-Purpose Flour

1 tablespoon finely chopped onion

2 garlic cloves, minced

1/2 cup whipping cream

1/4 cup grated Parmesan cheese

1 (8 oz.) can Pillsbury® Refrigerated Crescent Dinner Rolls

2 tablespoons chopped fresh parsley

1 Heat oven to 350°F. In 10-inch skillet, melt butter over medium heat. Stir in mushrooms, flour, onion and garlic. Cook 5 minutes, stirring frequently, until vegetables are tender.

2 Stir in cream and cheese. Cook 2 to 3 minutes, stirring frequently, until most of liquid has evaporated.

3 Unroll dough into 2 long rectangles; firmly press perforations to seal. Cut each rectangle into 12 squares. Place 1 square in each of 24 ungreased mini muffin cups. Firmly press in bottom and up sides, leaving corners of dough extended over edges of cups. Spoon 1 heaping teaspoon mushroom mixture into each cup.

4 Bake 9 to 12 minutes or until golden brown. Sprinkle with parsley. Cool in pan 5 minutes. Remove tartlets from muffin cups; serve warm. Store in refrigerator.

NUTRITIONAL INFORMATION PER SERVING: Calories 70 • Total Fat 5g • Saturated Fat 2.5g • Trans Fat 0.5g • Cholesterol 10mg • Sodium 100mg • Total Carbohydrate 5g • Dietary Fiber 0g • Sugars 0g • Protein 2g. DIETARY EXCHANGES: 1/2 Starch • 1 Fat.

chicago deep-dish sausage pizza

PREP TIME: 25 MINUTES
READY IN: 45 MINUTES
SERVINGS: 6

1 lb. bulk Italian pork sausage

1/2 cup chopped green bell pepper

1 cup sliced fresh mushrooms

1 (8 oz.) can pizza sauce

1 (13.8 oz.) can Pillsbury® Refrigerated Pizza Crust

1-1/2 cups shredded mozzarella cheese (6 oz.)

2 medium Italian plum tomatoes, chopped

1/4 cup sliced ripe olives

2 tablespoons chopped green onions

1 Heat oven to 400°F. Spray 9-inch glass pie pan and large nonstick skillet with nonstick cooking spray. Heat skillet over medium-high heat until hot. Add sausage and bell pepper; cook 7 to 9 minutes or until sausage is no longer pink, stirring frequently. Stir in mushrooms and pizza sauce. Keep warm over low heat.

2 Unroll dough into sprayed pie pan. Press in bottom and up sides of pan, folding edge under to form crust. Sprinkle 1/2 cup of the cheese evenly in bottom of crust. Spoon hot sausage mixture over cheese. Top with remaining 1 cup cheese, tomatoes and olives.

3 Bake at 400°F for 15 to 20 minutes or until crust is golden brown. Sprinkle with onions. Let stand 5 minutes. To serve, cut pizza into wedges with serrated knife.

HIGH ALTITUDE (3500-6500 FT): Bake at 400°F for 23 to 28 minutes.

NUTRITIONAL INFORMATION PER SERVING: Calories 410 • Total Fat 22g • Saturated Fat 8g • Cholesterol 60mg • Sodium 1,170mg • Total Carbohydrate 29g • Dietary Fiber 1g • Sugars 6g • Protein 24g. DIETARY EXCHANGES: 2 Starch • 2-1/2 High-Fat Meat • 1/2 Fat.

creamy chicken enchilada pot pies

PREP TIME: 30 MINUTES
READY IN: 1 HOUR
SERVINGS: 10

1 (12 oz.) can Pillsbury® Hungry Jack® Golden Layer™ Refrigerated Biscuits

2/3 cup shredded Monterey Jack cheese (2-2/3 oz.)

2/3 cup crisp rice cereal

1 tablespoon oil

1/2 lb. chicken breast strips for stir frying

1 (8 oz.) package cream cheese, softened

1 (4.5 oz.) can Old El Paso® Chopped Green Chiles

1 (10 oz.) can Old El Paso® Enchilada Sauce

2 tablespoons chopped fresh cilantro

1 Heat oven to 375°F. Separate dough into 10 biscuits. Press each biscuit to form 4-1/2-inch round. Place 1 biscuit round in ungreased muffin cup; firmly press in bottom and up sides, forming 1/4-inch rim. Repeat with remaining biscuits.

2 Spoon about 1 tablespoon each of cheese and cereal into each biscuit-lined cup; press mixture in bottom.

3 Heat oil in large skillet over medium-high heat until hot. Add chicken; cook and stir until no longer pink in center. Reduce heat to medium. Add cream cheese, chiles, 1/2 cup of the enchilada sauce and cilantro; cook and stir until blended and cream cheese is melted. Spoon about 1/3 cup chicken mixture into each cup. Cups will be full.

4 Bake at 375°F for 21 to 26 minutes or until edges of biscuits are deep golden brown. Heat remaining enchilada sauce. Spoon warm sauce over pies.

NUTRITIONAL INFORMATION PER SERVING: Calories 540 • Total Fat 34g • Saturated Fat 16g • Cholesterol 90mg • Sodium 1,300mg • Total Carbohydrate 36g • Dietary Fiber 2g • Sugars 5g • Protein 23g. DIETARY EXCHANGES: 2-1/2 Starch • 2-1/2 Other Carbohydrate • 2 Very Lean Meat • 6 Fat.

deep-dish ground beef pot pies

PREP TIME: 25 MINUTES
READY IN: 1 HOUR
SERVINGS: 4

1 lb. lean (at least 80%) ground beef

1/2 cup chopped onion (1 medium)

2 cups diced (1/2 inch) unpeeled russet potatoes

2 cups Green Giant® Frozen Mixed Vegetables (from 1 lb. bag)

1 (14.5 oz.) can diced tomatoes with basil, garlic and oregano, undrained

1 (12 oz.) jar beef gravy

1/8 teaspoon pepper

1 Pillsbury® Refrigerated Pie Crust (from 15 oz. box), softened as directed on box

1 egg white, beaten

1 to 2 tablespoons finely chopped fresh parsley

1 Heat oven to 425°F. Spray 4 (2-cup) individual oven-proof bowls with nonstick cooking spray; place bowls in 15x10x1-inch pan. In 12-inch nonstick skillet or 4-quart Dutch oven, cook ground beef and onion over medium-high heat, stirring frequently, until beef is thoroughly cooked; drain.

2 Stir in potatoes, frozen vegetables, tomatoes, gravy and pepper. Reduce heat to medium-low; cover and cook 8 to 10 minutes, stirring occasionally, until potatoes are almost tender.

3 Meanwhile, remove pie crust from pouch; unroll crust onto work surface. With 5-inch round cutter, cut 4 rounds from crust.

4 Spoon beef mixture evenly into bowls. Place crusts over beef mixture; seal to edges of bowls. Cut slits in several places in each crust. Brush crusts with egg white; sprinkle with parsley.

5 Bake 30 to 35 minutes or until the crusts are golden brown.

HIGH ALTITUDE (3500-6500 FT): In Step 2, reduce heat to medium; cover and cook 10 to 15 minutes. Continue as directed.

NUTRITIONAL INFORMATION PER SERVING: Calories 490 • Total Fat 23g • Saturated Fat 9g • Trans Fat 1g • Cholesterol 75mg • Sodium 1,100mg • Total Carbohydrate 43g • Dietary Fiber 4g • Sugars 12g • Protein 28g. DIETARY EXCHANGES: 1-1/2 Starch • 1 Other Carbohydrate • 1 Vegetable • 3 Medium-Fat Meat • 1-1/2 Fat.

greek-style shepherd's meat and potato cups

PREP TIME: 25 MINUTES
READY IN: 45 MINUTES
SERVINGS: 4

1 lb. lean ground beef

1/4 cup Progresso® Plain Bread Crumbs

1 to 2 garlic cloves, minced

1 teaspoon dried oregano leaves

1/2 teaspoon salt

1 egg

1-1/3 cups plain mashed potato mix (dry)

Water

Milk

Margarine or butter

Salt

1/3 cup crumbled garlic and herb feta cheese (1-1/3 oz.)

1/3 cup pitted kalamata olives, sliced

1/3 cup chopped seeded tomato

1/4 cup finely chopped green onions

1 Heat oven to 375°F. In large bowl, combine ground beef, bread crumbs, garlic, oregano, 1/2 teaspoon salt and egg; mix well. Divide mixture evenly into 8 ungreased muffin cups. Pat in bottom and up sides of each cup to form crust.

2 In medium saucepan, prepare potatoes as directed on package using water, milk, margarine and salt. Add feta cheese; stir gently to mix. Fill beef-lined cups with the potato mixture.

3 Place cookie sheet on oven rack below muffin pan in case of spillover. Bake at 375°F for 15 to 20 minutes or until beef is thoroughly cooked. Remove cups from pan; place on individual serving plates. Sprinkle with olives, tomato and onions.

HIGH ALTITUDE (3500-6500 FT):
Bake 20 to 25 minutes.

NUTRITIONAL INFORMATION PER SERVING:
Calories 620 • Total Fat 28g • Saturated Fat 10g • Cholesterol 125mg • Sodium 1,050mg • Total Carbohydrate 66g • Dietary Fiber 5g • Sugars 6g • Protein 31g.
DIETARY EXCHANGES: 4 Starch • 2-1/2 Medium-Fat Meat • 3 Fat.

philly cheese steak pizza

PREP TIME: 30 MINUTES
READY IN: 50 MINUTES
SERVINGS: 6

1 (13.8 oz.) can Pillsbury® Refrigerated Pizza Crust

1 tablespoon butter or margarine

1 small green bell pepper, cut into thin strips

1 medium onion, halved, thinly sliced

2 cups finely shredded Cheddar cheese (8 oz.)

1/2 lb. cooked roast beef (from deli), diced

3 medium plum (Roma) tomatoes, sliced

1 Heat oven to 425°F. Grease 12-inch pizza pan with shortening. Unroll dough; place in pan. Starting at center, press out dough to edge of pan, forming 1/2-inch rim. Bake 7 to 9 minutes or until light golden brown.

2 Meanwhile, in 8-inch skillet, melt butter over medium-high heat. Add bell pepper and onion; cook 3 to 5 minutes, stirring occasionally, until tender.

3 Remove partially baked crust from oven. Sprinkle with 1 cup of the cheese. Top with bell pepper mixture, beef, remaining 1 cup cheese and the tomato slices (be sure beef is completely covered with cheese).

4 Return to oven; bake 12 to 18 minutes longer or until crust is deep golden brown. Cut into wedges to serve.

NUTRITIONAL INFORMATION PER SERVING:
Calories 440 • Total Fat 22g • Saturated Fat 12g • Trans Fat 1g • Cholesterol 75mg • Sodium 740mg • Total Carbohydrate 35g • Dietary Fiber 2g • Sugars 6g • Protein 25g.
DIETARY EXCHANGES: 2 Starch • 1/2 Other Carbohydrate • 2-1/2 High-Fat Meat.

chicken divan pot pie

PREP TIME: 30 MINUTES
READY IN: 1 HOUR 5 MINUTES
SERVINGS: 6

1 (15 oz.) package Pillsbury® Refrigerated Pie Crusts, softened as directed on package

3 tablespoons butter

3 tablespoons Pillsbury BEST® All-Purpose Flour

1/4 teaspoon pepper

1/2 cup chicken broth

1/4 cup milk

1 cup shredded American cheese (4 oz.)

2 cups diced cooked chicken

1 (9 oz.) package Green Giant® Frozen Cut Broccoli, thawed, well drained

1 Heat oven to 425°F. Prepare pie crusts as directed on package for two-crust pie using 9-inch glass pie pan.

2 Melt butter in medium saucepan over medium-low heat. Stir in flour and pepper; cook until mixture is smooth and bubbly. Gradually add broth and milk, stirring constantly, until mixture boils and thickens.

3 Add cheese; stir until melted. Stir in chicken and broccoli. Pour mixture into crust-lined pan. Top with second crust; seal edges and flute. Cut small slits in several places in top crust.

4 Bake at 425°F for 30 to 35 minutes or until crust is golden brown and filling is bubbly. Cover edge of crust with strips of foil after first 15 to 20 minutes of baking to prevent excessive browning. Cool 10 minutes before serving.

NUTRITIONAL INFORMATION PER SERVING:
Calories 560 • Total Fat 34g • Saturated Fat 16g • Cholesterol 95mg • Sodium 780mg • Total Carbohydrate 41g • Dietary Fiber 2g • Sugars 4g • Protein 22g.
DIETARY EXCHANGES: 2-1/2 Starch • 2-1/2 Other Carbohydrate • 2 Lean Meat • 5-1/2 Fat.

quick beef stew in bread bowls

READY IN: 35 MINUTES
SERVINGS: 4

1 (11 oz.) can Pillsbury® Refrigerated Crusty French Loaf

1 (17 oz.) package refrigerated precooked beef tips with gravy

1 (9 oz.) box Green Giant® Frozen Roasted Potatoes with Garlic & Herbs

1 (9 oz.) box Green Giant® Frozen Sweet Peas & Pearl Onions

1/2 cup beef gravy (from 12 oz. jar)

1/3 cup water

1 tablespoon Worcestershire sauce

1 Heat oven to 350°F. Spray cookie sheet with nonstick cooking spray. Remove dough from can; do not unroll. Cut dough into 4 equal pieces. Shape each into ball, placing seam at bottom so dough is smooth on top. Place dough balls, seam side down, on cookie sheet.

2 Bake 18 to 20 minutes or until deep golden brown. Remove from cookie sheet; place on wire rack. Cool 10 minutes.

3 Meanwhile, heat beef tips with gravy, and cook potatoes and peas with onions in microwave as directed on package and boxes. In 2-quart microwavable bowl, mix beef with gravy and vegetables. Stir

in remaining ingredients. Microwave mixture on High 1 to 2 minutes or until thoroughly heated.

4 Cut top off each bread loaf. Lightly press center of bread down to form bowls. Place each bread bowl in individual shallow soup plate. Spoon about 1 cup stew into each. Place top of each bread bowl next to filled bowl.

HIGH ALTITUDE (3500-6500 FT):
Bake at 375°F for 18 to 20 minutes.

NUTRITIONAL INFORMATION PER SERVING:
Calories 530 • Total Fat 19g • Saturated Fat 6g • Trans Fat 0.5g • Cholesterol 50mg • Sodium 1,510mg • Total Carbohydrate 62g • Dietary Fiber 5g • Sugars 9g • Protein 26g.
DIETARY EXCHANGES: 4 Starch • 1 Vegetable • 1-1/2 High-Fat Meat • 1 Fat.

canadian bacon-apple pizza

READY IN: 30 MINUTES
SERVINGS: 16 APPETIZERS

Arlene Swiatek Gillen
Holland, NY

4 teaspoons sesame seed

1 (13.8 oz.) can Pillsbury® Refrigerated Pizza Crust

3/4 lb. thinly sliced Canadian bacon

2-1/2 tablespoons horseradish mustard

1/4 teaspoon dried thyme leaves

2 large tart green apples, peeled, sliced (3 cups)

1 (8 oz.) package deli-thin Swiss cheese slices

1 Heat oven to 400°F. Lightly spray large cookie sheet with nonstick cooking spray or grease with shortening. Sprinkle sesame seed onto sprayed cookie sheet. Unroll dough; place over seed. Cover with waxed paper. With rolling pin, roll dough into 16x13-inch rectangle; remove the paper.

2 Bake for 11 to 16 minutes or until lightly browned. Meanwhile, arrange Canadian bacon slices on large microwavable plate; cover with microwavable plastic wrap. Microwave on High for 30 seconds. Rearrange bacon; cover and microwave an additional 30 to 60 seconds or until thoroughly heated. If necessary, drain off any liquid.

3 Remove partially baked crust from oven. Set oven to broil. Spread mustard over crust; sprinkle evenly with thyme. Layer bacon, apples and cheese over the mustard, covering the entire surface.

4 Broil 5 to 6 inches from heat for 4 to 7 minutes or just until cheese begins to bubble and turns light brown. With pizza cutter, cut into 16 squares. Serve warm.

NUTRITIONAL INFORMATION PER SERVING:
Calories 160 • Total Fat 7g • Saturated Fat 3g • Cholesterol 25mg • Sodium 500mg • Total Carbohydrate 16g • Dietary Fiber 0g • Sugars 4g • Protein 10g.

cheeseburger spaghetti pie

PREP TIME: 15 MINUTES
READY IN: 1 HOUR
SERVINGS: 6

CRUST

- 6 oz. uncooked vermicelli or spaghetti
- 1 egg
- 1 tablespoon prepared mustard

FILLING

- 1 lb. lean (at least 80%) ground beef
- 1/2 cup chopped onion (1 medium)
- 1/2 teaspoon seasoned salt
- 1/2 cup cooked real bacon pieces
- 1 (15 oz.) can Italian-style tomato sauce
- 1 cup finely shredded Cheddar cheese (4 oz.)
- 9 dill pickle hamburger slices

1 Heat oven to 350°F. Spray 9-1/2-inch deep-dish or 10-inch glass pie pan with nonstick cooking spray. Cook vermicelli as directed on package. Drain.

2 In large bowl, beat egg and mustard until blended. Add cooked vermicelli; toss to coat evenly. Spoon mixture into sprayed pie pan, pushing mixture up sides of pan to form crust.

3 In 10-inch nonstick skillet, break up ground beef; add onion and sprinkle with seasoned salt. Cook over medium-high heat until beef is thoroughly cooked, stirring frequently. Drain.

4 Stir in bacon and tomato sauce. Spoon evenly into vermicelli-lined pie pan, pushing to edge almost covering vermicelli. Sprinkle with 1/2 cup of the cheese.

5 Bake at 350°F for 30 minutes. Top with pickle slices; sprinkle with remaining 1/2 cup cheese. Bake an additional 10 to 15 minutes or until thoroughly heated and cheese is melted. Let stand 5 minutes before serving.

HIGH ALTITUDE (3500-6500 FT):
Spray 10-inch glass pie pan with nonstick cooking spray. Bake pie at 350°F for 35 minutes. After topping with pickle slices and sprinkling with cheese, bake an additional 10 to 15 minutes.

NUTRITIONAL INFORMATION PER SERVING:
Calories 410 • Total Fat 20g • Saturated Fat 9g • Cholesterol 105mg • Sodium 1,090mg • Total Carbohydrate 30g • Dietary Fiber 2g • Sugars 5g • Protein 28g.
DIETARY EXCHANGES: 2 Starch • 3 Medium-Fat Meat • 1 Fat.

cheesy bean and chicken pizza

PREP TIME: 15 MINUTES
READY IN: 30 MINUTES
SERVINGS: 6

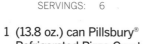

Patrice Kavanagh
Easton, PA

- 1 (13.8 oz.) can Pillsbury® Refrigerated Pizza Crust
- 3/4 cup regular or reduced-fat mayonnaise
- 1 teaspoon lime or lemon juice
- 1 (4.5 oz.) can Old El Paso® Chopped Green Chiles, drained
- 1 (15 oz.) can Progresso® Dark Red or Red Kidney Beans, well drained
- 1 cup shredded cooked chicken
- 1-1/2 cups shredded Mexican cheese blend (6 oz.)
- 2 tablespoons chopped fresh cilantro

1 Heat oven to 425°F. Lightly grease a 14-inch pizza pan with shortening or cooking spray. Unroll dough; place in pan. Starting at center, press out dough to edge of pan. Bake 8 to 10 minutes or just until crust begins to brown around edge.

2 Meanwhile, in small bowl, mix mayonnaise, lime juice and chiles.

3 Gently spread mayonnaise mixture over partially baked crust. Top with beans, chicken and cheese. Bake 10 to 14 minutes longer or until crust is golden brown. Sprinkle with cilantro before serving if desired.

NUTRITIONAL INFORMATION PER SERVING:
Calories 590 • Total Fat 34g • Saturated Fat 10g • Cholesterol 60mg • Sodium 900mg • Total Carbohydrate 47g • Dietary Fiber 4g • Sugars 6g • Protein 24g.
DIETARY EXCHANGES: 3 Starch • 2 Medium-Fat Meat • 4-1/2 Fat.

pizza bubble ring

PREP TIME: 20 MINUTES
READY IN: 1 HOUR 5 MINUTES
SERVINGS: 20 APPETIZERS

6 to 8 tablespoons butter or margarine, melted

1 teaspoon Italian seasoning

1/2 teaspoon garlic powder

2 (12 oz.) cans Pillsbury® Golden Layers® Refrigerated Original or Buttermilk Flaky Biscuits

40 small slices pepperoni (about 3 oz.)

8 oz. mozzarella cheese, cut into 20 pieces

1/4 cup grated Parmesan cheese

1-1/4 cups pizza sauce, heated

1 Heat oven to 350°F. Spray 12-cup fluted tube pan with cooking spray. In small bowl, mix melted butter, Italian seasoning and garlic powder.

2 Separate 1 can of dough into 10 biscuits; press or roll each into 3-inch round. Place 2 pepperoni slices in center of each biscuit round. Top each with piece of mozzarella cheese. Bring dough up around filling; press edge to seal and shape each into ball. Roll in butter mixture; place 10 balls in pan.

3 Sprinkle dough balls with Parmesan cheese. Repeat with remaining can of biscuits, placing balls over balls in pan. Pour remaining butter mixture over top.

4 Bake 33 to 38 minutes or until deep golden brown. Cool in pan 5 minutes. Gently loosen bread from side of pan. Place large heatproof plate upside down over pan; turn plate and pan over. Remove pan. Serve warm with warm pizza sauce for dipping. Store in refrigerator.

HIGH ALTITUDE (3500-6500 FT):
Bake at 350°F for 35 to 40 minutes.

NUTRITIONAL INFORMATION PER SERVING:
Calories 220 • Total Fat 14g • Saturated Fat 6g • Trans Fat 2.5g • Cholesterol 20mg • Sodium 610mg • Total Carbohydrate 16g • Dietary Fiber 0g • Sugars 4g • Protein 7g.
DIETARY EXCHANGES: 1 Starch • 1/2 High-Fat Meat • 2 Fat.

buffalo chicken pizzas

PREP TIME: 20 MINUTES
READY IN: 40 MINUTES
SERVINGS: 4

Pillsbury Bake-Off®

Kristin McLaughlin
Boyertown, PA

Olive oil

1 (13.8 oz.) can Pillsbury® Refrigerated Pizza Crust

3 tablespoons butter or margarine

1 lb. boneless skinless chicken breasts, cut into 1/2-inch pieces

1 medium sweet onion, chopped (1/2 cup)

3 tablespoons red pepper sauce

1 cup diced plum (Roma) tomatoes (about 3 medium)

1 cup shredded Monterey Jack cheese (4 oz.)

1 Heat oven to 425°F. Lightly coat cookie sheet with olive oil. Unroll dough; with sharp knife or pizza cutter, cut into 4 rectangles. Place rectangles on cookie sheet; press each into 6x5-inch rectangle.

2 In 10-inch skillet, melt butter over medium-high heat. Add chicken, onion and red pepper sauce; cook 4 to 6 minutes, stirring occasionally, until chicken is no longer pink in center. Remove from heat; stir in tomatoes.

3 With slotted spoon, spoon mixture over dough rectangles to within 1/4 inch of edges. Sprinkle evenly with the cheese.

4 Bake 13 to 16 minutes or until the crust is deep golden brown.

NUTRITIONAL INFORMATION PER SERVING:
Calories 590 • Total Fat 25g • Saturated Fat 12g • Cholesterol 115mg • Sodium 1,050mg • Total Carbohydrate 51g • Dietary Fiber 2g • Sugars 8g • Protein 40g.

southwestern & italian favorites

Brimming with incredible flavor and tongue-tingling satisfaction, few foods generate more excitement than south-of-the-border staples and Italian specialties. After all, tantalizing spices, hearty cheeses and aromatic herbs turn these savory mainstays into welcomed showpieces on any menu. Try the following casseroles and stovetop delights when you want to chase away the dinnertime doldrums.

Fiesta Enchilada
Bake
page 86

Mediterranean
Penne Pasta
and Beans
page 83

Chicken
Cheese
Enchiladas
page 81

pepperoni-ravioli supper
page 78

linguine chicken primavera

READY IN: 35 MINUTES
SERVINGS: 4

8 oz. uncooked linguine

1 lb. boneless skinless chicken breast halves, cut into 1-inch pieces

1 (1 oz.) package ranch salad dressing mix

1 tablespoon margarine or butter

1 garlic clove, minced

1 (1 lb.) package Green Giant Select® Frozen Broccoli, Carrots and Cauliflower

1 cup skim milk

1/4 cup light cream cheese (from 8 oz. tub)

1/2 cup shredded fresh Parmesan cheese (2 oz.)

1 Cook linguine to desired doneness as directed on package. Drain; cover to keep warm.

2 Meanwhile, in resealable food storage plastic bag, combine chicken and 2 tablespoons of the salad dressing mix; shake to coat.

3 Melt margarine in 12-inch nonstick skillet over medium-high heat. Add garlic; cook 1 minute. Add chicken; cook and stir 4 to 6 minutes or until chicken is lightly browned.

4 Add frozen vegetables; cover and cook 6 to 8 minutes or until chicken is no longer pink and vegetables are crisp-tender, stirring occasionally.

5 In small bowl, combine milk and remaining salad dressing mix; mix well. Reduce heat to medium; stir milk mixture and cream cheese into chicken mixture. Cook 1 to 2 minutes or until slightly thickened, stirring constantly. Add the cooked linguine and the Parmesan cheese; toss gently to mix.

NUTRITIONAL INFORMATION PER SERVING: Calories 500 • Total Fat 13g • Saturated Fat 5g • Cholesterol 85mg • Sodium 470mg • Total Carbohydrate 53g • Dietary Fiber 4g • Sugars 8g • Protein 42g.
DIETARY EXCHANGES: 3 Starch • 3 Other Carbohydrate • 1 Vegetable • 4-1/2 Very Lean Meat • 1-1/2 Fat.

italian spinach torta

PREP TIME: 15 MINUTES
READY IN: 1 HOUR 15 MINUTES
SERVINGS: 12

Larry Elder
Charlotte, NC

CRUST

1 (15 oz.) box Pillsbury® Refrigerated Pie Crusts, softened as directed on box

FILLING

1 (9 oz.) box Green Giant® Frozen Spinach, thawed, squeezed to drain

1 cup ricotta cheese

1/2 cup grated Parmesan cheese

1/4 to 1/2 teaspoon garlic salt

1/4 teaspoon pepper

1 egg, separated

1 teaspoon water

1 Make pie crusts as directed on box for two-crust pie using 10-inch tart pan with removable bottom or 9-inch glass pie pan. Place 1 pie crust in pan; press in bottom and up sides of pan. Trim the edges if necessary.

2 Place oven rack in lowest rack position; heat oven to 400°F. In medium bowl, mix spinach, ricotta cheese, Parmesan cheese, garlic salt, pepper and egg yolk until well blended; spread evenly in crust-lined pan.

3 To make lattice top, cut remaining pie crust into

3/4-inch-wide strips; arrange in lattice design over spinach mixture. Trim and seal edges. In small bowl with fork, beat egg white and water; gently brush over lattice.

4 Bake on lowest oven rack 45 to 50 minutes or until dark golden brown. If necessary, cover torta with foil during last 5 to 10 minutes of baking to prevent excessive browning. Cool 10 minutes; remove sides of pan.

NUTRITIONAL INFORMATION PER SERVING: Calories 200 • Total Fat 11g • Saturated Fat 4.5g • Cholesterol 30mg • Sodium 290mg • Total Carbohydrate 20g • Dietary Fiber 0g • Sugars 3g • Protein 6g.

stuffed poblano chile peppers

PREP TIME: 30 MINUTES
READY IN: 1 HOUR 10 MINUTES
SERVINGS: 6

Paula Blevins-Russell
Alabaster, AL

6 poblano chiles

1 lb. lean ground turkey

1 (1.25 oz.) package Old El Paso® Taco Seasoning Mix

1 (15 oz.) can Progresso® Black Beans, drained, rinsed

1 (11 oz.) can Green Giant® Mexicorn® Whole Kernel Corn, Red and Green Peppers, drained

2 cups shredded light Mexican cheese blend (8 oz.)

1 (14.5 oz.) can stewed tomatoes, undrained, chopped

1 (4.5 oz.) can Old El Paso® Chopped Green Chiles

1 Heat oven to 350°F. Spray 13x9-inch (3-quart) glass baking dish with nonstick cooking spray. Cut opening in one side of each chile. Carefully remove seeds and membranes, leaving top stem intact; rinse and drain well.

2 Spray large skillet with nonstick cooking spray. Add ground turkey; cook over medium-high heat for 7 minutes or until no longer pink and thoroughly cooked, stirring frequently. Add taco seasoning mix; mix well. Add beans, corn and 1 cup of the cheese; mix well. With small spoon, stuff chiles with turkey mixture. Place in sprayed baking dish. Lightly spray tops of chiles with nonstick cooking spray.

3 In small bowl, combine tomatoes and green chiles; mix well. Pour over stuffed chiles in baking dish.

4 Bake at 350°F for 30 to 40 minutes or until chiles are tender. Sprinkle with remaining 1 cup cheese. Bake an additional 3 minutes or until the cheese is melted.

NUTRITIONAL INFORMATION PER SERVING:
Calories 400 • Total Fat 15g • Saturated Fat 6g • Cholesterol 70mg • Sodium 1,390mg • Total Carbohydrate 33g • Dietary Fiber 7g • Sugars 6g • Protein 32g.
DIETARY EXCHANGES: 2 Starch • 2 Other Carbohydrate • 3-1/2 Lean Meat • 1 Fat.

pepperoni-ravioli supper

READY IN: 30 MINUTES
SERVINGS: 5

2 (9 oz.) packages refrigerated cheese-filled ravioli

1 (26 to 28 oz.) jar tomato pasta sauce

1 (4.5 oz.) jar Green Giant® Sliced Mushrooms, drained

1 (3.5 oz.) package sliced pepperoni, halved (about 1 cup)

1 cup shredded mozzarella cheese (4 oz.)

1 Cook ravioli as directed on package. Drain; cover to keep warm.

2 Meanwhile, in large saucepan, combine the pasta sauce, mushrooms and pepperoni; mix well. Bring to a boil. Reduce heat; simmer 8 to 10 minutes or until the sauce is slightly thickened, stirring occasionally.

3 Add cooked ravioli; stir gently to coat. Spoon onto serving platter. Sprinkle with cheese.

NUTRITIONAL INFORMATION PER SERVING: Calories 520 • Total Fat 26g • Saturated Fat 10g • Cholesterol 130mg • Sodium 2,200mg • Total Carbohydrate 47g • Dietary Fiber 3g • Sugars 13g • Protein 24g.
DIETARY EXCHANGES: 3 Starch • 2 High-Fat Meat • 2 Fat.

TIP: To turn this dish into Sausage-Ravioli Supper, prepare the recipe with 1 cup of cooked, crumbled Italian sausage in place of the pepperoni. Pillsbury® Refrigerated Garlic Breadsticks are perfect alongside this ravioli. Brownies and milk finish the meal.

light sour cream chicken enchiladas

PREP TIME: 15 MINUTES
READY IN: 45 MINUTES
SERVINGS: 6

1 (8 oz.) container light sour cream

1 (8 oz.) container nonfat plain yogurt

1 (10-3/4 oz.) can condensed 99%-fat-free cream of chicken soup with 1/3 less sodium

1 (4.5 oz.) can diced green chiles, undrained

12 (6- or 7-inch) white flour or corn tortillas

1 cup shredded reduced-fat Cheddar cheese (4 oz.)

1-1/2 cups chopped cooked chicken

1/4 cup sliced green onions

1 Heat oven to 350°F. Spray 13x9-inch (3-quart) baking dish with nonstick cooking spray. In medium bowl, combine sour cream, yogurt, soup and chiles; mix well.

2 Spoon about 3 tablespoons sour cream mixture down center of each tortilla. Reserve 1/4 cup of the cheese; sprinkle tortillas with remaining cheese, chicken and onions. Roll up; place in sprayed dish. Spoon remaining sour cream mixture over tortillas. Cover with foil.

3 Bake at 350°F for 25 to 30 minutes or until hot and bubbly. Remove foil; sprinkle with reserved 1/4 cup cheese. Bake uncovered for an additional 5 minutes or until cheese is melted. If desired, garnish with shredded lettuce and chopped tomatoes.

NUTRITIONAL INFORMATION PER SERVING: Calories 360 • Total Fat 11g • Saturated Fat 4g • Cholesterol 50mg • Sodium 1,060mg • Total Carbohydrate 41g • Dietary Fiber 2g • Sugars 9g • Protein 24g.
DIETARY EXCHANGES: 2-1/2 Starch • 1 Vegetable • 2 Lean Meat • 1/2 Fat.

chicken with dijon-tarragon cream sauce

READY IN: 25 MINUTES
SERVINGS: 4

8 oz. uncooked fettuccine

1 tablespoon butter or margarine

1 lb. boneless skinless chicken breasts, cut into 1/2-inch pieces

3/4 cup sour cream

1/2 cup milk

2 tablespoons Dijon mustard

1 tablespoon chopped fresh tarragon or 1 teaspoon dried tarragon leaves

2 tablespoons chopped fresh parsley, if desired

1 Cook and drain fettuccine as directed on package.

2 Meanwhile, in 10-inch skillet, melt butter over medium heat. Add chicken; cook 8 to 10 minutes, stirring frequently, until no longer pink in center.

3 In small bowl, mix sour cream, milk and mustard until smooth. Stir in tarragon. Pour into skillet with chicken. Cook about 5 minutes, stirring frequently, until thoroughly heated. Serve chicken mixture over fettuccine; sprinkle with parsley.

NUTRITIONAL INFORMATION PER SERVING: Calories 470 • Total Fat 18g • Saturated Fat 8g • Trans Fat 0.5g • Cholesterol 155mg • Sodium 310mg • Total Carbohydrate 41g • Dietary Fiber 2g • Sugars 3g • Protein 35g. DIETARY EXCHANGES: 2-1/2 Starch • 4 Lean Meat • 1 Fat.

penne with italian sausage and peppers

READY IN: 40 MINUTES
SERVINGS: 6

1 (16 oz.) package uncooked penne pasta

1 teaspoon dried basil leaves

6 hot or spicy Italian sausage links (about 1-1/2 lb.)

1 red bell pepper, cut into 1/2-inch pieces

1 green bell pepper, cut into 1/2-inch pieces

1 onion, cut into 1/2-inch pieces

1-1/2 cups diced Italian plum tomatoes

1 (15 oz.) can Italian-style tomato sauce

1/4 cup shredded fresh Asiago cheese (1 oz.)

1 Cook penne in large saucepan to desired doneness as directed on package. Drain; return to saucepan. Add the basil; toss to coat. Cover to keep warm.

2 Meanwhile, heat large nonstick skillet over medium heat until hot. Add sausage links, bell peppers and onion; cook 6 to 8 minutes or until sausage links are browned, stirring occasionally.

3 Add tomatoes and tomato sauce; mix well. Reduce heat to medium-low; cover and cook 13 to 15 minutes or until sausage links are thoroughly cooked and sauce is of desired consistency, stirring occasionally. Serve sauce over penne. Sprinkle with cheese.

NUTRITIONAL INFORMATION PER SERVING: Calories 660 • Total Fat 29g • Saturated Fat 10g • Cholesterol 80mg • Sodium 1,670mg • Total Carbohydrate 72g • Dietary Fiber 5g • Sugars 10g • Protein 33g. DIETARY EXCHANGES: 4-1/2 Starch • 4-1/2 Other Carbohydrate • 1 Vegetable • 2-1/2 High-Fat Meat • 2 Fat.

spinach pesto manicotti

PREP TIME: 35 MINUTES
READY IN: 1 HOUR 15 MINUTES
SERVINGS: 6

8 oz. uncooked manicotti

1 lb. extra-lean ground beef

1 (9 oz.) package Green Giant® Frozen Spinach, thawed, squeezed to drain and chopped

4 oz. mozzarella cheese, diced (about 1 cup)

1/2 cup purchased pesto

1 egg

1 (26 to 28 oz.) jar tomato pasta sauce

1 Heat oven to 400°F. Spray 13x9-inch (3-quart) glass baking dish with nonstick cooking spray. Cook manicotti to desired doneness as directed on package. Drain; rinse with cold water to cool. Drain well.

2 Meanwhile, in large bowl, combine ground beef, spinach, cheese, pesto and egg. If desired, add salt and pepper; mix well. For easier stuffing, place beef mixture in resealable freezer plastic bag; seal bag. Cut hole in bottom corner of bag.

3 Fill each manicotti by squeezing beef mixture into

manicotti; place in sprayed baking dish. Pour pasta sauce over manicotti. Cover with foil.

4 Bake at 400°F for 30 to 40 minutes or until filling is no longer pink in center.

HIGH ALTITUDE (3500-6500 FT):
Bake 35 to 45 minutes.

NUTRITIONAL INFORMATION PER SERVING:
Calories 610 • Total Fat 29g • Saturated Fat 8g • Cholesterol 95mg • Sodium 1,110mg • Total Carbohydrate 56g • Dietary Fiber 4g • Sugars 11g • Protein 31g.
DIETARY EXCHANGES: 4 Starch • 4 Other Carbohydrate • 2-1/2 Medium-Fat Meat • 3 Fat.

cheesy baked ravioli

PREP TIME: 5 MINUTES
READY IN: 1 HOUR 15 MINUTES
SERVINGS: 6

1 (26 to 28 oz.) jar tomato pasta sauce

1 (10-3/4 oz.) can condensed Cheddar cheese soup

1 (25 oz.) package frozen Italian sausage-filled ravioli

1-1/2 cups frozen bell pepper and onion stir fry

1-1/2 cups shredded mozzarella cheese (6 oz.)

1 Heat oven to 350°F. Spray 13x9-inch (3-quart) glass baking dish with nonstick cooking spray. In sprayed dish, combine pasta sauce and soup; mix well.

2 Add frozen ravioli, and bell pepper and onion stir fry; stir to coat. Cover with foil.

3 Bake at 350°F for 1 hour. Uncover baking dish; sprinkle with cheese. Bake uncovered an additional 5 to 10 minutes or until casserole is bubbly and cheese is melted.

HIGH ALTITUDE (3500-6500 FT):
After sprinkling with cheese, bake uncovered an additional 10 to 15 minutes.

NUTRITIONAL INFORMATION PER SERVING:
Calories 515 • Total Fat 22g • Saturated Fat 9g • Cholesterol 160mg • Sodium 2,080mg • Total Carbohydrate 55g • Dietary Fiber 3g • Sugars 11g • Protein 24g.
DIETARY EXCHANGES: 3-1/2 Starch • 3-1/2 Other Carbohydrate • 2 High-Fat Meat • 1 Fat.

chicken cheese enchiladas

PREP TIME: 15 MINUTES
READY IN: 40 MINUTES
SERVINGS: 6

Barbie Lee
Tavernier, FL

- 1 (1.25 oz.) package Old El Paso® Taco Seasoning Mix
- 1 tablespoon olive oil
- 1/2 cup water
- 1 lb. boneless skinless chicken breasts, cut into bite-sized pieces or strips
- 3 cups shredded Monterey Jack cheese (12 oz.)
- 1/3 cup chopped fresh cilantro
- 1/2 teaspoon salt
- 1 (15 oz.) container ricotta cheese
- 1 (4.5 oz.) can Old El Paso® Chopped Green Chiles
- 1 egg
- 1 (16 oz.) jar Old El Paso® Thick 'n Chunky Salsa
- 1 (10.5 oz.) package Old El Paso® Flour Tortillas (12 tortillas)

1 Heat oven to 350°F. In resealable food storage plastic bag, combine taco seasoning mix, oil and 1/4 cup of the water; seal bag and mix well. Add chicken pieces; turn to mix. Refrigerate 5 minutes or up to 12 hours.

2 In medium bowl, combine 2-1/2 cups of the Monterey Jack cheese, cilantro, salt, ricotta cheese, chiles and egg; mix well.

3 Heat large nonstick skillet over medium-high heat until hot. Add chicken with marinade; cook and stir 5 to 10 minutes or until chicken is no longer pink in center.

4 In ungreased 13x9-inch (3-quart) glass baking dish, combine 1/2 cup of the salsa and remaining 1/4 cup water;

mix well. Spread evenly in bottom of baking dish. Spoon 1/3 cup cheese mixture down center of each tortilla. Top with chicken; roll up. Place filled tortillas, seam side down, over salsa mixture in baking dish. Drizzle enchiladas with remaining salsa. Sprinkle with remaining 1/2 cup Monterey Jack cheese.

5 Bake at 350°F for 20 to 25 minutes or until the cheese is melted.

NUTRITIONAL INFORMATION PER SERVING: Calories 630 • Total Fat 33g • Saturated Fat 17g • Cholesterol 150mg • Sodium 2,160mg • Total Carbohydrate 40g • Dietary Fiber 2g • Sugars 6g • Protein 44g.
DIETARY EXCHANGES: 2-1/2 Starch • 2-1/2 Other Carbohydrate • 5 Medium-Fat Meat • 1 Fat.

mediterranean penne pasta and beans

mediterranean penne pasta and beans

READY IN: 30 MINUTES
SERVINGS: 4

- 6 oz. uncooked penne (1-3/4 cups)
- 1 tablespoon olive or vegetable oil
- 2 garlic cloves, minced
- 2 (14.5 oz.) cans no-salt-added tomatoes, undrained, cut up
- 1 (15 oz.) can Green Giant®, Joan of Arc® or Old El Paso® Garbanzo Beans or Progresso® Chick Peas, drained, rinsed
- 1-1/2 teaspoons dried Italian seasoning
- 1 teaspoon sugar
- 1 (10 oz.) package prewashed fresh spinach, stems removed, chopped (about 8 cups)
- 1/2 cup crumbled feta cheese (2 oz.)
- 1/4 cup sliced ripe olives

1 Cook penne to desired doneness as directed on package. Drain; cover to keep warm.

2 Meanwhile, heat oil in large skillet or Dutch oven over medium-high heat until hot. Add garlic; cook and stir 30 seconds. Add tomatoes, beans, Italian seasoning and sugar; mix well. Bring to a boil. Reduce heat; simmer 10 minutes.

3 Add spinach; cook 3 minutes or until spinach wilts, stirring frequently.

4 To serve, arrange cooked penne on large serving platter. Top with tomato mixture. Sprinkle with cheese and olives.

NUTRITIONAL INFORMATION PER SERVING: Calories 400 • Total Fat 10g • Saturated Fat 3g • Cholesterol 15mg • Sodium 470mg • Total Carbohydrate 61g • Dietary Fiber 10g • Sugars 8g • Protein 16g. **DIETARY EXCHANGES:** 3 Starch • 3 Other Carbohydrate • 3 Vegetable, 2 Fat.

HEALTHY HINT: Cans of no-salt-added tomatoes can reduce the sodium in this recipe by about 280 milligrams per serving. Complete the dinner with a few pineapple slices.

southwest chicken and fettuccine

READY IN: 20 MINUTES
SERVINGS: 4

- 1 (9 oz.) package refrigerated fettuccine
- 1 (14-1/2 oz.) can diced tomatoes with green chiles or jalapeno chiles, undrained
- 1 (9 oz.) package frozen southwestern-flavored cooked chicken breast strips, thawed
- 1 cup shredded Monterey Jack cheese (4 oz.)
- 1 medium avocado, pitted, peeled and chopped, if desired

1 Cook fettuccine to desired doneness as directed on package. Drain in colander.

2 In same saucepan, combine tomatoes and chicken; mix well. Cook over medium heat until thoroughly heated, stirring occasionally. Stir in fettuccine. Sprinkle individual servings with cheese and avocado.

NUTRITIONAL INFORMATION PER SERVING: Calories 405 • Total Fat 19g • Saturated Fat 8g • Cholesterol 100mg • Sodium 830mg • Total Carbohydrate 27g • Dietary Fiber 3g • Sugars 6g • Protein 31g. **DIETARY EXCHANGES:** 1-1/2 Starch • 1 Vegetable, 3-1/2 Lean Meat • 1-1/2 Fat.

taco steak pasta

READY IN: 30 MINUTES
SERVINGS: 4

Kathi Manzagol
Monterey, CA

- 1 tablespoon vegetable oil
- 1 lb. boneless lean beef sirloin steak, cut into bite-size strips
- 3 cups hot water
- 1 (7.1 oz.) box Hamburger Helper® Beef Taco
- 1/4 cup milk
- 1/2 cup finely chopped red bell pepper
- 1/2 teaspoon ground chipotle chiles
- 1/4 cup whipping cream
- 1 (11 oz.) can Green Giant® Super Sweet Yellow and White Corn, drained
- 1/2 cup sliced almonds

1 In 10- or 12-inch skillet, heat oil over medium-high heat. Add beef strips; cook and stir until browned. Drain. Stir in water and sauce mix. Increase heat to high; heat to boiling, stirring occasionally. Stir in pasta. Reduce heat to medium-low; cover and simmer about 10 minutes, stirring occasionally, until pasta is tender (sauce will thicken as it stands).

2 Meanwhile, in small bowl, stir milk and topping mix 30 seconds until blended; set aside.

3 Stir bell pepper, ground chipotle chiles, whipping cream and corn into pasta mixture. Cook about 2 minutes, stirring occasionally, until thoroughly heated. Remove from heat. Spoon topping over beef mixture. Sprinkle with almonds.

NUTRITIONAL INFORMATION PER SERVING:
Calories 540 • Total Fat 20g • Saturated Fat 5g • Trans Fat 0g • Cholesterol 80mg • Sodium 1,250mg • Total Carbohydrate 53g • Dietary Fiber 5g • Sugars 9g • Protein 36g.
DIETARY EXCHANGES: 3 Starch • 1/2 Other Carbohydrate • 4 Lean Meat • 1 Fat.

ground beef and spinach lasagna rollups

PREP TIME: 35 MINUTES
READY IN: 1 HOUR 15 MINUTES
SERVINGS: 2

- 1/2 lb. lean ground beef
- 1/4 cup chopped onion
- 1 (14 oz.) jar tomato pasta sauce
- 1 egg
- 3/4 cup ricotta cheese
- 2 tablespoons grated Parmesan cheese
- 2 teaspoons dried oregano leaves
- 1-1/4 cups shredded mozzarella cheese (5 oz.)
- 4 (8x2-1/2-inch) frozen precooked lasagna noodles, thawed
- 1 cup fresh baby spinach leaves, washed, stems removed

1 Heat oven to 350°F. In medium skillet, cook ground beef and onion over medium-high heat until beef is thoroughly cooked, stirring frequently. Drain. Stir in 1/2 cup of the pasta sauce. Remove skillet from heat.

2 Spread 3 tablespoons of the remaining pasta sauce in bottom of ungreased 8-inch square (2-quart) glass baking dish.

3 Beat egg in medium bowl. Add ricotta cheese, Parmesan cheese, oregano and 3/4 cup of the mozzarella cheese; mix well.

4 Spread 1/4 each of ricotta mixture, spinach leaves and beef mixture over each lasagna noodle. Starting with short side, gently and loosely roll each noodle; place seam side down over sauce in baking dish. Top rollups with remaining sauce. Cover with foil.

5 Bake at 350°F for 30 to 40 minutes or until bubbly and thoroughly heated. Remove foil; sprinkle with remaining 1/2 cup mozzarella cheese. Bake an additional 2 to 4 minutes or until cheese is melted. Let stand 5 minutes before serving.

NUTRITIONAL INFORMATION PER SERVING:
Calories 985 • Total Fat 48g • Saturated Fat 22g • Cholesterol 240mg • Sodium 1,840mg • Total Carbohydrate 78g • Dietary Fiber 5g • Sugars 19g • Protein 65g.
DIETARY EXCHANGES: 5 Starch • 5 Other Carbohydrate • 7 Medium-Fat Meat • 2-1/2 Fat.

southwestern spaghetti pie

PREP TIME: 40 MINUTES
READY IN: 1 HOUR 10 MINUTES
SERVINGS: 6

6 oz. uncooked spaghetti, broken into thirds

1/2 lb. lean ground turkey

1-1/4 cups Old El Paso® Thick 'n Chunky Salsa

3/4 cup Green Giant® Niblets® Frozen Corn, thawed

1 (15 oz.) can black beans, drained, rinsed

1 teaspoon cumin

1-1/2 cups shredded Cheddar cheese (6 oz.)

2 eggs

1 Cook spaghetti as directed on package. Drain.

2 Meanwhile, heat oven to 350°F. Spray 9-1/2-inch deep-dish glass pie pan with nonstick cooking spray. Cook ground turkey in large nonstick skillet over medium heat until no longer pink, stirring frequently. Drain. Stir in salsa, corn, beans and cumin. Cook 2 minutes or until thoroughly heated. Stir in 1/2 cup of the cheese.

3 Beat eggs in large bowl until well blended and foamy. Add cooked spaghetti; toss to coat. Spoon spaghetti mixture into sprayed pie pan, pushing mixture slightly up sides of pan to form crust. Spoon turkey mixture evenly into spaghetti-lined pie pan.

4 Bake at 350°F for 15 minutes. Sprinkle remaining 1 cup cheese over pie. Bake an additional 10 to 15 minutes or until crust is light golden brown. Let stand 10 minutes before serving.

NUTRITIONAL INFORMATION PER SERVING: Calories 415 • Total Fat 14g • Saturated Fat 7g • Cholesterol 125mg • Sodium 840mg • Total Carbohydrate 49g • Dietary Fiber 6g • Sugars 6g • Protein 29g.
DIETARY EXCHANGES: 3 Starch • 3 Lean Meat • 1 Fat.

fiesta enchilada bake

PREP TIME: 25 MINUTES
READY IN: 1 HOUR 10 MINUTES
SERVINGS: 6

1-1/4 lb. lean ground turkey

1 (10.35 oz.) box Old El Paso® Taco Dinner Kit

2/3 cup water

2 (10 oz.) cans Old El Paso® Enchilada Sauce

1/2 cup sliced green onions (8 medium)

2 cups shredded Cheddar cheese (8 oz.)

3 cups shredded lettuce

1/2 cup sour cream

1 Heat oven to 325°F. Spray 13x9-inch (3-quart) glass baking dish with nonstick cooking spray. In 2-quart saucepan, cook ground turkey over medium-high heat 4 to 6 minutes, stirring occasionally, until no longer pink; drain. Stir in seasoning mix from dinner kit and water. Cook as directed on the box.

2 Pour 1 can of the enchilada sauce into baking dish. Break taco shells from kit in half; layer half of the shells over sauce, overlapping if necessary. Top with turkey, onions and 1 cup of the cheese. Layer remaining shells over cheese. Pour remaining can of enchilada sauce over shells, coating well. Cover dish with foil.

3 Bake about 30 minutes or until hot and bubbly. Remove foil; sprinkle remaining 1 cup cheese over top. Bake uncovered about 15 minutes longer or until cheese is melted. Top individual servings with lettuce, sour cream and salsa from kit.

HIGH ALTITUDE (3500-6500 FT):
Heat oven to 350°F. Bake about 40 minutes or until hot and bubbly. Remove foil; sprinkle remaining 1 cup cheese over top. Bake uncovered 5 minutes longer or until the cheese is melted.

NUTRITIONAL INFORMATION PER SERVING:
Calories 480 • Total Fat 28g • Saturated Fat 13g • Trans Fat 0.5g • Cholesterol 115mg • Sodium 1,460mg • Total Carbohydrate 25g • Dietary Fiber 1g • Sugars 5g • Protein 33g.
DIETARY EXCHANGES: 1-1/2 Starch • 4 Very Lean Meat • 5 Fat.

---

black beans, chicken and rice

READY IN: 30 MINUTES
SERVINGS: 4

2 teaspoons oil

1 cup uncooked regular long-grain white rice

1-1/2 teaspoons cumin

1 teaspoon chili powder

2 cups cubed cooked chicken

2 cups frozen bell pepper and onion stir fry, coarsely chopped

1 (15 oz.) can black beans, drained, rinsed

1 (14 oz.) can chicken broth

2 tablespoons water

1/2 cup shredded Cheddar cheese (2 oz.)

1 Heat oil in large skillet over medium-high heat until hot. Add rice, cumin and chili powder; cook and stir 1 minute.

2 Stir in all remaining ingredients except cheese. Bring to a boil. Reduce heat; cover and simmer 15 to 18 minutes or until liquid is absorbed and rice is tender, stirring occasionally.

3 Remove skillet from heat. Uncover; fluff mixture with fork. Sprinkle with cheese. Cover; let stand 1 to 2 minutes or until the cheese is melted before serving.

HIGH ALTITUDE (3500-6500 FT):
Increase water to 3/4 cup. Increase simmer time covered to 30 to 35 minutes.

NUTRITIONAL INFORMATION PER SERVING:
Calories 550 • Total Fat 14g • Saturated Fat 5g • Cholesterol 75mg • Sodium 1,010mg • Total Carbohydrate 75g • Dietary Fiber 8g • Sugars 5g • Protein 39g.
DIETARY EXCHANGES: 4 Starch • 1 Vegetable • 3-1/2 Lean Meat • 1/2 Fat.

buffalo chicken enchiladas with creamy ranch sauce

PREP TIME: 25 MINUTES
READY IN: 1 HOUR 10 MINUTES
SERVINGS: 6 (2 ENCHILADAS EACH)

1 (10-3/4 oz.) can condensed cream of chicken soup

1 cup purchased sour cream ranch dip

2/3 cup chopped green onions (about 10 medium)

3 cups chopped cooked chicken

3/4 cup purchased buffalo wing sauce

1 (10.5 oz.) package Old El Paso® Flour Tortillas for Soft Tacos & Fajitas (twelve 6-inch tortillas)

3 cups shredded Cheddar cheese (12 oz.)

1 Heat oven to 350°F. Spray 13x9-inch (3-quart) glass baking dish with nonstick cooking spray. In medium bowl, mix soup, dip and 1/3 cup of the onions. In large bowl, mix chicken and buffalo wing sauce until coated.

2 Spoon 2 tablespoons soup mixture down center of each tortilla; set remaining mixture aside. Reserve 1/2 cup cheese for garnish. Top each tortilla with about 1/4 cup chicken mixture and scant 1/4 cup cheese. Fold sides of tortillas over filling; place seam side down in baking dish. Spoon remaining soup mixture over filled tortillas. Cover tightly with foil.

3 Bake 40 to 45 minutes or until hot and bubbly.

4 Remove from oven. Uncover; sprinkle with reserved 1/2 cup cheese and remaining 1/3 cup onions. Return to oven; bake uncovered about 5 minutes longer or until cheese is melted.

HIGH ALTITUDE (3500-6500 FT): Bake at 350°F for 45 to 50 minutes. Continue as directed above.

NUTRITIONAL INFORMATION PER SERVING: Calories 685 • Total Fat 37g • Saturated Fat 19g • Cholesterol 135mg • Sodium 1,600mg • Total Carbohydrate 47g • Dietary Fiber 2g • Sugars 12g • Protein 41g.
DIETARY EXCHANGES: 3 Starch • 4-1/2 Lean Meat • 4-1/2 Fat.

pork chop skillet and confetti salsa

READY IN: 30 MINUTES
SERVINGS: 5

PORK CHOPS

5 (4 oz.) boneless pork loin chops

1/2 teaspoon salt

1 cup water

1 (14 oz.) can chicken broth

1-1/2 cups uncooked regular long-grain white rice

1 cup Old El Paso® Thick 'n Chunky Salsa

CONFETTI SALSA

1 (11 oz.) can Green Giant® Mexicorn® Whole Kernel Corn, Red and Green Peppers, drained

1 avocado, pitted, peeled and chopped

1 papaya, peeled, seeded and chopped

1 tablespoon olive or vegetable oil

4 teaspoons fresh lime juice

1 Heat 12-inch nonstick skillet or Dutch oven over medium-high heat until hot. Sprinkle pork chops with salt; add to skillet. Cook 1 to 2 minutes or just until pork begins to brown, turning once.

2 Add water and broth. Bring to a boil. Stir in rice. Reduce heat to medium-low; cover and simmer 20 minutes or until pork is no longer pink in center, rice is tender and liquid is absorbed.

3 Meanwhile, in medium bowl, combine all confetti salsa ingredients; mix well.

4 Stir thick 'n chunky salsa into rice mixture in skillet; cook 1 minute or until thoroughly heated.

5 To serve, spoon confetti salsa over pork chops and rice. If desired, sprinkle with chopped fresh cilantro.

HIGH ALTITUDE (3500-6500 FT): Increase water to 1-1/4 cups; cover and simmer pork chops and rice 22 minutes.

NUTRITIONAL INFORMATION PER SERVING: Calories 565 • Total Fat 18g • Saturated Fat 5g • Cholesterol 70mg • Sodium 1,020mg • Total Carbohydrate 72g • Dietary Fiber 5g • Sugars 7g • Protein 34g.
DIETARY EXCHANGES: 5 Starch • 5 Other Carbohydrate • 2-1/2 Lean Meat • 2 Fat.

macaroni and cheese italian

PREP TIME: 30 MINUTES
READY IN: 55 MINUTES
SERVINGS: 4

8 oz. uncooked ziti (2-1/4 cups)

2 cups Green Giant Select® Frozen Broccoli Florets

2 cups milk

1/4 cup Pillsbury BEST® All-Purpose Flour

1/2 teaspoon salt

1/4 teaspoon hot pepper sauce

1 garlic clove, minced

1-1/2 cups shredded provolone cheese (6 oz.)

1/2 cup roasted red bell peppers (from a jar), drained, chopped

2 tablespoons Progresso® Italian Style Bread Crumbs

2 teaspoons butter or margarine, melted

1 Cook ziti in large saucepan as directed on package, adding broccoli during last minute of cooking time. Drain; return to saucepan and cover to keep warm.

2 Meanwhile, heat oven to 350°F. Spray 2-quart casserole with nonstick cooking spray. In medium saucepan, combine 1/2 cup of the milk, flour, salt, hot pepper sauce and garlic; stir with wire whisk until smooth. Stir in remaining 1-1/2 cups milk. Cook over medium heat until mixture boils and thickens, stirring constantly. Remove from heat. Add cheese; stir until melted.

3 Add cheese sauce to cooked ziti and broccoli; mix well. Stir in roasted peppers. Spoon into sprayed casserole. In small bowl, mix bread crumbs and butter. Sprinkle over top.

4 Bake at 350°F for 20 to 25 minutes or until the casserole is bubbly and the crumbs are golden brown.

NUTRITIONAL INFORMATION PER SERVING: Calories 505 • Total Fat 17g • Saturated Fat 10g • Cholesterol 45mg • Sodium 800mg • Total Carbohydrate 66g • Dietary Fiber 5g • Sugars 12g • Protein 27g. DIETARY EXCHANGES: 3-1/2 Starch • 1 Vegetable • 2 High-Fat Meat.

italian chicken sauté

READY IN: 30 MINUTES
SERVINGS: 4

- 1 tablespoon olive oil
- 1-1/4 lb. boneless skinless chicken thighs
- 2 garlic cloves, minced
- 1 (14.5 oz.) can diced tomatoes with Italian herbs, undrained
- 1 (15 or 19 oz.) can cannellini beans, drained, rinsed
- 1 tablespoon chopped fresh basil or 1 teaspoon dried basil leaves

1 Heat oil in large skillet over medium-high heat until hot. Add chicken thighs; cook until lightly browned on all sides.

2 Reduce heat to medium-low. Add garlic to skillet; cook about 1 minute or until tender. Add tomatoes; cover and cook 10 to 15 minutes or until chicken is fork-tender and juices run clear, stirring occasionally.

3 Stir in beans; cook until thoroughly heated. Sprinkle with basil.

HIGH ALTITUDE (3500-6500 FT): After adding tomatoes, cover and cook over medium-low heat for 15 to 20 minutes, stirring occasionally.

NUTRITIONAL INFORMATION PER SERVING: Calories 385 • Total Fat 15g • Saturated Fat 4g • Cholesterol 90mg • Sodium 480mg • Total Carbohydrate 29g • Dietary Fiber 7g • Sugars 3g • Protein 40g.
DIETARY EXCHANGES: 1-1/2 Starch • 5 Lean Meat.

shortcut sausage-stuffed manicotti

PREP TIME: 20 MINUTES
READY IN: 2 HOURS
SERVINGS: 7 (2 SHELLS EACH)

- 1 (26 oz.) jar sun-dried tomato pasta sauce
- 1/2 cup water
- 1-1/2 lb. uncooked Italian sausage links (7 links)
- 14 uncooked manicotti pasta shells (8 oz.)
- 2 cups shredded mozzarella cheese (8 oz.)
- 1/4 cup shredded Parmesan cheese (1 oz.)

1 Heat oven to 350°F. Spray 13x9-inch (3-quart) glass baking dish with nonstick cooking spray. Spread 1 cup of the pasta sauce in dish. To remaining sauce in jar, add water and mix well.

2 Cut sausage links in half lengthwise; remove casings. Shape each piece of sausage into roll; stuff into uncooked pasta shell. Place stuffed shells on sauce in dish. Pour remaining pasta sauce mixture over shells.

3 Cover tightly with foil; bake 1 hour 20 minutes. Sprinkle with mozzarella and Parmesan cheeses; bake uncovered 10 minutes longer or until cheeses are melted and pasta is tender. Let stand 10 minutes before serving.

NUTRITIONAL INFORMATION PER SERVING: Calories 530 • Total Fat 29g • Saturated Fat 12g • Trans Fat 0g • Cholesterol 75mg • Sodium 1,240mg • Total Carbohydrate 37g • Dietary Fiber 4g • Sugars 5g • Protein 30g.
DIETARY EXCHANGES: 2 Starch • 1 Vegetable • 3 Medium-Fat Meat • 2-1/2 Fat.

SIMPLE SUBSTITUTION: If you have bulk Italian sausage, divide it into 14 pieces. Shape each piece into a roll and stuff into a manicotti shell. Do not use smoked or precooked sausage.

fish & seafood

Crab-stuffed manicotti, sesame-ginger shrimp, old-fashioned tuna casseroles and scallops dressed in creamy sauces...these are a few of the enticing dinner opportunities that seafood offers. Whether you wish to lighten up summer meals with a refreshing fish entree or you prefer to chase away winter blues with a buttery seafood bake, the following dishes lead to truly enjoyable meals.

Smoked Salmon
and Asparagus
Primavera Pasta
page 96

Salmon with
Vegetable Pilaf
page 92

Seafood
Manicotti
page 102

fennel shrimp and fusilli
page 95

skillet fish and vegetables

READY IN: 20 MINUTES
SERVINGS: 4

1 (14-1/2 oz.) can ready-to-serve chicken broth

1 cup fresh baby carrots, quartered lengthwise

1/2 cup chopped celery

1 tablespoon dried parsley flakes

1-3/4 cups uncooked instant brown rice

1 lb. orange roughy fillets

1/4 teaspoon garlic-pepper blend

1 In 12-inch nonstick skillet, combine broth, carrots, celery and parsley flakes. Bring to a boil. Reduce heat to medium-low; cover and cook 3 minutes.

2 Uncover skillet; return to a boil. Stir in rice. Top with orange roughy fillets; sprinkle with garlic-pepper blend. Reduce heat to medium-low; cover and cook 10 to 15 minutes or until liquid is absorbed and center of fish flakes easily with fork. Garnish with fresh parsley sprigs if desired.

NUTRITIONAL INFORMATION PER SERVING: Calories 250 • Total Fat 3g • Saturated Fat 0g • Cholesterol 25mg • Sodium 460mg • Total Carbohydrate 33g • Dietary Fiber 3g • Sugars 2g • Protein 23g.
DIETARY EXCHANGES: 2 Starch • 2 Other Carbohydrate • 2-1/2 Very Lean Meat.

salmon with vegetable pilaf

READY IN: 20 MINUTES
SERVINGS: 2

SALMON

1 small carrot, thinly sliced (about 1/3 cup)

1-1/2 teaspoons chicken-flavor instant bouillon

1 teaspoon dried dill weed

1-1/2 cups water

1 cup uncooked instant brown rice

1 cup frozen french-style green beans

1 (8 oz.) salmon fillet (1/2 to 3/4 inch thick), halved

1/4 teaspoon lemon-pepper seasoning

SAUCE

2 tablespoons light sour cream

1 tablespoon mayonnaise or salad dressing

1/2 teaspoon Dijon mustard

1/4 teaspoon dried dill weed

Fresh dill

1 In large nonstick skillet, combine carrot, bouillon, 1 teaspoon dill and water. Bring to a boil. Reduce heat; cover and simmer 2 minutes.

2 Uncover skillet; stir in rice and green beans. Top with salmon, skin side down. Sprinkle salmon only with lemon-pepper seasoning. Return to a boil. Reduce heat to medium-low; cover and cook 8 to 10 minutes or until liquid is absorbed and thickest part of fish flakes easily with fork.

3 Meanwhile, in small bowl, combine all sauce ingredients; mix well.

4 To serve, remove salmon from skillet; place on serving platter. Fluff rice mixture with fork before serving. Serve sauce with salmon. Garnish with fresh dill if desired.

NUTRITIONAL INFORMATION PER SERVING: Calories 575 • Total Fat 16g • Saturated Fat 4g • Cholesterol 85mg • Sodium 1,180mg • Total Carbohydrate 81g • Dietary Fiber 8g • Sugars 6g • Protein 35g.
DIETARY EXCHANGES: 4-1/2 Starch • 1 Vegetable • 2-1/2 Lean Meat • 1-1/2 Fat.

tuna and linguine toss

READY IN: 30 MINUTES
SERVINGS: 4

8 oz. uncooked linguine

1-1/2 cups Green Giant Select® Frozen Whole Green Beans

1-1/2 cups fresh baby carrots, cut in half lengthwise if large

1/2 cup purchased pesto

2 tablespoons finely chopped red onion

2 (6 oz.) cans albacore tuna in spring water, drained, flaked

1/4 cup shredded fresh Parmesan cheese (1 oz.)

1 Cook linguine in large saucepan to desired doneness as directed on package. Drain; return to saucepan. Cover to keep warm.

2 Meanwhile, cook green beans and carrots together as directed on green bean package. Drain.

3 Add warm vegetables, pesto and onion to linguine; toss to mix. Add tuna; stir gently to mix. Sprinkle with cheese.

NUTRITIONAL INFORMATION PER SERVING:
Calories 535 • Total Fat 21g • Saturated Fat 5g • Cholesterol 35mg • Sodium 940mg • Total Carbohydrate 55g • Dietary Fiber 5g • Sugars 6g • Protein 36g.
DIETARY EXCHANGES: 3 Starch • 3 Other Carbohydrate • 1 Vegetable • 3-1/2 Very Lean Meat • 4 Fat.

caesar tuna and fettuccine

READY IN: 20 MINUTES
SERVINGS: 4

- 1 (9 oz.) package refrigerated fettuccine
- 1-1/2 cups Green Giant® Frozen Cut Green Beans
- 2 (6 oz.) cans water-packed white albacore tuna, drained, flaked
- 1/4 cup sliced ripe olives
- 1/2 cup purchased light creamy Caesar salad dressing
- 1/4 cup fat-free half-and-half
- 2 Italian plum tomatoes, coarsely chopped
- 2 tablespoons shredded fresh Parmesan cheese

1 Bring 2 quarts water (8 cups) to a boil in large saucepan or Dutch oven. Add fettuccine and green beans; cook to desired doneness as directed on fettuccine package. Drain; return to saucepan.

2 Add tuna, olives, salad dressing and half-and-half; stir gently to mix. Cook over medium-low heat just until thoroughly heated, stirring occasionally. Stir in tomatoes. Spoon into serving bowl; sprinkle with cheese.

NUTRITIONAL INFORMATION PER SERVING:
Calories 380 • Total Fat 12g • Saturated Fat 3g • Cholesterol 100mg • Sodium 990mg • Total Carbohydrate 42g • Dietary Fiber 3g • Sugars 5g • Protein 27g.
DIETARY EXCHANGES: 2-1/2 Starch • 2-1/2 Other Carbohydrate • 1 Vegetable • 2-1/2 Very Lean Meat • 1-1/2 Fat.

SIMPLE SUBSTITUTION: Try canned salmon instead of tuna in this dish. Regular tomatoes can replace the Italian variety, but squeeze out the juice first.

salmon en papillote

PREP TIME: 30 MINUTES
READY IN: 50 MINUTES
SERVINGS: 4

- Parchment paper or heavy-duty foil
- 2 teaspoons olive oil
- 2 medium potatoes, thinly sliced
- 1/2 teaspoon salt
- 1/4 teaspoon pepper
- 1 lb. salmon fillets, cut into 4 pieces
- 1 cup julienne-cut (2x1/8x1/8-inch) carrots
- 2 medium tomatoes, seeded, diced
- 8 sprigs of fresh herbs (such as dill, oregano or basil)

1 Heat oven to 400°F. Cut four 15-inch rounds of parchment paper. Fold each in half; unfold. Lightly brush 1/2 teaspoon oil onto each parchment round to within 1 inch of edge.

2 Arrange potato slices evenly on half of each parchment round. Sprinkle with half of the salt and pepper. Top each with salmon; sprinkle with remaining salt and pepper. Top each with carrots, tomatoes and 2 herb sprigs.

3 To seal each packet, fold untopped side of parchment round over topped side. Fold open edge over several times, folding and twisting until packet is completely sealed. Place the packets on an ungreased cookie sheet.

4 Bake at 400°F for 15 to 20 minutes, depending on thickness of fillets. Carefully unwrap 1 packet to check if fish flakes easily with fork; re-wrap and continue baking if not done.

5 Remove packets from oven; let stand 5 minutes before serving. Place packets on individual serving plates. Cut X-shaped slit in top of each packet; carefully tear back the paper to serve.

HIGH ALTITUDE (3500-6500 FT):
Bake at 425°F for 20 to 25 minutes.

NUTRITIONAL INFORMATION PER SERVING:
Calories 250 • Total Fat 7g • Saturated Fat 2g • Cholesterol 75mg • Sodium 380mg • Total Carbohydrate 21g • Dietary Fiber 3g • Sugars 4g • Protein 26g.
DIETARY EXCHANGES: 1-1/2 Starch • 3 Lean Meat.

crab, broccoli and roasted red pepper quiche

PREP TIME: 35 MINUTES
READY IN: 1 HOUR 35 MINUTES
SERVINGS: 6

1 Pillsbury® Refrigerated Pie Crust (from 15 oz. pkg.), softened as directed on package

1 (6 oz.) can white crabmeat, well drained

1 cup Green Giant® Frozen Cut Broccoli, thawed, drained well on paper towel

1 cup shredded provolone cheese (4 oz.)

1/3 cup chopped roasted red bell peppers (from a jar), well drained

2 tablespoons shredded fresh Parmesan cheese

4 eggs

1 cup milk

1/4 teaspoon salt

1/8 teaspoon ground red pepper (cayenne)

1 Heat oven to 425°F. Prepare pie crust as directed on package for one-crust baked shell using 9-inch glass pie pan. Bake at 425°F for 9 to 11 minutes or until light golden brown.

2 Remove baked shell from oven. Reduce oven temperature to 350°F. Layer crabmeat, broccoli, provolone cheese, roasted peppers and Parmesan cheese in baked shell.

3 Beat eggs in medium bowl until well blended. Add milk, salt and ground red pepper; blend well. Pour over mixture in shell. Cover crust with strips of foil to prevent excessive browning.

4 Bake at 350°F for 50 to 60 minutes or until knife inserted in center comes out clean. Let stand 5 to 10 minutes before serving.

NUTRITIONAL INFORMATION PER SERVING:
Calories 345 • Total Fat 20g • Saturated Fat 9g • Cholesterol 190mg • Sodium 610mg • Total Carbohydrate 22g • Dietary Fiber 1g • Sugars 5g • Protein 19g.
DIETARY EXCHANGES: 1-1/2 Starch • 2 Medium-Fat Meat • 2 Fat.

TIP: Instead of using regular provolone cheese, consider using smoked provolone. It will give this quiche a unique flavor and dimension.

fennel shrimp and fusilli

READY IN: 30 MINUTES
SERVINGS: 6

12 oz. uncooked fusilli (curly spaghetti) (3-1/2 cups)

2 tablespoons olive oil

1-1/2 lb. shelled deveined uncooked medium shrimp

1/2 teaspoon garlic salt

1/4 teaspoon pepper

1 (14.5 oz.) can diced tomatoes, undrained

1 cup coarsely chopped Italian plum tomatoes

1/2 cup sliced pitted kalamata or ripe olives

3/4 teaspoon fennel seed, crushed

2 tablespoons chopped fresh parsley

1 Cook fusilli to desired doneness as directed on package. Drain; cover pasta to keep warm.

2 Meanwhile, heat oil in large nonstick skillet over medium-high heat until hot. Add shrimp; sprinkle with garlic salt and pepper. Cook 2 to 3 minutes or until shrimp turn pink, stirring frequently.

3 Add canned tomatoes, fresh tomatoes, olives and fennel seed; mix well. Cook 2 to 3 minutes or just until thoroughly heated, stirring occasionally. Stir in fusilli. Sprinkle with parsley.

NUTRITIONAL INFORMATION PER SERVING:
Calories 370 • Total Fat 8g • Saturated Fat 1g • Cholesterol 160mg • Sodium 690mg • Total Carbohydrate 49g • Dietary Fiber 3g • Sugars 4g • Protein 26g.
DIETARY EXCHANGES: 3 Starch • 3 Other Carbohydrate • 2-1/2 Very Lean Meat • 1-1/2 Fat.

smoked salmon and asparagus primavera pasta

READY IN: 20 MINUTES
SERVINGS: 3

1 (9 oz.) package refrigerated fettuccine

1/3 cup water

1 lb. asparagus spears, trimmed, cut into 2-inch pieces

1 (10 oz.) container refrigerated reduced-fat Alfredo sauce

1 (4.5 oz.) package smoked salmon, skin removed, broken into bite-sized pieces

1 Cook fettuccine to desired doneness as directed on package. Drain; cover pasta to keep warm.

2 Meanwhile, place 1/3 cup water in medium saucepan. Bring just to a boil over medium heat. Reduce heat to medium-low. Add asparagus; cover and cook 4 to 6 minutes or until tender. Do not drain. Add the Alfredo sauce and salmon; cover and cook an additional 2 to 3 minutes or just until mixture is thoroughly heated.

3 Place fettuccine in large serving bowl. Add asparagus mixture; toss to coat.

NUTRITIONAL INFORMATION PER SERVING:
Calories 340 • Total Fat 14g • Saturated Fat 7g • Cholesterol 70mg • Sodium 920mg • Total Carbohydrate 33g • Dietary Fiber 2g • Sugars 4g • Protein 20g.
DIETARY EXCHANGES: 2 Starch • 2 Other Carbohydrate • 2 Lean Meat • 1-1/2 Fat.

shrimp with thai noodles and peanut sauce

READY IN: 25 MINUTES
SERVINGS: 4

3/4 cup water

1/2 cup creamy peanut butter

1/4 cup purchased Italian salad dressing

1 tablespoon brown sugar

2 tablespoons soy sauce

1 teaspoon grated gingerroot

1/2 teaspoon crushed red pepper flakes

1 (7 to 8 oz.) package Thai rice noodles or 8 oz. uncooked linguine

1 lb. shelled deveined cooked medium shrimp, tails removed

1 medium red bell pepper, cut into thin bite-sized strips

1/4 cup sliced green onions including tops

1 medium lime, cut into wedges

Green onions

1 In small saucepan, combine water, peanut butter, salad dressing, brown sugar, soy sauce, gingerroot and red pepper flakes. Cook over medium-low heat until smooth and warm, stirring frequently. Set aside.

2 Cook rice noodles as directed on package, adding shrimp during last minute of cooking time. Drain well; return to saucepan.

3 Add bell pepper, onions and peanut butter mixture to rice noodles and shrimp; toss gently to mix. Serve with lime wedges. If desired, garnish with additional green onion tops.

NUTRITIONAL INFORMATION PER SERVING:
Calories 590 • Total Fat 24g • Saturated Fat 4g • Cholesterol 225mg • Sodium 1,180mg • Total Carbohydrate 58g • Dietary Fiber 4g • Sugars 10g • Protein 35g.
DIETARY EXCHANGES: 3 Starch • 1 Other Carbohydrate • 3-1/2 Lean Meat • 2-1/2 Fat.

TIP: Let children help when cooking the rice noodles. They will be fascinated to see the noodles become transparent during cooking. Or, have the kids help you create a no-fuss side dish. Stir fried vegetables, such as spinach, broccoli or green beans, make a nice addition to this entree.

potato-topped tuna primavera bake

PREP TIME: 25 MINUTES
READY IN: 55 MINUTES
SERVINGS: 6

- 1 (10 oz.) container refrigerated Alfredo pasta sauce
- 2 tablespoons Pillsbury BEST® All-Purpose Flour
- 3 cups Green Giant Select® Frozen Broccoli, Carrots & Cauliflower, thawed, drained
- 1 cup Green Giant® Frozen Sweet Peas, thawed, drained
- 1 (12 oz.) can water-packed tuna, drained, flaked
- 1 (1 lb. 4 oz.) package refrigerated prepared mashed potatoes
- 2 tablespoons shredded fresh Parmesan cheese

  Chopped fresh parsley

1 Heat oven to 350°F. Spray 11x7-inch (2-quart) glass baking dish or deep-dish glass pie pan with nonstick cooking spray. In large bowl, combine Alfredo sauce and flour; mix well. Stir in vegetables and tuna. Spoon into sprayed baking dish.

2 Microwave mashed potatoes as directed on package. Stir with fork to soften. Spoon potatoes over tuna mixture; spread to cover.

3 Bake at 350°F for 30 minutes. Sprinkle cheese over potatoes; bake an additional 10 to 15 minutes or until mixture is bubbly and cheese is light golden brown. If desired, sprinkle with chopped parsley.

NUTRITIONAL INFORMATION PER SERVING:
Calories 390 • Total Fat 21g • Saturated Fat 11g • Cholesterol 65mg • Sodium 650mg • Total Carbohydrate 27g • Dietary Fiber 4g • Sugars 4g • Protein 23g.
DIETARY EXCHANGES: 1-1/2 Starch • 1 Vegetable • 2-1/2 Lean Meat • 2-1/2 Fat.

salsa cod with white beans

PREP TIME: 25 MINUTES
READY IN: 50 MINUTES
SERVINGS: 4

- 1 (16 oz.) jar Old El Paso® Thick 'n Chunky Salsa
- 2 (15 oz.) cans great northern beans, drained, rinsed
- 1 small green or red bell pepper, cut into thin strips
- 1 lb. cod, red snapper or skinless halibut fillets, cut into 4 pieces
- 1/4 cup sliced green onions
- 1/3 cup finely chopped fresh flat-leaf or curly parsley
- 1 tablespoon grated lime or orange peel
- 3 garlic cloves, finely chopped

1 Heat oven to 425°F. Spray 13x9-inch (3-quart) glass baking dish with nonstick cooking spray. Reserve 1/2 cup salsa for top. In sprayed baking dish, combine beans, bell pepper and remaining salsa; mix well.

2 Arrange fish over bean mixture. Spoon reserved 1/2 cup salsa over fish. Sprinkle with onions. Cover tightly with foil.

3 Bake for 25 minutes or until fish flakes easily with fork.

4 Meanwhile, in small bowl, combine parsley, lime peel and garlic; mix well. Serve fish and bean mixture sprinkled with parsley mixture.

NUTRITIONAL INFORMATION PER SERVING:
Calories 310 • Total Fat 2g • Saturated Fat 0g • Cholesterol 50mg • Sodium 1,250mg • Total Carbohydrate 41g • Dietary Fiber 11g • Sugars 6g • Protein 32g.
DIETARY EXCHANGES: 2-1/2 Starch • 2-1/2 Other Carbohydrate • 1 Vegetable • 3 Very Lean Meat.

old-time tuna bake

PREP TIME: 25 MINUTES
READY IN: 55 MINUTES
SERVINGS: 6

7 oz. uncooked wide egg noodles (4 cups)

1-1/2 cups Green Giant® Frozen Sweet Peas

1 (10-3/4 oz.) can condensed cream of celery soup

1 (12 oz.) can evaporated milk or 1-1/2 cups half-and-half

1 tablespoon instant minced onion

1 teaspoon seasoned salt

2 (6 oz.) cans water-packed tuna, drained, flaked

1 (2.8 oz.) can french fried onions

1 Cook noodles to desired doneness as directed on package, adding peas during last minute of cooking time. Drain.

2 Meanwhile, heat oven to 350°F. In ungreased 2-quart casserole, combine soup, milk, onion and salt; blend well. Add cooked noodles and tuna; mix well. Cover and bake for 30 minutes.

3 Remove casserole from oven; stir well. Uncover; sprinkle with french fried onions.

4 Return to oven; bake uncovered an additional 5 minutes or until onions are golden brown.

NUTRITIONAL INFORMATION PER SERVING:
Calories 420 • Total Fat 16g • Saturated Fat 6g • Cholesterol 70mg • Sodium 820mg • Total Carbohydrate 45g • Dietary Fiber 3g • Sugars 9g • Protein 24g.
DIETARY EXCHANGES: 3 Starch • 3 Other Carbohydrate • 2 Very Lean Meat • 2-1/2 Fat.

creamy scallops with angel hair pasta

READY IN: 25 MINUTES
SERVINGS: 4

8 oz. uncooked angel hair pasta (capellini)

2 tablespoons olive oil

3/4 lb. fresh or frozen small scallops, thawed, drained

2 medium tomatoes, peeled, seeded and diced

2 garlic cloves, minced

1/4 teaspoon salt

1/4 teaspoon freshly ground black pepper

1 cup whipping cream

1 tablespoon chopped fresh oregano or 1 teaspoon dried oregano leaves

1 cup crumbled feta cheese (4 oz.)

Fresh oregano

1 Cook pasta as directed on package. Drain; place in large serving bowl.

2 Meanwhile, heat oil in large skillet over medium-high heat until hot. Add scallops, tomatoes and garlic; sprinkle with salt and pepper. Cook about 2 minutes or just until surface of scallops turns opaque, stirring occasionally.

3 Stir in cream and oregano. Bring just to a boil. Add to hot pasta in bowl; toss gently to mix. Sprinkle with cheese. If desired, garnish each serving with sprig of fresh oregano.

NUTRITIONAL INFORMATION PER SERVING:
Calories 600 • Total Fat 33g • Saturated Fat 17g • Cholesterol 105mg • Sodium 830mg • Total Carbohydrate 53g • Dietary Fiber 2g • Sugars 6g • Protein 23g.
DIETARY EXCHANGES: 3-1/2 Starch • 2 Lean Meat • 5 Fat.

TIP: If using large scallops in this dish, cut them into halves or quarters before cooking. Be sure not to overcook scallops as they can become a bit rubbery.

salmon scrambled eggs

READY IN: 15 MINUTES
SERVINGS: 2

4 eggs

1 tablespoon milk

1/4 teaspoon dried dill weed

1/8 teaspoon pepper

Dash salt

1 tablespoon butter or margarine

1/4 cup sliced green onions

1 (7-1/4 oz.) can red salmon, drained, bones and skin removed, flaked

1/4 cup shredded Jarlsberg or Swiss cheese (1 oz.)

1 Beat eggs in medium bowl. Add milk, dill, pepper and salt; beat well.

2 Melt butter in medium nonstick skillet over medium-low heat. Add onions; cook and stir 2 to 3 minutes or until crisp-tender. Add egg mixture; gently stir in salmon. Cook until eggs are set but still moist, stirring constantly.

3 Sprinkle cheese over eggs. Cover; cook 1 minute or until cheese is melted.

NUTRITIONAL INFORMATION PER SERVING:
Calories 380 • Total Fat 26g • Saturated Fat 11g • Cholesterol 490mg • Sodium 730mg • Total Carbohydrate 3g • Dietary Fiber 0g • Sugars 2g • Protein 34g.
DIETARY EXCHANGE: 5 Medium-Fat Meat.

tuna with angel hair pasta and dill

READY IN: 20 MINUTES
SERVINGS: 4

8 oz. uncooked angel hair pasta (capellini)

1 teaspoon salt

1 tablespoon olive oil

1 cup diced red onion

2 medium carrots, sliced

1 (14 oz.) can fat-free chicken broth with 1/3 less sodium

2 tablespoons lemon juice

2 (7.06 oz.) pouches albacore tuna

2 cups fresh sugar snap peas, halved

3 tablespoons chopped fresh dill

1/2 teaspoon lemon-pepper seasoning

1 Cook pasta to desired doneness as directed on package adding 1 teaspoon salt to cooking water. Drain; cover to keep warm.

2 Meanwhile, heat oil in 12-inch skillet over medium heat until hot. Add onion and carrots; cook 3 minutes, stirring frequently. Add broth and lemon juice; cook 3 to 4 minutes or until mixture boils. Reduce heat to medium-low; add tuna. Cook 2 minutes, stirring occasionally. Add sugar snap peas; cook an additional 4 to 6 minutes or until carrots and peas are crisp-tender, stirring occasionally. Stir in dill and lemon-pepper seasoning.

3 Place pasta in individual serving bowls. Top each serving with tuna mixture.

NUTRITIONAL INFORMATION PER SERVING: Calories 420 • Total Fat 6g • Saturated Fat 1g • Cholesterol 30mg • Sodium 1,420mg • Total Carbohydrate 55g • Dietary Fiber 4g • Sugars 7g • Protein 37g.
DIETARY EXCHANGES: 3 Starch • 3 Other Carbohydrate • 1 Vegetable • 3-1/2 Very Lean Meat • 1 Fat.

tarragon fish and vegetables

READY IN: 35 MINUTES
SERVINGS: 4

2 tablespoons olive or vegetable oil

2 carrots, cut into julienne strips (1-1/2x1/4x1/4 inch)

1 zucchini, cut into julienne strips (1-1/2x1/4x1/4 inch)

1 small red bell pepper, cut into thin strips

1/2 cup sliced red onion

4 (6 oz.) orange roughy fillets

Salt

Pepper

4 teaspoons chopped fresh tarragon or 1-1/2 teaspoons dried tarragon leaves

2 tablespoons butter or margarine, chilled

1 Heat oven to 400°F. Heat oil in medium skillet over medium-high heat until hot. Add carrots, zucchini, bell pepper and onion; cook and stir 2 to 3 minutes or until vegetables are crisp-tender.

2 Arrange orange roughy fillets in ungreased 13x9-inch (3-quart) glass baking dish. If desired, sprinkle each fillet with salt and pepper. Top each with 1/4 of vegetable mixture, tarragon and butter.

3 Bake for 15 to 20 minutes or until fish flakes easily with fork.

NUTRITIONAL INFORMATION PER SERVING: Calories 305 • Total Fat 15g • Saturated Fat 5g • Cholesterol 110mg • Sodium 200mg • Total Carbohydrate 7g • Dietary Fiber 2g • Sugars 4g • Protein 35g.
DIETARY EXCHANGES: 1 Vegetable • 4-1/2 Very Lean Meat • 2-1/2 Fat.

TIP: Orange roughy is a mild-flavored fish, making it a great choice for this oven entree. You could also try it with sole, flounder, haddock or red snapper.

roast salmon provencal

PREP TIME: 20 MINUTES
READY IN: 40 MINUTES
SERVINGS: 4

4 (1/2-inch-thick) salmon fillets or steaks (4 to 6 ounces each)

3 cups refrigerated unpeeled potato wedges (from 1 lb. 4 oz. pkg.)

1-1/2 cups small whole fresh mushrooms

1/2 red bell pepper, cut into 1-inch pieces

1 medium zucchini, cut into 1/2-inch pieces

1/2 cup purchased Italian salad dressing

1/2 teaspoon dried basil leaves

1/2 cup large pitted kalamata or ripe olives

1 Heat oven to 425°F. Spray 15x10-inch baking pan with sides with nonstick cooking spray. Place salmon, potatoes, mushrooms, red pepper and zucchini in sprayed pan. Brush with half of the salad dressing. Sprinkle with basil. Bake for 20 minutes.

2 Remove pan from oven. Add olives to pan and stir vegetables slightly. Drizzle remaining salad dressing over salmon and vegetables.

3 Return to oven; bake an additional 5 to 10 minutes or until fish flakes easily with fork and potatoes are tender.

NUTRITIONAL INFORMATION PER SERVING:
Calories 445 • Total Fat 21g • Saturated Fat 3g • Cholesterol 80mg • Sodium 490mg • Total Carbohydrate 35g • Dietary Fiber 4g • Sugars 6g • Protein 29g.
DIETARY EXCHANGES: 2 Starch • 1 Vegetable • 3 Lean Meat • 2 Fat.

sesame-ginger shrimp and vegetable stir fry

READY IN: 20 MINUTES
SERVINGS: 4

2 cups uncooked instant rice

2 cups water

1 tablespoon oil

1 (16 oz.) package fresh stir fry vegetables, cut into bite-sized pieces (4 cups)

12 oz. shelled deveined uncooked medium shrimp, tails removed

1/2 cup purchased sesame-ginger stir fry seasoning sauce (from 12 oz. bottle)

1 Cook rice in water as directed on package.

2 Meanwhile, heat oil in 12-inch nonstick skillet or wok over medium-high heat until hot. Add vegetables; cook and stir 3 minutes. Add shrimp; cook and stir an additional 3 to 4 minutes or until the shrimp turn pink and the vegetables are crisp-tender.

3 Add seasoning sauce to shrimp and vegetables; cook and stir 1 to 2 minutes or until thoroughly heated. Serve over the rice.

NUTRITIONAL INFORMATION PER SERVING:
Calories 375 • Total Fat 5g • Saturated Fat 1g • Cholesterol 120mg • Sodium 2,430mg • Total Carbohydrate 60g • Dietary Fiber 3g • Sugars 6g • Protein 22g.
DIETARY EXCHANGES: 3-1/2 Starch • 1 Vegetable • 1-1/2 Very Lean Meat • 1/2 Fat.

seafood manicotti

PREP TIME: 50 MINUTES
READY IN: 1 HOUR 20 MINUTES
SERVINGS: 4

8 uncooked manicotti

1 cup whole-milk ricotta cheese

1 (3 oz.) package cream cheese, softened

1/4 cup chopped green onions

6 oz. frozen cooked small shrimp, thawed, tails removed and shrimp cut in half crosswise (about 25)

1 (6 oz.) can crabmeat, drained, flaked

1-1/2 cups meatless tomato pasta sauce

1/2 cup shredded mozzarella cheese (2 oz.)

1 Cook manicotti as directed on package. Drain; rinse with cold water to cool.

2 Meanwhile, heat oven to 375°F. In medium bowl, combine ricotta cheese and cream cheese; mix well. Gently stir in onions, shrimp and crabmeat.

3 Spread 1/2 cup of the pasta sauce in ungreased 11x7-inch (2-quart) glass baking dish. Fill each cooked manicotti with seafood mixture; place over sauce. Spoon remaining pasta sauce over manicotti. Cover tightly with foil.

4 Bake for 25 to 30 minutes or until bubbly. Uncover baking dish; sprinkle with mozzarella cheese. Bake uncovered an additional 5 to 8 minutes or until cheese is melted. Let stand 5 minutes before serving.

NUTRITIONAL INFORMATION PER SERVING:
Calories 535 • Total Fat 23g • Saturated Fat 12g • Cholesterol 185mg • Sodium 1,020mg • Total Carbohydrate 46g • Dietary Fiber 2g • Sugars 10g • Protein 36g.
DIETARY EXCHANGES: 3 Starch • 4 Lean Meat • 2 Fat.

shrimp and vegetables

READY IN: 20 MINUTES
SERVINGS: 4

- 2 cups uncooked instant white rice
- 2 cups water
- 2 tablespoons light sesame or vegetable oil
- 1 lb. shelled deveined uncooked medium shrimp (about 30 shrimp), tails removed
- 1 (1 lb.) package precut stir fry vegetables
- 2 tablespoons water
- 2/3 cup purchased stir fry sauce

1 Cook rice in 2 cups water as directed on package.

2 Meanwhile, heat 1 tablespoon of the oil in wok or 12-inch skillet over medium-high heat until hot. Add shrimp; cook and stir 4 to 6 minutes or until shrimp turn pink. Remove shrimp from wok; place on plate and cover to keep warm.

3 Add remaining tablespoon oil to wok. Add vegetables; cook and stir 2 minutes. Add 2 tablespoons water; cover and cook 6 to 8 minutes or until vegetables are crisp-tender, stirring occasionally.

4 Add stir fry sauce and return shrimp to wok; cook and stir 1 to 2 minutes or until sauce has thickened. Serve over rice.

NUTRITIONAL INFORMATION PER SERVING:
Calories 430 • Total Fat 8g • Saturated Fat 1g • Cholesterol 160mg • Sodium 2,940mg • Total Carbohydrate 62g • Dietary Fiber 3g • Sugars 8g • Protein 27g.
DIETARY EXCHANGES: 4 Starch • 2 Very Lean Meat • 1 Fat.

crab and corn cobbler

PREP TIME: 15 MINUTES
READY IN: 50 MINUTES
SERVINGS: 4

- 2 cups skim milk
- 1/3 cup Pillsbury BEST® All-Purpose Flour
- 1/4 teaspoon salt
- 1/8 teaspoon pepper
- 1 (10 oz.) package Green Giant® Frozen Southwestern Style Corn & Roasted Red Peppers
- 1 (8 oz.) package chunk-style imitation crabmeat (surimi)
- 3 tablespoons chopped green onions
- 1 (4 oz.) can Pillsbury® Refrigerated Crescent Dinner Rolls

1 Heat oven to 350°F. Spray 1-1/2-quart casserole with nonstick cooking spray. In medium saucepan, combine milk, flour, salt and pepper; blend well. Cook over medium-high heat until thickened and bubbly, stirring constantly.

2 Add corn with peppers, imitation crabmeat and onions. Cook and stir until thoroughly heated. Pour into sprayed casserole.

3 Remove dough from can; do not unroll. Cut into 8 slices; cut each in half crosswise. Arrange over hot mixture.

4 Bake for 30 to 35 minutes or until casserole is bubbly and rolls are deep golden brown.

NUTRITIONAL INFORMATION PER SERVING:
Calories 300 • Total Fat 7g • Saturated Fat 2g • Cholesterol 15mg • Sodium 980mg • Total Carbohydrate 44g • Dietary Fiber 1g • Sugars 16g • Protein 16g.
DIETARY EXCHANGES: 3 Starch • 3 Other Carbohydrate • 1 Very Lean Meat • 1 Fat.

meatless entrees

For some, meat-free meals are a way of life. Other family cooks simply bulk up on vegetable dishes occasionally. Regardless of your preference, you've come to the right spot! Whether you're always on the lookout for meatless specialties or merely wish to incorporate new tastes into your culinary repertoire, these hot bakes are guaranteed to become staples in your dinnertime lineup.

Creamy Spinach
Enchiladas
page 112

Cheesy Tortilla
Lasagna
page 114

Chile and
Basil
Vegetable
Stir Fry
page 113

impossibly easy chiles rellenos pie
page 106

three-cheese rotini bake

PREP TIME: 25 MINUTES
READY IN: 50 MINUTES
SERVINGS: 4

- 8 oz. uncooked rainbow rotini (3 cups)
- 3 tablespoons margarine or butter
- 1 garlic clove, minced
- 1/4 cup Pillsbury BEST® All-Purpose Flour
- 1/4 teaspoon pepper
- 2 cups milk
- 1 cup shredded American cheese (4 oz.)
- 1 cup shredded mozzarella cheese (4 oz.)
- 1/4 cup crumbled blue cheese (1 oz.)

1 Heat oven to 350°F. Spray 2-quart casserole with nonstick cooking spray. Cook rotini as directed on package. Drain.

2 Meanwhile, melt margarine in large saucepan over medium heat. Add garlic; cook and stir 30 to 60 seconds. Stir in flour and pepper; cook and stir until mixture is bubbly. Gradually add milk, stirring constantly, until mixture boils and thickens. Remove from heat. Reserve 1 tablespoon each American and mozzarella cheese for top. Add remaining cheeses to sauce; stir until melted.

3 Add cooked rotini to cheese sauce; stir gently to coat. Pour into sprayed casserole. Sprinkle with reserved cheeses.

4 Bake at 350°F for 20 to 25 minutes or until bubbly around edges.

NUTRITIONAL INFORMATION PER SERVING:
Calories 595 • Total Fat 28g • Saturated Fat 13g • Cholesterol 55mg • Sodium 830mg • Total Carbohydrate 58g • Dietary Fiber 2g • Sugars 9g • Protein 28g.
DIETARY EXCHANGES: 3 Starch • 1 Low-Fat Milk • 2 High-Fat Meat • 2 Fat.

SIMPLE SUBSTITUTION: For kids, omit the blue cheese and add hot dogs. Slice one or two hot dogs and stir them into the cheese sauce with the rotini. Serve the dish with a green salad tossed with a vinaigrette.

impossibly easy chiles rellenos pie

PREP TIME: 15 MINUTES
READY IN: 45 MINUTES
SERVINGS: 6

- 2 (4 oz.) cans whole green chiles, drained
- 1-1/2 cups shredded Mexican cheese blend (6 oz.)
- 3 eggs
- 3/4 cup original all-purpose baking mix
- 1/4 teaspoon garlic powder
- 1-1/2 cups milk
- 3/4 cup Old El Paso® Thick 'n Chunky Salsa
- Sour cream

1 Heat oven to 400°F. Spray 9-inch glass pie pan with nonstick cooking spray. Slit chiles lengthwise; remove seeds. Arrange chiles in single layer in bottom and up side of pie pan. Sprinkle 1 cup of the cheese over the chiles.

2 Beat eggs in medium bowl with wire whisk. Add baking mix, garlic powder and milk; beat until well blended. Pour over cheese.

3 Bake at 400°F for 25 to 30 minutes or until knife inserted in center comes out clean. Sprinkle with remaining 1/2 cup cheese. Let stand 5 minutes before serving. Serve with salsa and, if desired, sour cream.

NUTRITIONAL INFORMATION PER SERVING:
Calories 255 • Total Fat 15g • Saturated Fat 8g • Cholesterol 140mg • Sodium 740mg • Total Carbohydrate 16g • Dietary Fiber 1g • Sugars 7g • Protein 14g.
DIETARY EXCHANGES: 1 Starch • 1-1/2 High-Fat Meat • 1/2 Fat.

cheesy baked supper omelet

PREP TIME: 10 MINUTES
READY IN: 35 MINUTES
SERVINGS: 6

1 tablespoon butter or margarine

1/2 cup chopped red or green bell pepper (1 small)

1/4 cup chopped onion (1/2 medium)

12 eggs

1 (8 oz.) container sour cream

1/2 teaspoon salt

1/8 teaspoon pepper

1-1/2 cups shredded Cheddar-Monterey Jack cheese blend (6 oz.)

1 Heat oven to 325°F. Spray 12x8-inch (2-quart) glass baking dish with nonstick cooking spray. In 8-inch skillet, melt butter over medium heat. Add bell pepper and onion; cook 2 to 3 minutes, stirring occasionally, until tender.

2 In large bowl, beat eggs, sour cream, salt and pepper with wire whisk until well blended. Stir in bell pepper mixture and cheese. Pour into baking dish.

3 Bake uncovered 20 to 25 minutes or until eggs are set. Cut omelet into squares to serve.

HIGH ALTITUDE (3500-6500 FT):
Heat oven to 325°F. Bake uncovered 30 to 35 minutes.

NUTRITIONAL INFORMATION PER SERVING:
Calories 360 • Total Fat 29g • Saturated Fat 14g • Trans Fat 0.5g • Cholesterol 480mg • Sodium 510mg • Total Carbohydrate 4g • Dietary Fiber 0g • Sugars 4g • Protein 21g.
DIETARY EXCHANGES: 3 Medium-Fat Meat • 3 Fat.

lentil-barley-vegetable skillet

PREP TIME: 35 MINUTES
READY IN: 55 MINUTES
SERVINGS: 6

1 tablespoon oil

1 cup dried lentils, sorted, rinsed

1 medium carrot, sliced (1/2 cup)

1 small onion, coarsely chopped (about 1/3 cup)

3/4 cup uncooked quick-cooking barley

1 teaspoon dried basil leaves

1/4 teaspoon pepper

2 (14 oz.) cans vegetable or chicken broth

1 medium green bell pepper, cut into thin bite-sized strips

1 medium stalk celery, sliced (1/2 cup)

1 cup Green Giant® Niblets® Frozen Whole Kernel Corn

1 (14.5 oz.) can diced tomatoes with Italian herbs, undrained

1 Heat oil in 12-inch skillet over medium heat until hot. Add lentils, carrot and onion; cook 3 minutes, stirring frequently.

2 Add barley, basil, pepper and broth. Bring to a boil. Reduce heat to medium-low; cover and simmer 20 minutes or until lentils are tender but still firm.

3 Stir in all remaining ingredients. Increase heat to medium; cover and simmer an additional 10 to 15 minutes or until lentils and vegetables are tender and liquid is almost absorbed, stirring occasionally.

NUTRITIONAL INFORMATION PER SERVING:
Calories 225 • Total Fat 3g • Saturated Fat 0g • Cholesterol 0mg • Sodium 700mg • Total Carbohydrate 51g • Dietary Fiber 13g • Sugars 6g • Protein 12g.
DIETARY EXCHANGES: 2 Starch • 1 Vegetable • 1/2 Very Lean Meat • 1/2 Fat.

summer squash
and bean sauté

rotini, broccoli and cheese

PREP TIME: 20 MINUTES
READY IN: 50 MINUTES
SERVINGS: 4

- 8 oz. uncooked rotini (2-1/2 cups)
- 2 (10 oz.) packages Green Giant® Frozen Broccoli in Cheese Flavored Sauce
- 1/2 cup shredded Italian cheese blend (2 oz.)
- 1/4 cup sliced ripe olives
- 1 teaspoon dried Italian seasoning
- 2 Italian plum tomatoes, thinly sliced
- 2 tablespoons shredded fresh Parmesan cheese

1 Heat oven to 350°F. Spray 8-inch square or oval (2-quart) glass baking dish or casserole with nonstick cooking spray. Cook rotini to desired doneness as directed on package. Drain; return to saucepan.

2 Meanwhile, cook broccoli as directed on package.

3 Add broccoli in cheese sauce, Italian cheese blend, olives and 1/2 teaspoon of the Italian seasoning to rotini; mix well. Spoon into sprayed baking dish. Arrange tomatoes around outside edge of dish. Sprinkle with remaining 1/2 teaspoon Italian seasoning and Parmesan cheese.

4 Bake at 350°F for 25 to 30 minutes or until thoroughly heated and bubbly.

NUTRITIONAL INFORMATION PER SERVING:
Calories 380 • Total Fat 10g • Saturated Fat 4g • Cholesterol 20mg • Sodium 980mg • Total Carbohydrate 56g • Dietary Fiber 4g • Sugars 9g • Protein 16g.
DIETARY EXCHANGES: 2-1/2 Starch • 1/2 Fruit • 3 Other Carbohydrate • 2 Vegetable • 1/2 High-Fat Meat • 1 Fat.

summer squash and bean sauté

READY IN: 40 MINUTES
SERVINGS.   4

- 1 cup uncooked regular long-grain white rice
- 3 cups water
- 2 extra-large vegetarian vegetable bouillon cubes
- 2 teaspoons cornstarch
- 1 tablespoon olive or vegetable oil
- 1 medium onion, cut into thin wedges
- 8 oz. fresh green beans, trimmed, cut into 2-inch pieces (2 cups)
- 1 garlic clove, minced
- 1 medium yellow summer squash, halved lengthwise, sliced
- 1 medium zucchini, halved lengthwise, sliced
- 1/4 cup sliced fresh basil
- 1 (15.5 oz.) can butter beans, drained, rinsed

1 Cook rice in 2 cups of the water as directed on package. Stir bouillon cubes into remaining 1 cup water. In small bowl, combine cornstarch with 2 tablespoons of the bouillon mixture; blend well. Set aside.

2 Meanwhile, heat oil in large skillet over medium-high heat until hot. Add onion; cook and stir 2 minutes. Add green beans, garlic and remaining bouillon mixture; cover and cook 5 minutes.

3 Add squash and zucchini; cook 2 to 3 minutes or until vegetables are crisp-tender, stirring occasionally. Stir in cornstarch mixture; cook and stir until mixture is bubbly and slightly thickened.

4 Add basil and butter beans; cook 1 to 3 minutes or until thoroughly heated, stirring occasionally. Season to taste with salt and pepper. Serve over rice. If desired, garnish with additional basil sprigs.

NUTRITIONAL INFORMATION PER SERVING:
Calories 340 • Total Fat 5g • Saturated Fat 1g • Cholesterol 0mg • Sodium 1,530mg • Total Carbohydrate 63g • Dietary Fiber 9g • Sugars 7g • Protein 11g.
DIETARY EXCHANGES: 3 Starch • 1/2 Fruit • 3-1/2 Other Carbohydrate • 2 Vegetable • 1/2 Fat.

garden vegetable lasagna

PREP TIME: 50 MINUTES
READY IN: 1 HOUR 40 MINUTES
SERVINGS: 8

8 uncooked lasagna noodles

1 tablespoon olive or vegetable oil

1 garlic clove, minced

3 cups Green Giant® Frozen Broccoli Cuts

1-1/2 cups sliced fresh mushrooms (about 4 oz.)

1 medium red, yellow or orange bell pepper, coarsely chopped (about 1 cup)

1 egg

1 (15 oz.) container ricotta cheese

1 teaspoon dried Italian seasoning

1 (26 to 28 oz.) jar chunky vegetable tomato pasta sauce

2 cups shredded 6-cheese Italian cheese blend (8 oz.)

1 Cook lasagna noodles as directed on package. Drain; place in cold water to cool.

2 Meanwhile, heat oven to 350°F. Heat oil in large skillet over medium-high heat until hot. Add garlic, broccoli, mushrooms and bell pepper; cook 3 to 4 minutes or until vegetables are crisp-tender, stirring frequently. Remove from heat. If necessary, cut broccoli into smaller pieces.

3 Beat egg in small bowl with wire whisk. Add ricotta cheese and Italian seasoning; mix well.

4 Drain cooled lasagna noodles. Spread 1/2 cup of the pasta sauce in ungreased 13x9-inch (3-quart) glass baking dish. Top with 4 noodles, overlapping as necessary, half of ricotta mixture, half of cooked vegetables, half of remaining pasta sauce (about 2-1/4 cups) and 1 cup of the shredded cheese. Repeat layers, starting with noodles.

5 Bake at 350°F for 45 to 50 minutes or until hot and bubbly. If cheese is getting too brown, cover baking dish loosely with foil. Let stand 15 minutes before serving.

HIGH ALTITUDE (3500-6500 FT):
Thaw frozen broccoli before use.

NUTRITIONAL INFORMATION PER SERVING:
Calories 410 • Total Fat 18g • Saturated Fat 8g • Cholesterol 60mg • Sodium 800mg • Total Carbohydrate 41g • Dietary Fiber 4g • Sugars 11g • Protein 21g.
DIETARY EXCHANGES: 2-1/2 Starch • 1 Vegetable • 1-1/2 Medium-Fat Meat • 2 Fat.

teriyaki vegetable stir fry with ramen noodles

READY IN: 25 MINUTES
SERVINGS: 4

4 stalks bok choy

2 carrots, thinly sliced

1 medium green bell pepper, cut into thin bite-sized strips

1 cup water

1 (3 or 3.5 oz.) package any flavor ramen noodle soup mix

1 cup fresh bean sprouts

1 (14 oz.) can baby corn nuggets, drained, rinsed

1/2 cup purchased teriyaki baste and glaze

1 Separate bok choy leaves from stems. Cut leaves into 2-inch pieces; cut stems into 1/4-inch slices. Set aside.

2 Spray large nonstick skillet with nonstick cooking spray. Heat over medium-high heat until hot. Add carrots, bell pepper and bok choy stems; cook and stir 3 minutes. Add water; increase heat to high. Break noodles into small pieces; add to skillet. Discard seasoning packet from soup mix or reserve for another use. Cover; cook 3 minutes.

3 Add bok choy leaves, bean sprouts and corn. Stir in teriyaki baste and glaze. Cook and stir 1 to 2 minutes or until vegetables are crisp-tender and mixture is thoroughly heated.

NUTRITIONAL INFORMATION PER SERVING:
Calories 210 • Total Fat 5g • Saturated Fat 2g • Cholesterol 0mg • Sodium 1,060mg • Total Carbohydrate 34g • Dietary Fiber 5g • Sugars 14g • Protein 6g.
DIETARY EXCHANGES: 1/2 Starch • 1 Fruit • 1-1/2 Other Carbohydrate • 2 Vegetable • 1 Fat.

italian rice and veggie supper

READY IN: 45 MINUTES
SERVINGS: 4

1 tablespoon olive or vegetable oil

1 cup thinly sliced fresh carrots

1/2 cup chopped onion

1 stalk celery, thinly sliced

1 small zucchini or yellow summer squash, halved lengthwise, cut into 1/4-inch slices

3/4 cup uncooked regular long-grain white rice

1-1/2 cups water

1 (15 or 15.5 oz.) can kidney beans, drained, rinsed

1 (14.5 oz.) can diced tomatoes with basil, garlic and oregano, undrained

1/2 teaspoon salt

1 Heat oil in large saucepan or Dutch oven over medium-high heat until hot. Add carrots, onion and celery; cook and stir 3 minutes. Add zucchini; cook and stir 2 minutes.

2 Stir in all remaining ingredients. Bring to a boil. Reduce heat to low; cover and simmer 15 to 20 minutes or until vegetables are tender and liquid is absorbed, stirring occasionally.

NUTRITIONAL INFORMATION PER SERVING:
Calories 290 • Total Fat 4g • Saturated Fat 1g • Cholesterol 0mg • Sodium 640mg • Total Carbohydrate 55g • Dietary Fiber 7g • Sugars 7g • Protein 9g.
DIETARY EXCHANGES: 2 Starch • 1 Fruit • 3 Other Carbohydrate • 2 Vegetable • 1/2 Fat.

fettuccine and spinach bake

PREP TIME: 35 MINUTES
READY IN: 1 HOUR
SERVINGS: 6

1 (12 oz.) package uncooked fettuccine

2 tablespoons butter or margarine

1 medium onion, chopped (1/2 cup)

2 garlic cloves, minced

1/2 teaspoon salt

1 (14.5 oz.) can stewed tomatoes, undrained

1 (14.5 oz.) can diced tomatoes with Italian-style herbs, undrained

1 (1 lb.) bag Green Giant® Frozen Cut Leaf Spinach, thawed, squeezed to drain

1 cup whipping cream

1 cup shredded Swiss cheese (4 oz.)

1 Heat oven to 400°F. Cook and drain fettuccine as directed on package.

2 Meanwhile, in 10-inch skillet, melt butter over medium heat. Add onion; cook 3 to 4 minutes, stirring frequently, until tender. Stir in garlic, salt and both cans of tomatoes. Cook 5 minutes, stirring occasionally, until tomatoes are thoroughly heated.

3 In ungreased 13x9-inch (3-quart) glass baking dish, spread half of the fettuccine. Layer with all of the spinach and half of the tomato mixture. Repeat with layers of remaining fettuccine and tomato mixture.

4 Pour cream over top; sprinkle evenly with cheese.

5 Bake uncovered 20 to 25 minutes or until thoroughly heated and cheese is melted.

HIGH ALTITUDE (3500-6500 FT):
In Step 5, cover dish with foil sprayed with nonstick cooking spray, sprayed side down. Bake covered 25 to 30 minutes.

NUTRITIONAL INFORMATION PER SERVING:
Calories 490 • Total Fat 24g • Saturated Fat 13g • Trans Fat 0.5g • Cholesterol 120mg • Sodium 1,020mg • Total Carbohydrate 53g • Dietary Fiber 4g • Sugars 10g • Protein 16g.
DIETARY EXCHANGES: 2-1/2 Starch • 1/2 Other Carbohydrate • 2 Vegetable • 1/2 High-Fat Meat • 3-1/2 Fat.

creamy spinach enchiladas

PREP TIME: 40 MINUTES
READY IN: 1 HOUR
SERVINGS: 6

- 1 tablespoon margarine or butter
- 1/2 cup sliced green onions
- 1 (9 oz.) package Green Giant® Frozen Spinach, thawed, well drained
- 1 cup small-curd cottage or ricotta cheese
- 1/2 cup sour cream
- 1-1/2 cups shredded Monterey Jack cheese (6 oz.)
- 12 (6-inch) corn tortillas, heated
- 1 (10 oz.) can Old El Paso® Mild Enchilada Sauce

  Sliced green onions, if desired

1 Heat oven to 375°F. Melt margarine in large skillet over medium-high heat. Add 1/2 cup onions; cook and stir 2 minutes or until crisp-tender. Add spinach; cook 1 minute or until spinach is thoroughly heated, stirring occasionally. Remove from heat. Stir in cottage cheese, sour cream and 1 cup of the cheese.

2 Spoon 1/4 cup filling down center of each tortilla; roll up. Place, seam side down, in ungreased 13x9-inch (3-quart) glass baking dish. Pour enchilada sauce evenly over tortillas; sprinkle with remaining cheese.

3 Bake at 375°F for 15 to 20 minutes or until bubbly and thoroughly heated. Sprinkle with sliced green onions.

HIGH ALTITUDE (3500-6500 FT):
Bake at 375°F for 30 to 35 minutes.

NUTRITIONAL INFORMATION PER SERVING:
Calories 330 • Total Fat 17g • Saturated Fat 9g • Cholesterol 45mg • Sodium 670mg • Total Carbohydrate 32g • Dietary Fiber 5g • Sugars 4g • Protein 17g.
DIETARY EXCHANGES: 2 Starch • 1-1/2 High-Fat Meat • 1/2 Fat.

garden veggie frittata

READY IN: 40 MINUTES
SERVINGS: 4

- 6 eggs, beaten
- 1/3 cup milk
- 1 tablespoon chopped fresh chives
- 1 teaspoon chopped fresh marjoram
- 1/2 teaspoon salt
- 1/8 teaspoon pepper
- 1 tablespoon oil
- 1/3 cup chopped onion
- 1 small zucchini, halved lengthwise, sliced
- 1 garlic clove, minced
- 2 cups fresh small broccoli florets
- 1 cup Green Giant® Niblets® Frozen Corn
- 2 teaspoons oil
- 1/2 cup shredded Cheddar cheese (2 oz.)
- 2 Italian plum tomatoes, thinly sliced

1 In medium bowl, combine eggs, milk, chives, marjoram, salt and pepper; mix well. Set aside.

2 Heat 1 tablespoon oil in 12-inch nonstick skillet over medium-high heat until hot. Add onion, zucchini and garlic; cook and stir 1 minute. Reduce heat to medium. Add broccoli, corn and 1/4 cup water; cover and cook 4 to 6 minutes or until vegetables are crisp-tender, stirring occasionally. Remove vegetables from skillet.

3 Add 2 teaspoons oil to skillet. Return vegetables to skillet; pour egg mixture over vegetables. Cover loosely; cook over medium heat for 10 to 15 minutes or until center is set, lifting edges occasionally to allow uncooked egg mixture to flow to bottom of skillet.

4 Sprinkle frittata with cheese; arrange tomato slices on top. Cover; cook 1 to 2 minutes or until cheese is melted. If desired, garnish with additional chives or sprigs of marjoram. To serve, cut into wedges.

NUTRITIONAL INFORMATION PER SERVING:
Calories 290 • Total Fat 19g • Saturated Fat 6g • Cholesterol 335mg • Sodium 480mg • Total Carbohydrate 14g • Dietary Fiber 3g • Sugars 6g • Protein 16g.
DIETARY EXCHANGES: 1/2 Starch • 1/2 Other Carbohydrate • 1 Vegetable • 2 Medium-Fat Meat • 1-1/2 Fat.

chile and basil vegetable stir fry

READY IN: 35 MINUTES
SERVINGS: 4

RICE

1 cup uncooked basmati rice

2 cups water

SAUCE

1 (4.5 oz.) can Old El Paso® Chopped Green Chiles

1/4 cup chopped fresh basil

2 teaspoons chopped fresh mint

1/4 cup soy sauce

1/4 cup water

1 teaspoon sugar

2 teaspoons cornstarch

STIR FRY

1 tablespoon oil

2 cups fresh small cauliflower florets

1 small onion, cut into thin wedges

2 medium zucchini, quartered lengthwise, cut into 1/4-inch slices

1 medium red bell pepper, cut into thin strips

2 cups shredded Chinese (napa) cabbage

1 Cook rice in 2 cups water as directed on package. Cover to keep warm.

2 Meanwhile, in small bowl, combine all sauce ingredients; blend well. Set aside.

3 Heat oil in 12-inch nonstick skillet over medium-high heat until hot. Add cauliflower and onion; cook and stir 2 minutes. Add zucchini and bell pepper; cook and stir 4 to 6 minutes or until vegetables are crisp-tender.

4 Stir sauce well. Add to vegetables in skillet; cook 2 to 4 minutes or until sauce is bubbly and thickened, stirring frequently. Stir in cabbage. Serve over rice. If desired, garnish with additional basil or mint.

NUTRITIONAL INFORMATION PER SERVING:
Calories 230 • Total Fat 4g • Saturated Fat 1g • Cholesterol 0mg • Sodium 1,140mg • Total Carbohydrate 41g • Dietary Fiber 5g • Sugars 7g • Protein 7g.
DIETARY EXCHANGES: 1 Starch • 1 Fruit • 2 Other Carbohydrate • 2 Vegetable • 1 Fat.

TIP: The combination of sweet and hot flavors in this stir fry is inspired by Thai cuisine. Not hot enough? Add a dab of Thai curry paste or a pinch of crushed red pepper flakes to the sauce.

cheesy tortilla lasagna

PREP TIME: 40 MINUTES
READY IN: 1 HOUR 15 MINUTES
SERVINGS: 6

1 cup chopped Italian plum tomatoes (3 medium)

1 cup julienne-cut zucchini (2x1/4x1/4-inch slices)

1/2 cup finely chopped green onions

1 (15 oz.) can black beans, drained, rinsed

1 (10 oz.) can Old El Paso® Enchilada Sauce

1 (8 oz.) container southwest-flavor sour cream dip

8 (6-inch) corn tortillas, halved

2 cups shredded colby-Monterey Jack cheese blend (8 oz.)

1 tablespoon chopped fresh cilantro

1 Heat oven to 375°F. Spray 13x9-inch (3-quart) glass baking dish with nonstick cooking spray. In medium bowl, combine tomatoes, zucchini, onions and beans; mix well. Reserve 1/3 cup enchilada sauce; set aside. In another medium bowl, combine remaining enchilada sauce and sour cream dip; blend well.

2 Spoon 2 tablespoons enchilada sauce mixture in bottom of sprayed baking dish. Arrange 8 tortilla pieces over sauce, overlapping as necessary. Spoon half of vegetable-bean mixture over tortillas; sprinkle with 2/3 cup of the cheese. Spoon half of remaining sauce mixture over cheese. Repeat layers, reserving 2/3 cup cheese for top. Top with the reserved 1/3 cup enchilada sauce. Cover with foil.

3 Bake at 375°F for 30 to 35 minutes or until thoroughly heated. Uncover; sprinkle with reserved 2/3 cup cheese. Bake uncovered an additional 5 minutes or until cheese is melted. Let stand 10 minutes before serving. Sprinkle with cilantro.

NUTRITIONAL INFORMATION PER SERVING: Calories 400 • Total Fat 20g • Saturated Fat 11g • Cholesterol 50mg • Sodium 1,040mg • Total Carbohydrate 42g • Dietary Fiber 7g • Sugars 7g • Protein 20g. DIETARY EXCHANGES: 2 Starch • 2 Other Carbohydrate • 2 High-Fat Meat • 1 Fat.

portobello-broccoli stir fry

READY IN: 25 MINUTES
SERVINGS: 4

RICE
- 1-1/3 cups uncooked regular long-grain white rice
- 2-2/3 cups water

SAUCE
- 1/4 cup water
- 2 tablespoons soy sauce
- 1 tablespoon hoisin sauce
- 2 teaspoons cornstarch
- 1 teaspoon honey

STIR FRY
- 1 (6 oz.) package portobello mushroom caps
- 1 medium onion, cut into thin wedges
- 1 small red bell pepper, cut into thin strips
- 1 garlic clove, minced
- 3 cups fresh broccoli florets (about 6 oz.)
- 1/4 cup water

1 Cook rice in 2-2/3 cups water as directed on package. Cover to keep warm.

2 Meanwhile, in small nonmetal bowl, combine all sauce ingredients; blend well. Set aside.

3 With small metal spoon, scrape underside of mushroom caps to remove dark gills and stems. Cut mushroom caps into 3/4-inch pieces.

4 Spray large nonstick skillet with nonstick cooking spray. Heat over medium-high heat until hot. Add mushrooms, onion, bell pepper and garlic; cook and stir 3 minutes.

5 Add broccoli and 1/4 cup water; cover and cook 3 to 5 minutes or until vegetables are crisp-tender, stirring occasionally. Add sauce; cook and stir 2 to 3 minutes or until bubbly and thickened. Serve stir fry over rice.

NUTRITIONAL INFORMATION PER SERVING: Calories 300 • Total Fat 1g • Saturated Fat 0g • Cholesterol 0mg • Sodium 590mg • Total Carbohydrate 64g • Dietary Fiber 4g • Sugars 8g • Protein 9g.
DIETARY EXCHANGES: 2 Starch • 1-1/2 Fruit • 3-1/2 Other Carbohydrate • 2 Vegetable.

fagioli pasta

READY IN: 30 MINUTES
SERVINGS: 4

- 8 oz. uncooked rigatoni (3 cups)
- 2 tablespoons olive oil
- 1/2 cup chopped onion
- 1 large carrot, finely chopped (1 cup)
- 1 garlic clove, minced
- 1 (15 oz.) can Progresso® Cannellini Beans, drained, rinsed
- 1 (14.5 oz.) can diced tomatoes, undrained
- 1 tablespoon chopped fresh parsley or 1 teaspoon dried parsley flakes
- 1/2 teaspoon salt
- Dash pepper

1 Cook rigatoni to desired doneness as directed on package. Drain.

2 Meanwhile, heat oil in medium saucepan over medium-high heat until hot. Add onion, carrot and garlic; cook 5 to 6 minutes or until tender, stirring occasionally.

3 Add all remaining ingredients except rigatoni. Reduce heat to medium-low; simmer 5 minutes or until thoroughly heated. Serve over rigatoni.

NUTRITIONAL INFORMATION PER SERVING: Calories 400 • Total Fat 8g • Saturated Fat 1g • Cholesterol 0mg • Sodium 620mg • Total Carbohydrate 69g • Dietary Fiber 8g • Sugars 7g • Protein 13g.
DIETARY EXCHANGES: 4 Starch • 1/2 Fruit • 4-1/2 Other Carbohydrate • 1 Vegetable • 1 Fat.

zesty italian tortellini

PREP TIME: 20 MINUTES
READY IN: 45 MINUTES
SERVINGS: 4

1 (9 oz.) bag refrigerated cheese-filled tortellini

2 cups Green Giant Select® Frozen Broccoli Florets (from 14 oz. bag)

1/3 cup drained julienne-cut sun-dried tomatoes in oil

2 cups marinara sauce

1 tablespoon butter or margarine, melted

1/4 cup Progresso® Italian Style Bread Crumbs

1 Heat oven to 350°F. Cook tortellini as directed on package; drain and return to saucepan.

2 Stir in broccoli, tomatoes and marinara sauce; spoon into ungreased shallow 1-1/2-quart casserole. In small bowl, mix melted butter and bread crumbs; sprinkle over top.

3 Bake 20 to 25 minutes or until the mixture is hot and bubbly, and topping is golden brown.

HIGH ALTITUDE (3500-6500 FT):
Thaw frozen broccoli before use. Bake at 350°F for 25 to 30 minutes.

NUTRITIONAL INFORMATION PER SERVING: Calories 340 • Total Fat 14g • Saturated Fat 5g • Cholesterol 60mg • Sodium 770mg • Total Carbohydrate 44g • Dietary Fiber 4g • Sugars 12g • Protein 9g.
DIETARY EXCHANGES: 2-1/2 Starch • 1 Vegetable • 2-1/2 Fat.

mexican shells and cheese

PREP TIME: 35 MINUTES
READY IN: 1 HOUR 5 MINUTES
SERVINGS: 4

CASSEROLE

7 oz. small shell pasta, uncooked (2-1/2 cups)

3 tablespoons butter

3 tablespoons Pillsbury BEST® All-Purpose Flour

2 cups milk

1/3 cup chopped green onions

1 (4.5 oz.) can Old El Paso® Chopped Green Chiles

1 tablespoon Old El Paso® Taco Seasoning Mix (from 1.25 oz. pkg.)

2 cups shredded Mexican cheese blend (8 oz.)

TOPPING

2 tablespoons butter, melted

1 tablespoon Old El Paso® Taco Seasoning Mix (from 1.25 oz. pkg.)

1 cup fresh bread crumbs

1 Heat oven to 375°F. Spray 8-inch square (2-quart) glass baking dish with nonstick cooking spray. Cook pasta to desired doneness as directed on package. Drain; cover to keep warm.

2 Meanwhile, melt 3 tablespoons butter in large saucepan over medium heat. Add flour; cook and stir 1 to 2 minutes or until smooth and bubbly. Gradually add milk, stirring constantly, until mixture boils and thickens. Add onions, chiles and 1 tablespoon taco seasoning mix; mix well. Remove from heat.

3 Add cooked pasta; toss to coat. Spread half of pasta mixture evenly in bottom of sprayed baking dish. Top with half of the cheese. Repeat layers.

4 In small bowl, combine all topping ingredients; mix well. Sprinkle over top of casserole.

5 Bake at 375°F for 25 to 30 minutes or until the mixture is bubbly and the topping is golden brown.

NUTRITIONAL INFORMATION PER SERVING: Calories 660 • Total Fat 36g • Saturated Fat 23g • Cholesterol 100mg • Sodium 1,210mg • Total Carbohydrate 59g • Dietary Fiber 3g • Sugars 9g • Protein 25g.
DIETARY EXCHANGES: 3-1/2 Starch • 1/2 Fruit • 4 Other Carbohydrate • 2 High-Fat Meat • 3-1/2 Fat.

cheese-topped veggie supper

READY IN: 30 MINUTES
SERVINGS: 5

- 1 cup uncooked regular long-grain white rice
- 2 cups water
- 2 teaspoons oil
- 1/2 cup chopped onion
- 2 garlic cloves, minced
- 1 medium green bell pepper, chopped (1 cup)
- 1/2 teaspoon dried oregano leaves
- 1/4 teaspoon salt
- 1/8 teaspoon pepper
- 2 medium tomatoes, coarsely chopped (2 cups)
- 1 medium zucchini, coarsely chopped (1 cup)
- 1 (15.5 or 15 oz.) can kidney beans, drained, rinsed
- 1 cup shredded reduced-fat Cheddar cheese (4 oz.)

1 Cook rice in water as directed on package.

2 Meanwhile, heat oil in large nonstick skillet over medium heat until hot. Add onion and garlic; cook about 5 minutes or until onion is tender, stirring frequently. Add bell pepper, oregano, salt and pepper; cook about 5 minutes or until bell pepper is crisp-tender, stirring frequently.

3 Add cooked rice, tomatoes, zucchini and kidney beans; mix well. Bring to a boil. Reduce heat; cover and simmer 5 to 8 minutes or until vegetables are tender. Remove from heat. Sprinkle with cheese. Cover; let stand 1 to 2 minutes or until cheese melts.

NUTRITIONAL INFORMATION PER SERVING:
Calories 320 • Total Fat 8g • Saturated Fat 4g • Cholesterol 15mg • Sodium 410mg • Total Carbohydrate 48g • Dietary Fiber 5g • Sugars 4g • Protein 14g.
DIETARY EXCHANGES: 3 Starch • 3 Other Carbohydrate • 1 Vegetable • 1/2 Lean Meat • 1 Fat.

chow mein stir fry

READY IN: 30 MINUTES
SERVINGS: 4

- 1 tablespoon oil
- 2 cups fresh small broccoli florets
- 2 cups diagonally sliced celery
- 1 cup fresh baby carrots, quartered lengthwise
- 1 large onion, cut into thin wedges
- 1 (8 oz.) package sliced mushrooms (3 cups)
- 1 cup purchased sesame-ginger stir fry seasoning sauce (from 12 oz. bottle)
- 4 oz. fresh snow pea pods, trimmed, cut in half diagonally (1 cup)
- 4 cups chow mein noodles

1 Heat oil in 12-inch skillet or wok over medium-high heat until hot. Add broccoli, celery, carrots, onion and mushrooms; cook and stir 6 to 8 minutes or until carrots are crisp-tender.

2 Add stir fry sauce and pea pods; cook and stir 2 to 3 minutes or until sauce is bubbly and thickened. Serve over chow mein noodles.

NUTRITIONAL INFORMATION PER SERVING:
Calories 410 • Total Fat 18g • Saturated Fat 3g • Cholesterol 0mg • Sodium 1,400mg • Total Carbohydrate 54g • Dietary Fiber 7g • Sugars 19g • Protein 9g.
DIETARY EXCHANGES: 1-1/2 Starch • 1-1/2 Fruit • 3 Other Carbohydrate • 2 Vegetable • 3-1/2 Fat.

herbed pasta
and beans

linguine with
tarragon vegetables

herbed pasta and beans

READY IN: 25 MINUTES
SERVINGS: 4

- 6 oz. uncooked rainbow rotini (2 cups)
- 1 (15 or 19 oz.) can cannellini beans, drained, rinsed
- 2 medium tomatoes, seeded, chopped
- 2 tablespoons chopped fresh chives
- 2 tablespoons chopped fresh parsley
- 2 tablespoons extra-virgin olive oil
- 2 tablespoons capers, if desired
- 1/4 teaspoon salt
- 1/2 cup shredded fresh Parmesan cheese (2 oz.)

1 Cook rotini as directed on package, adding beans during last minute of cooking time. Cook until the rotini is tender. Drain.

2 Meanwhile, in large bowl, combine all remaining ingredients except cheese.

3 Add cooked rotini and beans; toss gently to coat.

Add cheese; toss gently. If desired, garnish with additional chives or parsley, and season to taste with pepper.

NUTRITIONAL INFORMATION PER SERVING: Calories 390 • Total Fat 12g • Saturated Fat 3g • Cholesterol 10mg • Sodium 780mg • Total Carbohydrate 54g • Dietary Fiber 7g • Sugars 3g • Protein 16g.
DIETARY EXCHANGES: 3-1/2 Starch • 3-1/2 Other Carbohydrate • 1 Very Lean Meat • 2 Fat.

SIMPLE SUBSTITUTION:
The clean, pickled flavor of capers brightens pasta, sauces and salads. If you don't have any on hand, replace them with an equal amount of chopped pickles or green olives.

linguine with tarragon vegetables

READY IN: 30 MINUTES
SERVINGS: 4

- 8 oz. uncooked linguine
- 12 oz. fresh asparagus spears, trimmed, cut into 1-inch pieces (about 2 cups)
- 2 medium tomatoes, seeded, chopped
- 1/4 cup sliced green onions
- 2 tablespoons chopped fresh tarragon
- 2 tablespoons olive or vegetable oil
- 1/2 teaspoon salt
- 1/2 teaspoon finely grated lemon peel
- 1/8 teaspoon coarse ground black pepper
- 1 garlic clove, minced
- 1 cup shredded Asiago cheese (4 oz.)

1 In large saucepan, cook linguine as directed on package, adding asparagus during last 4 to 6 minutes of cooking time. Cook until linguine and asparagus are tender. Drain.

2 Meanwhile, in large bowl, combine all remaining ingredients except cheese.

3 Add cooked linguine and asparagus; toss gently to coat. Add cheese; toss to mix.

NUTRITIONAL INFORMATION PER SERVING: Calories 410 • Total Fat 16g • Saturated Fat 6g • Cholesterol 25mg • Sodium 620mg • Total Carbohydrate 50g • Dietary Fiber 4g • Sugars 5g • Protein 17g.
DIETARY EXCHANGES: 2-1/2 Starch • 2-1/2 Other Carbohydrate • 2 Vegetable • 1 Lean Meat • 2-1/2 Fat.

side dish casseroles

You'll be thrilled to spoon out hearty helpings of these dinner accompaniments because they're perfect alongside any main course. Cheesy vegetables, baked rice dishes and savory dressings are just a sampling of the versatile classics you'll find here. And if you're looking to mix up mealtime routines, be sure to see the recipes for dishes such as stuffed zucchini boats and chipotle hash browns.

Wild Rice Stuffing
page 137

Oven-Roasted
Potatoes and
Vegetables
page 135

Hassle-Free
Vegetable-
Rice Pilaf
page 127

cheddary vegetable gratin page 136

cheesy broccoli stuffed zucchini

PREP TIME: 30 MINUTES
READY IN: 50 MINUTES
SERVINGS: 4

1 tablespoon oil

1/2 cup chopped onion

1/4 cup roasted red bell peppers (from 7.25 oz. jar), drained, chopped

2 (10 oz.) packages Green Giant® Frozen Broccoli in Cheese Flavored Sauce, thawed

1 (4.5 oz.) jar Green Giant® Sliced Mushrooms, drained

2 (9-inch) zucchini

1/2 cup Progresso® Plain Bread Crumbs

2 tablespoons butter, melted

1 Heat oven to 350°F. Heat oil in medium skillet over medium heat until hot. Add onion; cook and stir 3 minutes or until tender. Add roasted peppers, broccoli in sauce and mushrooms; cook 2 to 3 minutes or until broccoli is crisp-tender, stirring occasionally.

2 Cut each zucchini in half lengthwise. Scoop out center, leaving 1/4-inch shell. Spoon broccoli mixture into each zucchini half. Place in ungreased 12x8-inch (2-quart) glass baking dish.

3 In small bowl, combine bread crumbs and butter; mix well. Sprinkle over stuffed zucchini. Cover with foil.

4 Bake at 350°F for 20 minutes. Uncover; bake an additional 8 to 12 minutes or until topping is golden brown and vegetables are tender.

NUTRITIONAL INFORMATION PER SERVING:
Calories 270 • Total Fat 13g • Saturated Fat 5g • Cholesterol 20mg • Sodium 990mg • Total Carbohydrate 30g • Dietary Fiber 6g • Sugars 11g • Protein 9g.
DIETARY EXCHANGES: 1/2 Starch • 1/2 Fruit • 1 Other Carbohydrate • 3 Vegetable • 2-1/2 Fat.

southwest green bean casserole

PREP TIME: 10 MINUTES
READY IN: 1 HOUR 5 MINUTES
SERVINGS: 14

4 (14.5 oz.) cans Green Giant® Cut Green Beans, drained

1 (18 oz.) can Progresso® Vegetable Classics Creamy Mushroom Soup

1 (8 oz.) container southwestern ranch sour cream dip

1 teaspoon chopped chipotle chiles in adobo sauce (from 7 oz. can)

1 cup crushed corn chips (3 oz.)

1 Heat oven to 350°F. In ungreased 2-1/2-quart casserole, place green beans. In medium bowl, mix soup, dip and chiles; stir into the beans. Bake 20 minutes.

2 Remove from oven. Stir mixture; bake 15 to 25 minutes longer or until hot and bubbly. Sprinkle with corn chips; bake 5 to 10 minutes longer or until bubbly around edge.

HIGH ALTITUDE (3500-6500 FT):
Heat oven to 375°F. Continue as directed.

NUTRITIONAL INFORMATION PER SERVING:
Calories 105 • Total Fat 6g • Saturated Fat 2g • Cholesterol 5mg • Sodium 590mg • Total Carbohydrate 10g • Dietary Fiber 2g • Sugars 3g • Protein 3g.
DIETARY EXCHANGES: 1/2 Starch • 1 Vegetable • 1 Fat.

mexican cheesy potatoes

PREP TIME: 20 MINUTES
READY IN: 1 HOUR 30 MINUTES
SERVINGS: 20

1 (16 oz.) container sour cream

1 (10-3/4 oz.) can condensed cream of chicken soup

1 (4.5 oz.) can Old El Paso® Chopped Green Chiles

1/2 cup chopped onion (1 medium)

1 (32 oz.) bag frozen southern-style diced hash-brown potatoes, thawed

2 cups cubed mild Mexican pasteurized prepared cheese product with jalapeño peppers (12 oz.)

1 cup shredded hot pepper Monterey Jack cheese (4 oz.)

1 cup shredded mozzarella cheese (4 oz.)

2 cups crushed gold or yellow tortilla chips (about 6 oz.)

1 Heat oven to 350°F. Spray 13x9-inch (3-quart) glass baking dish with cooking spray. In large bowl, mix sour cream, soup, green chiles and onion. Stir in hash browns. Fold in cubed and shredded cheeses; pour into baking dish.

2 Bake 1 hour or until potatoes are tender and mixture is hot and bubbly. Sprinkle with crushed chips;

bake 5 to 10 minutes longer or until chips are light golden brown.

HIGH ALTITUDE (3500-6500 FT):
Heat oven to 375°F. Continue as directed.

NUTRITIONAL INFORMATION PER SERVING:
Calories 240 • Total Fat 13g • Saturated Fat 7g • Cholesterol 38mg • Sodium 530mg • Total Carbohydrate 23g • Dietary Fiber 1g • Sugars 4g • Protein 8g.
DIETARY EXCHANGES: 1-1/2 Starch • 1/2 High-Fat Meat • 1-1/2 Fat.

rösti potatoes with peppers and onions

READY IN: 25 MINUTES
SERVINGS: 6

1 tablespoon margarine or butter

1/2 cup finely chopped onion

1/4 cup finely chopped green bell pepper

1 (1 lb. 4 oz.) package refrigerated shredded hash-brown potatoes

1/2 teaspoon seasoned salt

1/8 teaspoon pepper

1/2 cup shredded Swiss cheese (2 oz.)

1 Melt margarine in 12-inch nonstick skillet over medium heat. Add onion and bell pepper; cook and stir 2 minutes.

2 Add potatoes. Sprinkle with seasoned salt and pepper; mix well. Spread mixture evenly and firmly in skillet. Cover; cook over medium heat for 6 to 8 minutes or until golden brown on bottom.

3 Stir potatoes; press evenly and firmly in skillet. Cover;

cook an additional 4 to 6 minutes or until golden brown on bottom. Stir again if necessary. Cook until potatoes are cooked and mostly golden brown. Sprinkle with cheese. Cover; let stand 1 to 2 minutes or until cheese melts.

NUTRITIONAL INFORMATION PER SERVING: Calories 140 • Total Fat 5g • Saturated Fat 2g • Cholesterol 10mg • Sodium 250mg • Total Carbohydrate 19g • Dietary Fiber 2g • Sugars 1g • Protein 5g.
DIETARY EXCHANGES: 1-1/2 Starch • 1-1/2 Other Carbohydrate • 1 Fat.

TIP: Serve these delicious potatoes with pork chops or steaks. At brunch, try them with turkey sausage patties.

florentine risotto

READY IN: 45 MINUTES
SERVINGS: 4

3-1/2 to 4-1/2 cups vegetable broth

1 tablespoon olive or vegetable oil

1 (8 oz.) package whole mushrooms, quartered

1/2 cup finely chopped onion

1 garlic clove, minced

1-1/2 cups uncooked short-grain Arborio rice

1/2 teaspoon salt

4 cups baby spinach leaves, coarsely chopped

1 (14 oz.) can small artichoke hearts, drained, rinsed and quartered

1/2 cup shredded fresh Parmesan cheese (2 oz.)

1 Bring broth to a boil in medium saucepan over high heat. Reduce heat to low to keep broth barely simmering.

2 Meanwhile, heat oil in 3-quart saucepan over medium-high heat until hot. Add mushrooms, onion and garlic; cook and stir 2 minutes. Add rice; cook and stir 1 minute.

3 Carefully stir in 1 cup hot broth and salt. Bring to a boil. Reduce heat to medium-low; cook and stir until almost all of liquid is absorbed. Continue adding broth, 1/2 cup at a time, cooking and stirring after each addition until liquid is absorbed. Rice should be tender and creamy but still slightly firm in center.

4 Add spinach and artichoke hearts; cook and stir 2 to 3 minutes or until spinach is wilted and artichokes are thoroughly heated. Stir in cheese. If desired, garnish with additional Parmesan cheese.

NUTRITIONAL INFORMATION PER SERVING: Calories 370 • Total Fat 9g • Saturated Fat 3g • Cholesterol 10mg • Sodium 1,820mg • Total Carbohydrate 58g • Dietary Fiber 6g • Sugars 6g • Protein 14g.
DIETARY EXCHANGES: 3-1/2 Starch • 3-1/2 Other Carbohydrate • 1 Vegetable • 1-1/2 Fat.

cheesy winter vegetables casserole

PREP TIME: 15 MINUTES
READY IN: 7 HOURS 15 MINUTES
SERVINGS: 12

1 (1 lb. 4 oz.) package refrigerated new potato wedges

1 (16 oz.) package fresh baby carrots

1 medium stalk celery, cut into 1-inch pieces

1 (10-3/4 oz.) can condensed Cheddar cheese soup

2 teaspoons Worcestershire sauce

1/8 teaspoon ground red pepper (cayenne)

1 cup Green Giant® Frozen Sweet Peas, thawed

1 cup shredded Cheddar and American cheese blend (4 oz.)

1 In 3-1/2- or 4-quart slow cooker, combine potatoes, carrots and celery. In small bowl, combine soup, Worcestershire sauce and ground red pepper if desired; mix well. Pour soup mixture over vegetables; stir gently to coat.

2 Cover; cook on Low setting for 6 to 7 hours.

3 About 10 minutes before serving, gently stir thawed peas and cheese into vegetable mixture. Cover; cook an additional 10 minutes or until carrots are tender.

NUTRITIONAL INFORMATION PER SERVING:
Calories 135 • Total Fat 5g • Saturated Fat 3g • Cholesterol 15mg • Sodium 480mg • Total Carbohydrate 17g • Dietary Fiber 2g • Sugars 4g • Protein 5g.
DIETARY EXCHANGES: 1 Starch • 1/2 High-Fat Meat.

sweet corn potluck pudding

PREP TIME: 5 MINUTES
READY IN: 6 HOURS 5 MINUTES
SERVINGS: 14

1 (1 lb.) package Green Giant® Niblets® Frozen Corn

2 (11 oz.) cans Green Giant® Mexicorn® Whole Kernel Corn, Red and Green Peppers

1 (14.75 oz.) can Green Giant® Cream Style Sweet Corn

1 (6.5 oz.) package corn muffin and bread mix

3/4 cup water

1/4 cup butter or margarine, melted

1 teaspoon salt

1 In 3 to 4-quart slow cooker, combine all ingredients; mix well.

2 Cover; cook on Low setting for 3 hours.

3 Stir mixture; cover and cook an additional 2 to 3 hours or until pudding is slightly puffed in center.

NUTRITIONAL INFORMATION PER SERVING:
Calories 180 • Total Fat 5g • Saturated Fat 3g • Cholesterol 10mg • Sodium 470mg • Total Carbohydrate 30g • Dietary Fiber 2g • Sugars 6g • Protein 4g.
DIETARY EXCHANGES: 2 Starch • 1 Fat.

slow-cooked wild rice pilaf

hassle-free vegetable-rice pilaf

slow-cooked wild rice pilaf

PREP TIME: 10 MINUTES
READY IN: 5 HOURS 10 MINUTES
SERVINGS: 12

1-1/2 cups uncooked wild rice

1/2 cup sliced green onions

1 (4.5 oz.) jar Green Giant® Sliced Mushrooms, drained

1 garlic clove, minced

3/4 teaspoon salt

1 (14-1/2 oz.) can ready-to-serve chicken broth

2 cups water

1/2 cup dried cherries (3 oz.)

3/4 teaspoon dried thyme leaves

1/4 teaspoon nutmeg

2 tablespoons chopped fresh parsley

1 Spray 4- to 6-quart slow cooker with nonstick cooking spray. Rinse rice with cold water; place in sprayed slow cooker. Add onions, mushrooms, garlic, salt, broth and water.

2 Cover; cook on High setting for 3 to 4 hours.

3 Add cherries, thyme and nutmeg to rice; mix gently. Cook on Low setting for an additional 30 to 60 minutes or until rice is opened and tender.

4 Just before serving, stir in the parsley.

NUTRITIONAL INFORMATION PER SERVING: Calories 110 • Total Fat 1g • Saturated Fat 0g • Cholesterol 0mg • Sodium 180mg • Total Carbohydrate 21g • Dietary Fiber 2g • Sugars 4g • Protein 4g.
DIETARY EXCHANGES: 1 Starch • 1/2 Fruit • 1-1/2 Other Carbohydrate.

hassle-free vegetable-rice pilaf

PREP TIME: 10 MINUTES
READY IN: 2 HOURS 10 MINUTES
SERVINGS: 12

1 (14-1/2 oz.) can ready-to-serve chicken broth with roasted garlic

2/3 cup water

1-1/2 cups uncooked converted long-grain white rice

1 tablespoon olive oil

1-1/4 cups Green Giant® Frozen Cut Green Beans

1/2 cup sliced carrot

2 green onions, sliced

1/2 teaspoon salt

1/4 teaspoon lemon-pepper seasoning

1 In 4-cup glass measuring cup, combine broth and water. Microwave on High for 4 to 5 minutes or until steaming.

2 Meanwhile, spray 4- to 6-quart slow cooker with nonstick cooking spray. Combine rice and oil in sprayed slow cooker; mix well. Add all remaining ingredients and hot broth mixture.

3 Cover; cook on High setting for 1-1/2 to 2 hours.

NUTRITIONAL INFORMATION PER SERVING: Calories 110 • Total Fat 2g • Saturated Fat 0g • Cholesterol 0mg • Sodium 120mg • Total Carbohydrate 21g • Dietary Fiber 1g • Sugars 1g • Protein 2g.
DIETARY EXCHANGES: 1-1/2 Starch • 1-1/2 Other Carbohydrate.

TIP: This rice is perfect for a buffet table. To keep rice warm in a slow cooker, set it on Low. If you have a round slow cooker, twirl the lid to check on the rice instead of lifting it. Twirling will clear the drops of condensation from the lid so you can see inside the cooker.

orange-glazed carrots and sugar snap peas

READY IN: 15 MINUTES
SERVINGS: 6

2   cups ready-to-eat baby-cut carrots

1   cup Green Giant Select® Frozen Sugar Snap Peas (from 1 lb. bag)

2   tablespoons orange marmalade

1/4   teaspoon salt

Dash pepper

1 In 2-quart saucepan, heat 1 cup water to boiling. Add carrots; return to boiling. Reduce heat to low; cover and simmer 8 to 10 minutes or until carrots are tender, adding sugar snap peas during last 5 minutes of cooking time. Drain; return to saucepan.

2 Stir in marmalade, salt and pepper. Cook and stir over medium heat until marmalade is melted and vegetables are glazed.

NUTRITIONAL INFORMATION PER SERVING: Calories 45 • Total Fat 0g • Saturated Fat 0g • Cholesterol 0mg • Sodium 115mg • Total Carbohydrate 10g • Dietary Fiber 2g • Sugars 6g • Protein 1g.
DIETARY EXCHANGE: 1/2 Starch.

no-fuss party potatoes

PREP TIME: 10 MINUTES
READY IN: 4 HOURS 40 MINUTES
SERVINGS: 13

1 (10-3/4 oz.) can condensed 98% fat-free cream of mushroom soup

1 (8 oz.) container fat-free sour cream

1 (4.5 oz.) can Old El Paso® Chopped Green Chiles

1 cup shredded reduced-fat Cheddar cheese (4 oz.)

1 (32 oz.) package frozen southern-style cubed hash-brown potatoes

2-1/2 cups baked nacho-flavored taco chips, finely crushed (1/2 cup)

3 green onions, sliced (1/3 cup)

1 Spray 3-1/2- or 4-quart slow cooker with nonstick cooking spray. In medium bowl, combine soup, sour cream, chiles and cheese; mix well.

2 Arrange half of potatoes in sprayed slow cooker. Top with half of sour cream mixture, spreading evenly. Repeat layers.

3 Cover; cook on High setting for 3-1/2 to 4-1/2 hours.

4 Just before serving, sprinkle chips and onions over top.

NUTRITIONAL INFORMATION PER SERVING:
Calories 140 • Total Fat 2g • Saturated Fat 1g • Cholesterol 5mg • Sodium 360mg • Total Carbohydrate 26g • Dietary Fiber 2g • Sugars 3g • Protein 5g.
DIETARY EXCHANGE: 2 Starch.

roasted vegetable combo

READY IN: 55 MINUTES
SERVINGS: 6

1-1/2 cups fresh baby carrots

1 lb. small red potatoes, unpeeled, quartered (3 cups)

1 medium onion, cut into thin wedges

1 tablespoon olive or vegetable oil

1 teaspoon dried basil leaves

1 teaspoon dried thyme leaves

1/2 teaspoon garlic salt

1/4 teaspoon pepper

1 (14 oz.) package Green Giant Select® Frozen Whole Green Beans

1 Heat oven to 425°F. Spray 15x10x1-inch baking pan with nonstick cooking spray. In large bowl, combine carrots, potatoes and onion. Add oil, basil, thyme, garlic salt and pepper; mix well. Spread evenly in sprayed pan. Bake at 425°F for 20 minutes.

2 Remove vegetables from oven. Add green beans; toss to mix.

3 Return to oven; bake an additional 20 to 25 minutes or until vegetables are tender, stirring once.

NUTRITIONAL INFORMATION PER SERVING:
Calories 130 • Total Fat 3g • Saturated Fat 0g • Cholesterol 0mg • Sodium 180mg • Total Carbohydrate 23g • Dietary Fiber 4g • Sugars 5g • Protein 3g.
DIETARY EXCHANGES: 1/2 Starch • 1/2 Fruit • 1 Other Carbohydrate • 1 Vegetable • 1/2 Fat.

peachy glazed sweet potatoes

PREP TIME: 15 MINUTES
READY IN: 3 HOURS 45 MINUTES
SERVINGS: 10

SWEET POTATOES

2-1/4 lb. dark-orange sweet potatoes, peeled

1 cup peach pie filling (from 21 oz. can)

2 tablespoons margarine or butter, melted

1 teaspoon grated gingerroot

1/4 teaspoon salt

TOPPING

2 tablespoons brown sugar

1 tablespoon margarine or butter

1/8 teaspoon cinnamon

1/2 cup coarsely chopped pecans

1 Spray 4- to 6-quart slow cooker with nonstick cooking spray. Halve larger sweet potatoes lengthwise; cut each into 1/2-inch slices. Place in sprayed slow cooker. Add pie filling, 2 tablespoons margarine, gingerroot and salt; mix well to coat potatoes.

2 Cover; cook on High setting for 2-1/2 to 3-1/2 hours.

3 Meanwhile, line cookie sheet with foil. In small skillet, combine all topping ingredients. Cook over medium heat for 2 to 3 minutes or until bubbly and glazed, stirring frequently. Spoon onto foil-lined cookie sheet to cool.

4 Just before serving, gently stir the potatoes. Sprinkle with topping.

NUTRITIONAL INFORMATION PER SERVING: Calories 200 • Total Fat 8g • Saturated Fat 1g • Cholesterol 0mg • Sodium 110mg • Total Carbohydrate 29g • Dietary Fiber 3g • Sugars 12g • Protein 2g.
DIETARY EXCHANGES: 1 Starch • 1 Fruit • 2 Other Carbohydrate • 1-1/2 Fat.

TIP: Use any remaining pie filling to glaze fruit salads, or to garnish ice cream or pudding. Or simply spoon the filling into single-serving-sized, prepared crumb crusts and top them with whipped topping for a fast and tasty weeknight dessert.

mac 'n cheese with broccoli

READY IN: 10 MINUTES
SERVINGS: 3

1/2 cup uncooked elbow macaroni (2 oz.)

1 (10 oz.) box Green Giant® Frozen Broccoli & Cheese Flavored Sauce

1 In 2-quart saucepan, cook macaroni as directed on package. Drain; return to saucepan.

2 Meanwhile, cook broccoli as directed on box.

3 Stir broccoli with cheese sauce into macaroni.

NUTRITIONAL INFORMATION PER SERVING: Calories 135 • Total Fat 3g • Saturated Fat 0g • Cholesterol 5mg • Sodium 550mg • Total Carbohydrate 22g • Dietary Fiber 2g • Sugars 5g • Protein 5g.
DIETARY EXCHANGES: 1 Starch • 1 Vegetable • 1/2 Fat.

orzo-barley pilaf

PREP TIME: 5 MINUTES
READY IN: 25 MINUTES
SERVINGS: 4

1 (14 oz.) can fat-free chicken broth with 33% less sodium

1/4 cup water

1/2 teaspoon dried thyme leaves

1/4 teaspoon salt

1 cup sliced fresh mushrooms (about 3 oz.)

1/2 cup uncooked orzo or rosamarina (rice-shaped pasta)

1/2 cup uncooked quick-cooking barley

2 tablespoons sliced green onions (2 medium)

1/2 teaspoon grated lemon peel

Pepper

1 In 2-quart nonstick saucepan, heat broth, water, thyme and salt to boiling. Stir in mushrooms, orzo and barley. Return to boiling.

2 Reduce heat to low; cover and simmer 15 to 18 minutes or until the orzo and barley are tender and the liquid is absorbed.

3 Stir in onions and lemon peel. If desired, season to taste with pepper.

HIGH ALTITUDE (3500-6500 FT):
Increase water to 1/3 cup.

NUTRITIONAL INFORMATION PER SERVING:
Calories 160 • Total Fat 1g • Saturated Fat 0g • Cholesterol 0mg • Sodium 360mg • Total Carbohydrate 33g • Dietary Fiber 5g • Sugars 1g • Protein 7g.
DIETARY EXCHANGE: 2 Starch.

creamy garlic and parmesan potatoes

PREP TIME: 15 MINUTES
READY IN: 6 HOURS 15 MINUTES
SERVINGS: 12

1/2 teaspoon cream of tartar

3 lb. russet potatoes, peeled, sliced (about 8 medium)

1 (10-3/4 oz.) can condensed golden mushroom soup

1/2 cup water

1/4 cup Pillsbury BEST® All-Purpose Four

3 tablespoons butter or margarine, melted

1/2 teaspoon salt

1/4 teaspoon pepper

1/4 teaspoon garlic powder

1/3 cup shredded fresh Parmesan cheese (1-1/3 oz.)

1 In large bowl, combine 1 cup water and cream of tartar. Add sliced potatoes; toss to coat. Drain, discarding water. Place the potatoes in 3- to 4-quart slow cooker.

2 In medium bowl, combine soup, 1/2 cup water, flour, butter, salt, pepper and garlic powder; mix well. Pour mixture over potatoes; stir gently to coat.

3 Cover; cook on Low setting for 5 to 6 hours.

4 Just before serving, sprinkle Parmesan cheese over top if desired.

NUTRITIONAL INFORMATION PER SERVING:
Calories 160 • Total Fat 5g • Saturated Fat 3g • Cholesterol 10mg • Sodium 350mg • Total Carbohydrate 25g • Dietary Fiber 1g • Sugars 2g • Protein 4g.
DIETARY EXCHANGES: 1-1/2 Starch • 1 Fat.

potatoes alfredo with garden peas

PREP TIME: 10 MINUTES
READY IN: 4 HOURS 40 MINUTES
SERVINGS: 10

- 2 lb. small (2- to 3-inch) red potatoes, cut into 1/4-inch-thick slices (8 cups)
- 1/4 cup sliced green onions
- 2 garlic cloves, minced
- 1 (10 oz.) container refrigerated Alfredo sauce
- 1/2 cup half-and-half or milk
- 1/2 teaspoon salt
- 1/8 teaspoon pepper
- 1-1/2 cups Green Giant® Frozen Sweet Peas

1 Spray 3-1/2- to 4-quart slow cooker with nonstick cooking spray. Layer half each of potatoes, onions and garlic in sprayed slow cooker. In medium bowl, combine Alfredo sauce, half-and-half, salt and pepper; mix well. Spoon half of mixture over top. Layer with remaining potatoes, onions, garlic and sauce mixture. Do not stir.

2 Cover; cook on High setting for 3 to 4 hours.

3 About 30 minutes before serving, sprinkle peas over potato mixture. Cover; cook on High setting an additional 20 to 30 minutes. Stir gently to mix the peas with the potatoes before serving.

NUTRITIONAL INFORMATION PER SERVING:
Calories 215 • Total Fat 11g • Saturated Fat 7g • Cholesterol 30mg • Sodium 270mg • Total Carbohydrate 24g • Dietary Fiber 2g • Sugars 3g • Protein 5g.
DIETARY EXCHANGES: 1-1/2 Starch • 1-1/2 Other Carbohydrate • 2 Fat.

smoky cheese and potato bake

PREP TIME: 10 MINUTES
READY IN: 6 HOURS 10 MINUTES
SERVINGS: 14

- 1 (10-3/4 oz.) can condensed cream of mushroom soup
- 1 (8 oz.) container sour cream (about 1 cup)
- 1 (7 oz.) round hickory-smoked Gouda cheese, cut into 1/2-inch cubes
- 1/3 cup roasted red bell pepper strips (from a jar)
- 1 (32 oz.) package frozen southern-style cubed hash-brown potatoes (8 cups), thawed

1 Spray 3-1/2- to 4-quart slow cooker with nonstick cooking spray. In medium bowl, combine soup, sour cream and cheese; mix well. Gently stir in roasted pepper strips.

2 Arrange half of potatoes in sprayed slow cooker. Top with half of sour cream mixture; spread evenly. Top with remaining potatoes and sour cream mixture, spreading evenly. Do not stir.

3 Cover; cook on Low setting for 5 to 6 hours.

NUTRITIONAL INFORMATION PER SERVING:
Calories 180 • Total Fat 8g • Saturated Fat 5g • Cholesterol 25mg • Sodium 320mg • Total Carbohydrate 21g • Dietary Fiber 1g • Sugars 2g • Protein 6g.
DIETARY EXCHANGES: 1-1/2 Starch • 1-1/2 Other Carbohydrate • 1/2 High-Fat Meat • 1 Fat.

TIP:
Remove the red wax coating from the cheese before cutting it into cubes. To thaw the potatoes, microwave them in a covered, 2-quart, microwave-safe glass dish on High for 5 to 6 minutes or until thawed, stirring twice.

potatoes alfredo with garden peas

smoky cheese and potato bake

slow-cooked zesty pinto beans

PREP TIME: 30 MINUTES
READY IN: 12 HOURS
SERVINGS: 12

- 1 (16 oz.) package dried pinto beans, sorted, rinsed (3-1/4 cups)
- 2 cups water
- 1 cup chopped onions (2 medium)
- 1/2 cup finely chopped cooked ham
- 2 garlic cloves, minced
- 2 tablespoons brown sugar
- 1 tablespoon chili powder
- 1/2 teaspoon cumin
- 1/2 teaspoon salt
- 1 (14-1/2 oz.) can diced tomatoes with green chiles, undrained

1 In large saucepan, combine beans and 10 cups water. Bring to a boil. Reduce heat to medium-low; simmer 1 to 1-1/2 hours or until the beans are tender but still firm, stirring occasionally.

2 Drain beans, discarding water. Place beans in 3-1/2- to 4-quart slow cooker. Add 2 cups water and all remaining ingredients except the tomatoes; mix well.

3 Cover; cook on Low setting for 8 hours.

4 Add tomatoes; mix well. Cover; cook an additional 1 to 2 hours or until the beans are tender.

NUTRITIONAL INFORMATION PER SERVING: Calories 125 • Total Fat 1g • Saturated Fat 0g • Cholesterol 5mg • Sodium 240mg • Total Carbohydrate 28g • Dietary Fiber 8g • Sugars 5g • Protein 9g.
DIETARY EXCHANGES: 1 Starch • 1 Very Lean Meat • 1 Fat.

slow-cooked zesty pinto beans

monterey chipotle hash browns

monterey chipotle hash browns

PREP TIME: 10 MINUTES
READY IN: 1 HOUR
SERVINGS: 8

- 1 (20 oz.) package refrigerated hash-brown potatoes
- 1 cup shredded Monterey Jack cheese (4 oz.)
- 1/2 cup sliced green onions
- 1-1/4 cups milk
- 2 chipotle chiles in adobo sauce, finely chopped
- 2 teaspoons adobo sauce from a can
- 2 garlic cloves, minced
- 1/2 teaspoon seasoned salt
- 1/4 teaspoon pepper

1 Heat oven to 350°F. Spray shallow 1-1/2-quart casserole or gratin dish with nonstick cooking spray. In sprayed casserole, combine potatoes, cheese and onions; mix well.

2 In medium bowl, combine all remaining ingredients; blend well. Pour over potato mixture; mix well.

3 Bake at 350°F for 45 to 50 minutes or until the potatoes are tender and the top is golden brown.

NUTRITIONAL INFORMATION PER SERVING:
Calories 165 • Total Fat 5g • Saturated Fat 3g • Cholesterol 15mg • Sodium 270mg • Total Carbohydrate 23g • Dietary Fiber 2g • Sugars 4g • Protein 7g.
DIETARY EXCHANGES: 1-1/2 Starch • 1/2 High-Fat Meat • 5 Fat.

TIP: These flavorful hash browns are perfect for brunch or supper. At brunch, serve them with scrambled eggs, sausage and fresh fruit. For supper, try them with sautéed chicken breasts or pork chops.

oven-roasted potatoes and vegetables

PREP TIME: 10 MINUTES
READY IN: 30 MINUTES
SERVINGS: 6

- 2-1/2 cups refrigerated new potato wedges (from 1 lb. 4 oz. bag)
- 1 medium red bell pepper, cut into 1-inch pieces
- 1 small zucchini, cut into 1/2-inch pieces
- 4 oz. fresh whole mushrooms, quartered (about 1 cup)
- 2 teaspoons olive oil
- 1/2 teaspoon dried Italian seasoning
- 1/4 teaspoon garlic salt

1 Heat oven to 450°F. Spray 15x10x1-inch pan with nonstick cooking spray. In large bowl, toss all ingredients to coat. Spread evenly in pan.

2 Bake 15 to 20 minutes, stirring once halfway through baking time, until the vegetables are tender and lightly browned.

NUTRITIONAL INFORMATION PER SERVING:
Calories 70 • Total Fat 2g • Saturated Fat 0g • Cholesterol 0mg • Sodium 200mg • Total Carbohydrate 14g • Dietary Fiber 2g • Sugars 2g • Protein 2g.
DIETARY EXCHANGE: 1 Starch.

cheddary vegetable gratin

PREP TIME: 10 MINUTES
READY IN: 45 MINUTES
SERVINGS: 10

1 (10-3/4 oz.) can condensed Cheddar cheese soup

1/2 cup shredded Cheddar cheese (2 oz.)

1/2 cup sour cream

1 medium red bell pepper, coarsely chopped

1 (1 lb.) package Green Giant Select® Frozen Broccoli, Carrots and Cauliflower, thawed, drained

1-1/2 cups Cheddar cheese crackers, crushed

2 tablespoons butter, melted

1 Heat oven to 375°F. Spray shallow 1-1/2-quart casserole or gratin dish with nonstick cooking spray. In large bowl, combine soup, cheese and sour cream; mix well. Stir in bell pepper and thawed vegetables. Spoon into sprayed casserole.

2 In small bowl, combine crushed crackers and butter; mix well. Sprinkle over the vegetable mixture.

3 Bake at 375°F for 30 to 35 minutes or until mixture is bubbly and vegetables are crisp-tender.

NUTRITIONAL INFORMATION PER SERVING:
Calories 165 • Total Fat 11g • Saturated Fat 6g • Cholesterol 25mg • Sodium 440mg • Total Carbohydrate 12g • Dietary Fiber 1g • Sugars 3g • Protein 5g.
DIETARY EXCHANGES: 1 Starch • 1/2 High-Fat Meat • 1 Fat.

harvest vegetable roast

PREP TIME: 20 MINUTES
READY IN: 1 HOUR 5 MINUTES
SERVINGS: 14

1 small butternut squash (about 2 lb.), peeled, seeded and cut into 1-inch pieces (about 3 cups)

4 small new red potatoes, unpeeled, quartered

1 medium red onion, cut into 1/2-inch wedges

1 medium parsnip, peeled, cut into 2x1/2x1/2-inch strips

2 cups small fresh Brussels sprouts (about 8 oz.)

2 tablespoons olive oil

1/2 teaspoon dried marjoram leaves

1/2 teaspoon garlic-pepper blend

1/2 teaspoon seasoned salt

1 Heat oven to 425°F. Spray 17x11- or 15x10-inch baking pan with sides with nonstick cooking spray. In large bowl, combine all vegetables. Add all remaining ingredients; toss to coat. Spread vegetables in sprayed pan.

2 Bake at 425°F for 30 to 45 minutes or until vegetables are tender, stirring and turning the vegetables several times during baking.

NUTRITIONAL INFORMATION PER SERVING:
Calories 90 • Total Fat 2g • Saturated Fat 0g • Cholesterol 0mg • Sodium 60mg • Total Carbohydrate 16g • Dietary Fiber 2g • Sugars 4g • Protein 2g.
DIETARY EXCHANGES: 1 Starch • 1/2 Fat.

TIP: To prepare the butternut squash in this side dish, halve it crosswise with a large, sharp knife. Place the squash, cut side down, on a work surface and cut each piece in half lengthwise. Remove the seeds. Use a vegetable peeler or sharp paring knife to trim away the peel. Cut the flesh into cubes.

texas-style barbecued beans

PREP TIME: 15 MINUTES
READY IN: 6 HOURS 15 MINUTES
SERVINGS: 24

6 slices bacon

4 (15.5 oz.) cans great
northern beans, drained,
rinsed

4 (15 oz.) cans black beans,
drained, rinsed

4 garlic cloves, minced

3/4 cup finely chopped onion

1-1/2 cups ketchup

1/2 cup firmly packed brown
sugar

1/2 cup barbecue sauce

2 tablespoons prepared
mustard

2 tablespoons
Worcestershire sauce

3 teaspoons chili powder

1/2 teaspoon hot pepper
sauce

1 Cook bacon in large skillet over medium heat until crisp. Remove bacon from skillet; drain on paper towels.

2 In 4- to 5-quart slow cooker, combine all remaining ingredients; mix gently. Crumble the bacon; sprinkle over bean mixture.

3 Cover; cook on Low setting for 4 to 6 hours.

NUTRITIONAL INFORMATION PER SERVING:
Calories 270 • Total Fat 2g • Saturated Fat
0g • Cholesterol 5mg • Sodium 5mg •
Total Carbohydrate 49g • Dietary Fiber 9g
• Sugars 13g • Protein 14g.
DIETARY EXCHANGES: 3 Starch • 3 Other
Carbohydrate • 1/2 Very Lean Meat •
1/2 Fat.

wild rice stuffing

PREP TIME: 20 MINUTES
READY IN: 6 HOURS 20 MINUTES
SERVINGS: 22

1 cup uncooked whole-grain
wild rice (not cracked or
broken)

1 cup sliced fresh
mushrooms

1 medium onion, chopped
(1/2 cup)

1 medium stalk celery,
chopped (about 1/2 cup)

1 medium carrot, chopped
(about 1/2 cup)

2 tablespoons butter or
margarine, cut into small
pieces

1 (32 oz.) container chicken
broth

5 cups herb-seasoned
cubed stuffing

1 In 5- to 6-quart slow cooker, combine all ingredients except stuffing; mix well.

2 Cover; cook on Low setting for 5 hours.

3 Gently stir stuffing into rice mixture. Cover; cook an additional 45 to 60 minutes or until the stuffing is moist and tender.

4 Just before serving, gently stir mixture.

NUTRITIONAL INFORMATION PER SERVING:
Calories 110 • Total Fat 2g • Saturated Fat
1g • Cholesterol 5mg • Sodium 440mg •
Total Carbohydrate 19g • Dietary Fiber 1g •
Sugars 1g • Protein 4g.
DIETARY EXCHANGES: 1 Starch • 1/2 Fat.

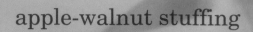
apple-walnut stuffing

ready-to-go green bean casserole

apple-walnut stuffing

PREP TIME: 10 MINUTES
READY IN: 5 HOURS 10 MINUTES
SERVINGS: 10

1/2 cup margarine or butter

1/2 cup chopped walnuts

1 tablespoon honey

1/8 teaspoon nutmeg

1 cup sliced celery

1 cup chopped onion

1 (14 oz.) package cubed herb-seasoned stuffing

1 (4.5 oz.) jar Green Giant® Sliced Mushrooms, drained

1-1/2 cups applesauce

2 cups water

1 In medium skillet, heat 2 tablespoons of the margarine and walnuts over medium heat until nuts are lightly toasted, stirring occasionally. With slotted spoon, remove nuts from skillet; place in small dish. Add honey and nutmeg to nuts; mix to glaze. Set aside.

2 Melt remaining 6 table-spoons margarine in same skillet over medium heat. Add celery and onion; cook over medium heat for 3 to 4 minutes or until almost tender, stirring occasionally.

3 Meanwhile, spray 4- to 6-quart slow cooker with nonstick cooking spray. Place stuffing cubes in sprayed slow cooker. Add mushrooms and cooked celery and onion with butter; mix lightly. Add apple-sauce and water; mix lightly.

4 Cover; cook on Low setting for 4 to 5 hours.

5 Just before serving, sprinkle with glazed walnuts.

NUTRITIONAL INFORMATION PER SERVING:
Calories 330 • Total Fat 15g • Saturated Fat 2g • Cholesterol 0mg • Sodium 710mg • Total Carbohydrate 43g • Dietary Fiber 4g • Sugars 11g • Protein 6g.
DIETARY EXCHANGES: 2 Starch • 1 Fruit • 3 Other Carbohydrate • 2-1/2 Fat.

ready-to-go green bean casserole

PREP TIME: 10 MINUTES
READY IN: 4 HOURS 10 MINUTES
SERVINGS: 10

1 (28 oz.) package Green Giant® Frozen Cut Green Beans

1 (8 oz.) can sliced water chestnuts, drained

1/2 cup roasted red bell pepper strips (from 7.25 oz. jar)

1/4 teaspoon salt

1 (10 oz.) container refrigerated Alfredo sauce

1 (2.8 oz.) can french fried onions

1 In 4- to 6-quart slow cooker, combine all ingredients except onions. Stir in half of the onions.

2 Cover; cook on High setting for 3 to 4 hours, stirring after 1 to 1-1/2 hours.

3 Just before serving, in small skillet, heat remaining half of onions over medium-high heat for 2 to 3 minutes or until hot, stirring frequently. Stir bean mixture; sprinkle with onions.

NUTRITIONAL INFORMATION PER SERVING:
Calories 160 • Total Fat 9g • Saturated Fat 4g • Cholesterol 15mg • Sodium 310mg • Total Carbohydrate 16g • Dietary Fiber 3g • Sugars 4g • Protein 4g.
DIETARY EXCHANGES: 1 Starch • 1 Other Carbohydrate • 1-1/2 Fat.

breakfast & brunch

Looking for a delicious way to welcome the morning? Bubbling egg bakes and steaming hash-brown casseroles offer the eye-opening appeal that families crave. In addition to make-ahead convenience, these dishes rely on kitchen staples for fast assembly. Whether prepared as a Sunday brunch or weekday treat, the following are sure to help you greet mornings with a kitchen full of smiles.

Country Scrambled Breakfast Burritos page 146

Ham and Chile Brunch Pizza page 143

Southwestern Brunch Eggs page 149

tex-mex breakfast bake
page 148

mexicorn® bread pudding

PREP TIME: 15 MINUTES
READY IN: 1 HOUR 5 MINUTES
SERVINGS: 6

Lillian Julow
Gainesville, FL

8   Pillsbury® Home Baked Classics® Frozen Soft White or Crusty French Dinner Rolls (from 12.4 oz. bag)

6   eggs

2   cups milk

1/4 teaspoon kosher (coarse) or regular salt

1/4 teaspoon dried thyme leaves

1/4 teaspoon coarse ground black pepper

    Dash nutmeg

1   cup shredded hot pepper Monterey Jack cheese (4 oz.)

1   (11 oz.) can Green Giant® Mexicorn® Whole Kernel Corn, Red and Green Peppers, drained

1   (4.5 oz.) can Old El Paso® Chopped Green Chiles, drained

1 Heat oven to 375°F. Spray 13x9-inch (3-quart) glass baking dish with nonstick cooking spray. Place frozen rolls on cutting board; let stand about 5 minutes to thaw.

2 Meanwhile, in large bowl, beat eggs, milk, salt, thyme, pepper and nutmeg with wire whisk until well blended.

3 Cut rolls into 3/4-inch cubes; place in bowl with egg mixture. Stir in cheese, corn and chiles. Pour into the sprayed dish.

4 Bake at 375°F for 30 to 40 minutes or until puffed, golden brown and knife inserted in center comes out clean. Let stand 10 minutes before serving. Cut into squares.

HIGH ALTITUDE (3500-6500 FT): Bake at 375°F for 40 to 45 minutes.

NUTRITIONAL INFORMATION PER SERVING: Calories 365 • Total Fat 15g • Saturated Fat 6g • Cholesterol 235mg • Sodium 670mg • Total Carbohydrate 39g • Dietary Fiber 2g • Sugars 10g • Protein 18g.

TIP: For fast assembly, beat the eggs, milk, salt, thyme, pepper and nutmeg the night before. Store the mixture covered in the refrigerator. In the morning, prepare the dish as directed.

crab quiche squares

PREP TIME: 30 MINUTES
READY IN: 1 HOUR 10 MINUTES
SERVINGS: 32

Jann Stricklin
Mena, AR

1 (8 oz.) can Pillsbury® Refrigerated Crescent Dinner Rolls

1 (8 oz.) package cream cheese, softened

1/2 cup sour cream

2 eggs

2 (6 oz.) cans crabmeat, drained, flaked

3/4 cup grated Parmesan cheese

8 green onions, finely chopped

Dash salt

Dash pepper

1 Heat oven to 350°F. Unroll dough into 2 long rectangles. Place in ungreased 13x9-inch pan; press over bottom to form crust. Firmly press perforations to seal.

2 Beat cream cheese in medium bowl until light and fluffy. Add sour cream and eggs; beat well. Add crabmeat, 1/2 cup of the cheese, onions, salt and pepper; mix well. Spoon and spread over dough in pan. Sprinkle with remaining 1/4 cup cheese.

3 Bake at 350°F for 35 to 40 minutes or until center is set and the edges are golden brown. Cool 10 minutes. Cut into squares.

NUTRITIONAL INFORMATION PER SERVING: Calories 90 • Total Fat 6g • Saturated Fat 3g • Cholesterol 30mg • Sodium 160mg • Total Carbohydrate 4g • Dietary Fiber 0g • Sugars 1g • Protein 4g.
DIETARY EXCHANGES: 1/2 Starch • 1/2 Other Carbohydrate • 1/2 Very Lean Meat • 1 Fat.

ham & chile brunch pizza

READY IN: 30 MINUTES
SERVINGS: 4

Jennifer Kavanagh
Easton, PA

1 (13.8-oz.) can Pillsbury® Refrigerated Pizza Crust

6 eggs

1/4 teaspoon salt

1/8 teaspoon pepper

1 tablespoon butter

1 cup julienne-cut strips or chopped cooked ham

1 (4.5-oz.) can Old El Paso® Chopped Green Chiles

1-1/2 cups shredded Monterey Jack cheese or hot pepper Monterey Jack cheese (6 oz.)

2 tablespoons chopped fresh cilantro

1 Heat oven to 425°F. Grease 14-inch pizza pan. Unroll dough; place in greased pan. Starting at center, press out dough to edge of pan. Bake for 6 to 8 minutes or until crust begins to brown.

2 Meanwhile combine eggs, salt and pepper; beat well. Melt butter in large skillet over medium heat. Add eggs; cook 1 to 2 minutes or until firm but moist, stirring often.

3 Remove partially baked crust from oven. Spoon and spread eggs over crust. Top with ham, chiles and cheese.

4 Return to oven; bake an additional 8 to 12 minutes or until crust is deep golden brown. Sprinkle with cilantro if desired.

NUTRITIONAL INFORMATION PER SERVING: Calories 520 • Total Fat 27g • Saturated Fat 13g • Cholesterol 380mg • Sodium 1,560mg • Total Carbohydrate 36g • Dietary Fiber 2g • Sugars 5g • Protein 33g.
DIETARY EXCHANGES: 2-1/2 Starch • 2-1/2 Other Carbohydrate • 3-1/2 Very Lean Meat • 4-1/2 Fat.

italian garden frittata

italian garden frittata

READY IN: 20 MINUTES
SERVINGS: 4

8 eggs

1 tablespoon coarsely chopped fresh sage

1/2 teaspoon salt

1/4 teaspoon pepper

1/2 cup grated Romano cheese

1 teaspoon olive oil

1 small zucchini, sliced

2 green onions, sliced

2 Italian plum tomatoes, thinly sliced lengthwise

1 In medium bowl, combine eggs, sage, salt, pepper and 1/4 cup of the cheese; beat well. Set aside.

2 Heat oil in medium ovenproof nonstick skillet over medium heat until hot. Add zucchini and onions; cook and stir 2 minutes or until zucchini is tender. Add egg mixture; cook 2 minutes or until egg mixture is almost set, lifting edges occasionally to allow uncooked egg mixture to flow to bottom of skillet.

3 Top frittata with tomato slices; sprinkle with remaining 1/4 cup cheese. Broil 4 to 6 inches from heat for 1 to 3 minutes or until top is set and begins to brown.

NUTRITIONAL INFORMATION PER SERVING: Calories 220 • Total Fat 15g • Saturated Fat 5g • Cholesterol 440mg • Sodium 550mg • Total Carbohydrate 4g • Dietary Fiber 1g • Sugars 3g • Protein 17g. DIETARY EXCHANGES: 1/2 Fruit • 1/2 Other Carbohydrate • 2-1/2 Medium-Fat Meat • 1/2 Fat.

HEALTHY HINT: Substituting 8 egg whites for 4 of the whole eggs will reduce the cholesterol by about 215 milligrams and fat by about 5 grams per serving in this recipe.

broccoli strata

PREP TIME: 25 MINUTES
READY IN: 5 HOURS 20 MINUTES
SERVINGS: 6

1 medium onion, chopped

1 cup julienne-cut carrots (2x1/8x1/8-inch)

2 cups Green Giant Select® Frozen 100% Broccoli Florets, thawed

6 slices day-old sourdough, French or English muffin bread

1 cup shredded Italian cheese blend (4 oz.)

1-1/2 cups fat-free half-and-half or milk

1 cup refrigerated or frozen fat-free egg product, thawed, or 4 eggs

1 teaspoon garlic-pepper blend

2 tablespoons shredded fresh Parmesan cheese

1 Spray 8-inch square (2-quart) glass baking dish and large nonstick skillet with nonstick cooking spray. Heat skillet over medium-high heat until hot. Add onion and carrots; cook and stir 3 to 4 minutes. Add broccoli; cook and stir 2 to 3 minutes or until vegetables are crisp-tender.

2 Cut bread into large cubes; place in sprayed baking dish. Spoon broccoli mixture over bread. Sprinkle Italian cheese blend evenly over top.

3 In medium bowl, combine half-and-half, egg product and garlic-pepper blend; beat until smooth. Pour over broccoli mixture. Sprinkle with Parmesan cheese. Cover; refrigerate at least 4 hours or overnight.

4 Heat oven to 350°F. Uncover strata; bake 45 to 55 minutes or until knife inserted in center comes out clean. Let stand 5 minutes before cutting into squares.

NUTRITIONAL INFORMATION PER SERVING: Calories 220 • Total Fat 7g • Saturated Fat 5g • Cholesterol 15mg • Sodium 550mg • Total Carbohydrate 25g • Dietary Fiber 2g • Sugars 6g • Protein 15g. DIETARY EXCHANGES: 1-1/2 Starch • 1-1/2 Other Carbohydrate • 1 Vegetable • 1 Lean Meat • 1/2 Fat.

creamy swiss eggs on biscuits

READY IN: 25 MINUTES
SERVINGS: 4

4 Pillsbury® Oven Baked Frozen Buttermilk Biscuits (from 25 oz. bag)

1 can (10-3/4 oz.) condensed cream of chicken with herbs soup

2/3 cup milk

1 cup shredded Swiss cheese (4 oz.)

1/8 teaspoon pepper

6 eggs

2 medium green onions, sliced (2 tablespoons)

2 teaspoons butter or margarine

1 Heat oven to 375°F. Bake the frozen biscuits as directed on bag.

2 Meanwhile, in small bowl, mix soup, milk, cheese and pepper; set aside. In medium bowl, beat eggs with wire whisk. Stir in 1 tablespoon of the onions. In 8-inch skillet, melt butter over medium heat. Add egg mixture; cook 4 to 5 minutes, stirring occasionally, until eggs are thoroughly cooked but still moist.

3 Gently stir soup mixture into egg mixture. Cook and stir until thoroughly heated.

4 Split each warm biscuit; place on individual serving plate. Spoon egg mixture over biscuits. Sprinkle with the remaining onions.

NUTRITIONAL INFORMATION PER SERVING: Calories 520 • Total Fat 32g • Saturated Fat 13g • Trans Fat 4.5g • Cholesterol 355mg • Sodium 1,330mg • Total Carbohydrate 33g • Dietary Fiber 0g, Sugars 6g • Protein 25g.
DIETARY EXCHANGES: 1-1/2 Starch • 1/2 Other Carbohydrate • 3 High-Fat Meat • 1-1/2 Fat.

country scrambled breakfast burritos

READY IN: 30 MINUTES
SERVINGS: 4

1/4 lb. bulk turkey breakfast sausage

1/4 cup chopped onion

2 small red potatoes, unpeeled, diced (3/4 cup)

1 (8 oz.) carton refrigerated or frozen fat-free egg product, thawed (1 cup), or 4 eggs, beaten

4 (8 inch) flour tortillas

4 tablespoons reduced-fat smoky Cheddar cold pack cheese food

1 Heat oven to 375°F. Spray cookie sheet with nonstick cooking spray.

2 Spray large nonstick skillet with nonstick cooking spray. Heat over medium-high heat until hot. Add sausage, onion and potatoes; cook 8 to 10 minutes or until sausage is no longer pink and vegetables are tender, stirring frequently. Remove from skillet; cover to keep warm.

3 Add egg product to same skillet; cook 3 to 5 minutes or until firm but moist, stirring frequently.

4 Spread each tortilla with 1 tablespoon cheese food; spread to within 1/2 inch of edge. Place on sprayed cookie sheet. Spoon 1/4 of egg product and 1/4 of sausage mixture down center of each tortilla. Fold bottom of each tortilla up over filling; fold right side to center. Fold left side over right side. Secure with wooden toothpick.

5 Bake at 375°F for 3 to 4 minutes or until cheese is melted. If desired, serve with salsa.

NUTRITIONAL INFORMATION PER SERVING: Calories 310 • Total Fat 12g • Saturated Fat 4g • Cholesterol 35mg • Sodium 570mg • Total Carbohydrate 34g • Dietary Fiber 2g • Sugars 4g • Protein 17g.
DIETARY EXCHANGES: 2-1/2 Starch • 2-1/2 Other Carbohydrate.

cheesy fiesta quiche

PREP TIME: 25 MINUTES
READY IN: 1 HOUR 20 MINUTES
SERVINGS: 6

Gretchen Koch
Rocky River, OH

CRUST

1 (4.6 oz.) box Old El Paso® White Corn Taco Shells (12 shells)

3 tablespoons butter or margarine, melted

FILLING

3 eggs

1 cup small-curd cottage cheese

2 cups shredded Mexican 4-cheese blend (8 oz.)

1/2 cup milk

2 tablespoons butter or margarine, melted

1/3 cup all-purpose flour

1/2 teaspoon baking powder

2 tablespoons drained Old El Paso® Chopped Green Chiles (from 4.5 oz. can)

2 tablespoons chopped ripe olives

TOPPING

6 tablespoons sour cream

6 tablespoons Old El Paso® Thick 'n' Chunky Salsa

1 Heat oven to 325°F. In food processor or blender, crush taco shells until very fine. In medium bowl, mix crushed taco shells and 3 tablespoons melted butter. Press in bottom and up side of 9-inch glass pie pan. Bake at 325°F for 15 minutes.

2 Meanwhile, in large bowl, beat eggs. Add all remaining filling ingredients except chiles and olives; beat with electric mixer on medium speed until well blended. Stir in the chiles and olives.

3 Remove partially baked crust from oven; increase oven temperature to 400°F. Pour filling into crust.

4 Return to oven; bake at 400°F for 10 minutes. Reduce oven temperature to 325°F; bake an additional 25 to 35 minutes or until center is slightly puffed and light golden brown. Cool 10 minutes.

5 Cut quiche into wedges; place on individual serving plates. Top each with 1 tablespoon sour cream and 1 tablespoon salsa. If desired, garnish plates with tortilla chips.

HIGH ALTITUDE (3500-6500 FT):
Bake crust at 325°F for 15 minutes. Increase oven temperature to 400°F. After filling partially baked crust, bake at 400°F for 10 minutes. Reduce oven temperature to 325°F; bake an additional 30 to 40 minutes.

NUTRITIONAL INFORMATION PER SERVING:
Calories 470 • Total Fat 34g • Saturated Fat 18g • Cholesterol 185mg • Sodium 720mg • Total Carbohydrate 23g • Dietary Fiber 2g • Sugars 4g • Protein 20g.

potato frittata

READY IN: 25 MINUTES
SERVINGS: 4

6 eggs

1/3 cup milk

1/2 teaspoon salt

Dash black pepper

1/4 cup chopped roasted red bell peppers (from a jar)

2 tablespoons chopped fresh chives

2 tablespoons vegetable oil

3 cups frozen southern-style hash brown potatoes (from 32 oz. bag)

1 In medium bowl, beat eggs, milk, salt and black pepper with wire whisk until well blended. Stir in roasted peppers and chives; set aside.

2 In 12-inch nonstick skillet, heat oil over medium-high heat. Add potatoes; cook 4 to 5 minutes, stirring frequently, until thawed.

3 Reduce heat to medium-low. Stir egg mixture; pour over potatoes in skillet. Cover; cook

8 to 10 minutes or until eggs are set, lifting edges occasionally to allow uncooked egg mixture to flow to bottom of skillet. Cut into 8 wedges to serve.

NUTRITIONAL INFORMATION PER SERVING:
Calories 320 • Total Fat 15g • Saturated Fat 3.5g • Trans Fat 0g • Cholesterol 320mg • Sodium 430mg • Total Carbohydrate 33g • Dietary Fiber 3g • Sugars 4g • Protein 13g.
DIETARY EXCHANGES: 2 Starch • 1 Medium-Fat Meat • 2 Fat.

tex-mex breakfast bake

PREP TIME: 20 MINUTES
READY IN: 1 HOUR 15 MINUTES
SERVINGS: 6

Lynne Milliron
Austin, TX

- 1/4 lb. bulk lean breakfast sausage
- 1 (10 oz.) can Old El Paso® Red Enchilada Sauce
- 1/2 cup crumbled queso fresco (Mexican cheese) or farmer cheese (2-1/2 oz.)
- 1/3 cup sour cream
- 1/4 cup chopped green onions
- 1 (16.3 oz.) can Pillsbury® Grands!® Flaky Layers Refrigerated Original or Buttermilk Biscuits
- 1-1/4 cups shredded Colby-Monterey Jack cheese blend (5 oz.)
- 1/4 cup chopped fresh cilantro

1 Heat oven to 350°F. Spray 8x8- or 11x7-inch (2-quart) glass baking dish with cooking spray. In 10-inch skillet, cook sausage over medium-high heat, stirring frequently, until no longer pink.

2 Meanwhile, in small bowl, mix 1/4 cup of the enchilada sauce, the queso fresco, sour cream and onions; set aside. Pour remaining enchilada sauce into medium bowl. Separate dough into 8 biscuits; cut each into 8 pieces. Gently stir dough pieces into enchilada sauce to coat. Spoon mixture into sprayed dish; spread evenly.

3 Drain sausage on paper towels. Sprinkle sausage evenly on top of biscuit pieces. Spread sour cream mixture evenly over top.

4 Bake at 350°F for 30 to 35 minutes or until center is set and edges are deep golden brown. Remove from oven. Sprinkle Colby-Monterey Jack cheese over top.

5 Return to oven; bake an additional 10 minutes or until cheese is bubbly. Sprinkle with cilantro. Let stand 5 minutes before serving. Cut into squares.

HIGH ALTITUDE (3500-6500 FT):
Use 11x7-inch (2-quart) glass baking dish. Bake at 375°F for 45 to 50 minutes. Sprinkle Colby-Monterey Jack cheese over top; bake an additional 5 minutes.

NUTRITIONAL INFORMATION PER SERVING:
Calories 450 • Total Fat 25g • Saturated Fat 11g • Cholesterol 40mg • Sodium 1,400mg • Total Carbohydrate 41g • Dietary Fiber 2g • Sugars 13g • Protein 15g.

apple-cheddar strata

PREP TIME: 10 MINUTES
READY IN: 7 HOURS 10 MINUTES
SERVINGS: 4

- 4 slices white bread, cubed (3-1/2 cups)
- 1 (12 oz.) box frozen harvest apples, thawed
- 1 cup chopped cooked ham (about 6 oz.)
- 3/4 cup shredded sharp Cheddar cheese (3 oz.)
- 4 eggs
- 1/4 cup half-and-half
- Dash white pepper

1 Spray 9-1/2-inch deep-dish glass pie plate with cooking spray. Arrange bread cubes in bottom of pie plate. Spoon apples evenly over bread; sprinkle with ham and cheese.

2 In medium bowl, beat eggs, half-and-half and pepper with wire whisk until well blended. Carefully pour over apples, ham and cheese. Cover; refrigerate at least 6 hours or overnight.

3 Heat oven to 350°F. Bake uncovered 40 to 45 minutes or until top is lightly browned and center is set. Let stand 10 to 15 minutes before serving.

HIGH ALTITUDE (3500-6500 FT):
Bake uncovered 43 to 48 minutes.

NUTRITIONAL INFORMATION PER SERVING:
Calories 390 • Total Fat 19g • Saturated Fat 9g • Trans Fat 0g • Cholesterol 265mg • Sodium 980mg • Total Carbohydrate 31g • Dietary Fiber 1g • Sugars 16g • Protein 24g.
DIETARY EXCHANGES: 1 Starch • 1 Other Carbohydrate • 3 Medium-Fat Meat • 1/2 Fat.

southwestern brunch eggs

PREP TIME: 40 MINUTES
READY IN: 4 HOURS 40 MINUTES
SERVINGS: 12

5 cups frozen shredded hash-brown potatoes (from 30 oz. bag)

1 (15 oz.) can black beans, drained, rinsed

16 eggs

1 cup half-and-half

1/2 teaspoon salt

1/4 teaspoon pepper

2 tablespoons butter or margarine

1 (10-3/4 oz.) can condensed cream of mushroom soup

2 cups shredded Colby-Monterey Jack cheese blend (8 oz.)

1 cup Old El Paso® Thick 'n' Chunky Salsa

1 In microwavable 3- to 4-quart slow cooker insert or medium bowl, microwave potatoes on High 3-1/2 to 4 minutes, stirring once, until thawed. Stir in beans. With back of spoon, press mixture in bottom and 2 to 3 inches up side of slow cooker; set aside.

2 In large bowl, beat eggs, half-and-half, salt and pepper with wire whisk until well blended. In 10-inch non-stick skillet, melt butter over medium heat. Add egg mixture; cook, stirring occasionally, until eggs are almost set.

3 Spoon half of egg mixture into slow cooker; top with half each of the soup, cheese and salsa. Layer with the remaining egg mixture, soup, cheese and salsa.

4 Cover; cook on Low setting 3 to 4 hours.

NUTRITIONAL INFORMATION PER SERVING: Calories 360 • Total Fat 19g • Saturated Fat 9g • Cholesterol 315mg • Sodium 740mg • Total Carbohydrate 31g • Dietary Fiber 4g • Sugars 5g • Protein 19g.
DIETARY EXCHANGES: 2 Starch • 2 Medium-Fat Meat • 1-1/2 Fat.

wild rice and ham country tart

PREP TIME: 30 MINUTES
READY IN: 1 HOUR 5 MINUTES
SERVINGS: 8

1 Pillsbury® Refrigerated Pie Crust (from 15 oz. pkg.), softened as directed on package

1 cup diced cooked ham

1/2 cup cooked wild rice

1/3 cup finely chopped red bell pepper

1/4 cup thinly sliced green onion tops

1 (4.5 oz.) jar Green Giant® Sliced Mushrooms, well drained

3 eggs

1 (8 oz.) container sour cream

1 tablespoon country-style Dijon mustard

1/2 teaspoon salt

1/8 teaspoon pepper

2 cups shredded Swiss cheese (8 oz.)

8 pecan halves

1 Heat oven to 450°F. Place pie crust in 10-inch tart pan with removable bottom or 9-inch pie pan as directed on package for one-crust filled pie. Press in bottom and up sides of pan. Trim edges if necessary. Do not prick crust. Bake at 450°F for 9 to 11 minutes or until crust is light golden brown. Remove from oven. Reduce heat to 400°F.

2 In medium bowl, combine ham, wild rice, bell pepper, onions and mushrooms; mix well. Beat eggs in small bowl until well blended. Add sour cream, mustard, salt and pepper; blend well.

3 Sprinkle 1 cup of the cheese over bottom of baked crust. Spread ham mixture over cheese. Pour egg mixture over ham mixture. Sprinkle with remaining 1 cup cheese.

4 Bake at 400°F for 30 to 35 minutes or until knife inserted in center comes out clean, arranging pecan halves on top of tart during last 10 minutes of baking time. Let stand 10 minutes before serving.

HIGH ALTITUDE (3500-6500 FT):
Add 1 tablespoon all-purpose flour to ham mixture.

NUTRITIONAL INFORMATION PER SERVING: Calories 360 • Total Fat 24g • Saturated Fat 13g • Cholesterol 140mg • Sodium 770mg • Total Carbohydrate 19g • Dietary Fiber 0g • Sugars 3g • Protein 17g. **DIETARY EXCHANGES:** 1 Starch • 1 Other Carbohydrate • 2 High-Fat Meat • 1-1/2 Fat.

TIPS:
Wild rice is not rice but long-grain marsh grass native to the Great Lakes. It's famous for its nutty flavor and chewy texture.

Cooked wild rice is conveniently available canned and frozen. The cans are stocked near bags or raw wild rice. It isn't necessary to thaw frozen wild rice before use in this tart.

This recipe calls for 1 cup or about 6 ounces of ham. From the deli, order ham sliced 1/4 inch thick; these slices can be easily diced. We baked this pie in a 9-inch pie pan. For a simple, decorative crust edge, use a fork and make overlapping diagonal marks to form the design.

Enjoy this savory tart with fresh pear slices.

cheesy sausage pie

PREP TIME: 15 MINUTES
READY IN: 1 HOUR 20 MINUTES
SERVINGS: 8

Pillsbury
Bake-Off

Elizabeth Caulfield Felt
Stevens Point, WI

1 lb. bulk pork sausage

1 medium onion, chopped (1/2 cup)

1 tablespoon minced garlic

1/3 cup tomato paste (from 6 oz. can)

1 cup Green Giant® Niblets® Frozen Corn (from 1 lb. bag)

1 (14.5 oz.) can diced tomatoes with Italian-style herbs, undrained

1 (2.25 oz.) can sliced ripe olives, drained

1 Pillsbury® Refrigerated Pie Crust (from 15 oz. box), softened as directed on the box

1-1/2 cups shredded Cheddar cheese (6 oz.)

1 Heat oven to 350°F. In 12-inch skillet, cook sausage, onion and garlic over medium heat, stirring frequently, until sausage is no longer pink. Drain and discard any drippings. Stir in tomato paste, corn, tomatoes and olives.

2 Place pie crust in 9-inch glass pie pan as directed on box for one-crust filled pie. Spoon sausage mixture into pie crust-lined pan.

3 Bake at 350°F for 30 to 40 minutes or until crust is golden brown. Sprinkle cheese over top. Bake an additional 10 to 15 minutes or until cheese is melted and starts to brown. Let stand 10 minutes before serving. Cut into wedges.

HIGH ALTITUDE (3500-6500 FT): Prebake crust at 375°F for 8 minutes. After filling partially baked crust, bake pie for 40 to 50 minutes. Sprinkle cheese over top; bake about 5 minutes.

NUTRITIONAL INFORMATION PER SERVING: Calories 350 • Total Fat 23g • Saturated Fat 11g • Cholesterol 50mg • Sodium 820mg • Total Carbohydrate 24g • Dietary Fiber 2g • Sugars 4g • Protein 13g.

italian zucchini crescent pie

PREP TIME: 30 MINUTES
READY IN: 55 MINUTES
SERVINGS: 6

Millicent Caplan
Tamarac, FL

2 tablespoons margarine or butter

4 cups thinly sliced zucchini

1 cup chopped onions

2 tablespoons dried parsley flakes

1/2 teaspoon salt

1/2 teaspoon pepper

1/4 teaspoon garlic powder

1/4 teaspoon dried basil leaves

1/4 teaspoon dried oregano leaves

2 eggs, well beaten

2 cups shredded Muenster or mozzarella cheese (8 oz.)

1 (8 oz.) can Pillsbury® Refrigerated Crescent Dinner Rolls

2 teaspoons prepared mustard

1 Heat oven to 375°F. Melt margarine in 12-inch skillet over medium-high heat. Add zucchini and onions; cook and stir 6 to 8 minutes or until tender. Stir in the parsley flakes, salt, pepper, garlic powder, basil and oregano.

2 In large bowl, combine eggs and cheese; mix well. Stir in cooked vegetable mixture.

3 Separate dough into 8 triangles. Place in ungreased 10-inch pie pan or 11-inch quiche pan; press over bottom and up sides to form crust. Firmly press perforations to seal. Spread crust with mustard. Pour egg mixture evenly into crust-lined pan.

4 Bake at 375°F for 18 to 22 minutes or until knife inserted near center comes out clean. Cover edge of crust with strips of foil during last 10 minutes of baking if necessary to prevent excessive browning. Let stand 10 minutes before serving.

NUTRITIONAL INFORMATION PER SERVING: Calories 370 • Total Fat 25g • Saturated Fat 10g • Cholesterol 105mg • Sodium 790mg • Total Carbohydrate 21g • Dietary Fiber 2g • Sugars 7g • Protein 15g.
DIETARY EXCHANGES: 1 Starch • 1 Other Carbohydrate • 1 Vegetable • 1-1/2 High-Fat Meat • 2-1/2 Fat.

TIP: To make this crescent pie in a 12x8-inch (2-quart) baking dish, unroll the dough into 2 long rectangles. Press the dough over bottom and 1 inch up sides of pan to form crust. Firmly press perforations to seal. Continue with recipe as directed.

sour cream-ham enchiladas

PREP TIME: 15 MINUTES
READY IN: 55 MINUTES
SERVINGS: 6 (2 ENCHILADAS EACH)

3 cups chopped cooked ham

1 (8 oz.) container sour cream (about 1 cup)

1 (4.5 oz.) can Old El Paso® Chopped Green Chiles

3 cups shredded Cheddar cheese (12 oz.)

1 (10.5 oz.) package Old El Paso® Flour Tortillas, 6 inch (12 tortillas)

1 (10 oz.) can Old El Paso® Enchilada Sauce

1 Heat oven to 350°F. Spray 13x9-inch (3-quart) glass baking dish with cooking spray. In large bowl, mix ham, sour cream, green chiles and 2-1/2 cups of the cheese.

2 Spoon about 1/3 cup ham mixture evenly down center of each tortilla. Fold sides of tortilla over filling; place seam side down in baking dish. Pour enchilada sauce over filled tortillas.

3 Spray sheet of foil with cooking spray; cover dish tightly with foil, sprayed side down. Bake 30 to 35 minutes or until thoroughly heated. Uncover; sprinkle with remaining 1/2 cup cheese. Bake uncovered 5 minutes longer or until cheese is melted. If desired, serve with shredded lettuce and chopped tomatoes.

HIGH ALTITUDE (3500-6500 FT): Bake 35 to 40 minutes.

NUTRITIONAL INFORMATION PER SERVING: Calories 590 • Total Fat 37g • Saturated Fat 20g • Trans Fat 0.5g • Cholesterol 125mg • Sodium 2,030mg • Total Carbohydrate 31g • Dietary Fiber 0g • Sugars 3g • Protein 33g.
DIETARY EXCHANGES: 2 Starch • 4 Medium-Fat Meat • 3 Fat.

italian zucchini crescent pie

mushroom-crab-asparagus tart

PREP TIME: 20 MINUTES
READY IN: 1 HOUR 5 MINUTES
SERVINGS: 8

Linda Miranda
Wakefield, RI

1 (9 oz.) box Green Giant® Frozen Asparagus Cuts

1/4 cup butter or margarine

1 lb. fresh mushrooms, coarsely chopped

1/2 cup Progresso® Parmesan Bread Crumbs

1/4 teaspoon pepper

2 cups shredded sharp Cheddar or Swiss cheese (8 oz.)

1/2 lb. lump crabmeat or 1 (6 oz.) can lump crabmeat, drained

1 (8 oz.) container garlic-and-herb spreadable cheese

4 eggs

2 tablespoons chopped fresh parsley

1 Heat oven to 375°F. Spray bottom and side of 12-inch tart pan with removable bottom or 13x9-inch (3-quart) glass baking dish with cooking spray. Cook asparagus as directed on box; drain and cool.

2 Meanwhile, in 12-inch skillet, melt butter over medium heat. Add mushrooms; cook about 5 minutes, stirring frequently, just until tender. Stir in bread crumbs and pepper. Press mushroom mixture evenly in bottom and up side of sprayed tart pan or in bottom of sprayed baking dish. Sprinkle shredded cheese over mushrooms. Top with asparagus and crabmeat.

3 In medium bowl or blender, place spreadable cheese, eggs and 1 tablespoon of the parsley. Beat with electric mixer on medium speed or cover and blend on low speed until smooth. Pour evenly over crabmeat.

4 Bake at 375°F for 30 to 35 minutes or until set in center and edges are golden brown. Sprinkle remaining tablespoon parsley over top. Let stand 10 minutes before serving. Carefully remove side of pan. Cut into wedges or squares.

NUTRITIONAL INFORMATION PER SERVING: Calories 380 • Total Fat 29g • Saturated Fat 17g • Cholesterol 210mg • Sodium 460mg • Total Carbohydrate 10g • Dietary Fiber 1g • Sugars 3g • Protein 21g.

sausage and cheese crescent squares

PREP TIME: 20 MINUTES
READY IN: 1 HOUR
SERVINGS: 32

Becky McPherson
Birmingham, AL

2 (8 oz.) cans Pillsbury® Refrigerated Crescent Dinner Rolls

1 lb. hot or mild bulk pork sausage

1 (8 oz.) pkg. cream cheese

2 cups shredded sharp Cheddar cheese (8 oz.)

1 Heat oven to 375°F. Unroll 1 can of dough into 2 long rectangles. Place in ungreased 13x9-inch (3-quart) glass baking dish; press over bottom and 1/2 inch up sides to form crust.

2 Brown sausage in large skillet over medium heat until thoroughly cooked, stirring frequently. Remove sausage from skillet; discard drippings. Add cream cheese to same skillet. Cook over low heat until melted. Add cooked sausage; stir to coat. Spoon evenly over crust in the baking dish. Sprinkle with the cheese.

3 Unroll second can of dough on work surface. Press to form 13x9-inch rectangle; firmly press the perforations to seal. Carefully place over cheese.

4 Bake at 375°F for 21 to 26 minutes or until golden brown. Cool 15 minutes. Cut into small squares.

NUTRITIONAL INFORMATION PER SERVING: Calories 130 • Total Fat 10g • Saturated Fat 4g • Cholesterol 20mg • Sodium 260mg • Total Carbohydrate 6g • Dietary Fiber 0g, Sugars 1g • Protein 5g.
DIETARY EXCHANGES: 1/2 Starch • 1/2 Other Carbohydrate • 1/2 High-Fat Meat • 1 Fat.

quick corn and mushroom brunch squares

PREP TIME: 20 MINUTES
READY IN: 1 HOUR
SERVINGS: 12

- 2 (8 oz.) cans Pillsbury® Refrigerated Crescent Dinner Rolls
- 2 cups chopped cooked ham
- 1-1/2 cups shredded Monterey Jack cheese (6 oz.)
- 1-1/2 cups shredded Swiss cheese (6 oz.)
- 1 (11 oz.) can Green Giant® Mexicorn® Whole Kernel Corn, Red and Green Peppers, drained
- 1 (4.5 oz.) jar Green Giant® Sliced Mushrooms, drained
- 6 eggs
- 1 cup milk
- 1/2 teaspoon salt
- 1/4 to 1/2 teaspoon pepper

1 Heat oven to 375°F. Unroll both cans of dough into 4 long rectangles. Place crosswise in ungreased 15x10x1-inch baking pan; press firmly over bottom and 3/4 inch up sides to form crust. Press edges and perforations to seal.

2 Sprinkle ham, Monterey Jack cheese, Swiss cheese, corn and mushrooms evenly over crust. In medium bowl, beat eggs, milk, salt and pepper until well blended. Pour evenly over ham, cheeses and vegetables.

3 Bake at 375°F for 35 to 40 minutes or until crust is deep golden brown, egg mixture is set and knife inserted in center comes out clean. Cool 5 minutes. Cut into squares.

HIGH ALTITUDE (3500-6500 FT):
Bake 37 to 42 minutes.

NUTRITIONAL INFORMATION PER SERVING:
Calories 350 • Total Fat 19g • Saturated Fat 8g • Cholesterol 145mg • Sodium 1,060mg • Total Carbohydrate 25g • Dietary Fiber 1g • Sugars 7g • Protein 20g.
DIETARY EXCHANGES: 1-1/2 Starch • 1-1/2 Other Carbohydrate • 2 Medium-Fat Meat • 2 Fat.

ham and tomato quiche

PREP TIME: 15 MINUTES
READY IN: 1 HOUR
SERVINGS: 6

- 1 Pillsbury® Refrigerated Pie Crust (from 15 oz. box), softened as directed on box
- 3 eggs
- 3/4 cup milk
- 2 tablespoons Pillsbury BEST® All-Purpose Flour
- 1/4 cup grated Parmesan cheese
- 1 cup finely chopped cooked ham (about 6 oz.)
- 1 medium tomato, cut in half, seeded and cut into thin strips
- 3 tablespoons chopped green onions (3 medium)
- 1 cup shredded Cheddar cheese (4 oz.)

1 Heat oven to 400°F. Place pie crust in 9-inch glass pie plate as directed on box for One-Crust Filled Pie. Do not prick crust. Bake 8 to 10 minutes or just until edge begins to brown (if crust puffs up in center, gently push down with back of wooden spoon).

2 Meanwhile, in medium bowl, beat eggs, milk, flour and Parmesan cheese with wire whisk until well blended.

3 Layer ham, tomato, onions and Cheddar cheese in partially baked crust. Pour egg mixture over layers.

4 Cover crust edge with strips of foil to prevent excessive browning; bake 25 to 35 minutes or until golden brown and knife inserted in center comes out clean. Let stand 10 minutes before serving.

NUTRITIONAL INFORMATION PER SERVING:
Calories 370 • Total Fat 23g • Saturated Fat 10g • Trans Fat 0g • Cholesterol 155mg • Sodium 810mg • Total Carbohydrate 23g • Dietary Fiber 0g • Sugars 4g • Protein 18g.
DIETARY EXCHANGES: 1-1/2 Starch • 2 Medium-Fat Meat • 2-1/2 Fat.

skillet & stovetop suppers

Even when the kitchen clock is ticking, there's always time for a dash-in-the-pan specialty. Stop here when you are in the mood for a complete meal but simply can't afford the time to heat up the oven. Chicken dinners, pasta delights and savory stir fries come together at the drop of a hat with the following stovetop recipes. Best of all, many of the dishes found here are ready in 30 minutes or less.

Orzo with Bacon
and Asparagus
page 167

Beef Fried
Rice
page 158

Orange-
Cumin
Chicken and
Vegetables
page 162

louisiana chicken and pasta
page 177

beef fried rice

READY IN: 30 MINUTES
SERVINGS: 6

1 cup uncooked regular long-grain white rice

2 cups water

1 egg

1 lb. lean ground beef

1 cup sliced fresh mushrooms

1/2 cup sliced celery

1/3 cup soy sauce

1 tablespoon sesame oil

1/2 teaspoon hot pepper sauce

1-1/2 cups fresh snow pea pods, halved diagonally

1/2 cup chopped green onions

1 Cook rice in water as directed on package.

2 Meanwhile, spray 12-inch nonstick skillet with nonstick cooking spray. Heat over medium heat until hot. Beat egg in small bowl. Add egg to skillet; cook 1 minute or until firm but still moist. Remove from skillet; cut into thin strips. Cover to keep warm.

3 In same skillet, cook ground beef, mushrooms and celery over medium heat for 8 to 10 minutes or until beef is thoroughly cooked, stirring frequently.

4 In small bowl, combine soy sauce, sesame oil and hot pepper sauce; mix well. Stir soy sauce mixture into beef mixture. Add pea pods, onions, cooked egg and cooked rice; cook an additional 2 to 3 minutes or until thoroughly heated, stirring constantly.

NUTRITIONAL INFORMATION PER SERVING:
Calories 330 • Total Fat 14g • Saturated Fat 5g • Cholesterol 80mg • Sodium 880mg • Total Carbohydrate 31g • Dietary Fiber 1g • Sugars 2g • Protein 20g.
DIETARY EXCHANGES: 2 Starch • 2 Other Carbohydrate • 2 Medium-Fat Meat • 1/2 Fat.

tuscany pasta toss

READY IN: 20 MINUTES
SERVINGS: 4

Susan Burns
Trenton, NJ

1 (9 oz.) package refrigerated fettuccine

2 cups chopped tomatoes (about 2 large)

1/3 cup chopped fresh basil

1 (4.5 oz.) jar Green Giant® Sliced Mushrooms, drained

3 tablespoons olive or vegetable oil

2 tablespoons balsamic vinegar

1 tablespoon minced garlic in water (from 4.5 oz. jar)

1/2 teaspoon salt

1/4 teaspoon cracked black pepper

1 cup Gorgonzola or blue cheese, crumbled (4 oz.)

1/2 cup chopped walnuts

Fresh basil leaves

1 Cook fettuccine as directed on package; drain.

2 Meanwhile, in large serving bowl, mix tomatoes, chopped basil, mushrooms, oil, vinegar, garlic, salt and pepper.

3 Toss in cooked fettuccine to coat. Gently stir in cheese and walnuts. Garnish with basil leaves if desired.

NUTRITIONAL INFORMATION PER SERVING:
Calories 500 • Total Fat 30g • Saturated Fat 8g • Cholesterol 20mg • Sodium 960mg • Total Carbohydrate 43g • Dietary Fiber 5g • Sugars 4g • Protein 17g.

asian meatball and rice toss

READY IN: 35 MINUTES
SERVINGS: 6

2 tablespoons butter

1 (6.8 oz.) package beef-flavor rice and vermicelli mix

3 cups water

1/3 cup purchased Asian sesame marinade and salad dressing

1 (16 oz.) package frozen cooked meatballs, thawed

1 cup julienne-cut (2x1/8x1/8-inch) carrots

1/2 cup halved fresh snow pea pods

3 tablespoons dry-roasted peanuts, chopped

3 tablespoons chopped green onions

1 Melt butter in 12-inch nonstick skillet over medium heat. Stir in rice and vermicelli from mix; cook and stir 2 to 3 minutes or until rice is lightly browned.

2 Add water, Asian marinade and contents of seasoning packet from mix; bring to a boil. Reduce heat to medium-low. Add meatballs and carrots; cover and cook 15 to 18 minutes or until rice is tender, stirring occasionally.

3 Stir in pea pods. Cook uncovered an additional 2 to 3 minutes or until pea pods are crisp-tender. Garnish individual servings with peanuts and onions.

HIGH ALTITUDE (3500-6500 FT):
Cook rice and vermicelli over medium-high heat. Continue as directed.

NUTRITIONAL INFORMATION PER SERVING:
Calories 350 • Total Fat 20g • Saturated Fat 8g • Cholesterol 95mg • Sodium 870mg • Total Carbohydrate 24g • Dietary Fiber 1g • Sugars 7g • Protein 18g.
DIETARY EXCHANGES: 1-1/2 Starch • 1-1/2 Other Carbohydrate • 2 Medium-Fat Meat • 2 Fat.

spring chicken fricassee with peas

PREP TIME: 20 MINUTES
READY IN: 50 MINUTES
SERVINGS: 4

- 8 boneless skinless chicken thighs
- 1/2 teaspoon salt
- 1/8 teaspoon pepper
- 1 tablespoon oil
- 1 cup chopped sweet onions (such as Maui or Texas Sweet)
- 3/4 cup fat-free chicken broth with 1/3 less sodium
- 3/4 cup evaporated fat-free milk
- 3 tablespoons Pillsbury BEST® All-Purpose Flour
- 2 cups Green Giant® Frozen Sweet Peas
- 2 teaspoons chopped fresh tarragon or 1/2 teaspoon dried tarragon leaves

1 Sprinkle chicken thighs with salt and pepper. Heat oil in Dutch oven over medium-high heat until hot. Add chicken, in batches; cook 4 to 6 minutes or until browned on both sides. Remove the chicken from the Dutch oven.

2 Add onions to Dutch oven; cook 3 to 4 minutes or until tender, stirring frequently. Add chicken and broth; cover and cook over low heat for 25 to 30 minutes or until chicken is fork-tender and juices run clear. Remove the chicken; place on platter. Cover with foil to keep warm.

3 In small bowl, blend milk and flour until smooth.

Beating with wire whisk, add flour mixture to cooking juices in Dutch oven. Increase heat to medium. Add peas and tarragon; cook 5 minutes or until peas are tender and sauce has thickened slightly, stirring frequently. Pour mixture over chicken and onions.

HIGH ALTITUDE (3500-6500 FT)
Cook onions over medium-low heat.

NUTRITIONAL INFORMATION PER SERVING:
Calories 380 • Total Fat 15g • Saturated Fat 4g • Cholesterol 85mg • Sodium 570mg • Total Carbohydrate 23g • Dietary Fiber 4g • Sugars 10g • Protein 38g.
DIETARY EXCHANGES: 1-1/2 Starch • 1-1/2 Other Carbohydrate • 4-1/2 Lean Meat • 1/2 Fat.

spicy szechuan beef and vegetables

READY IN: 25 MINUTES
SERVINGS: 4

- 2 cups uncooked instant white rice
- 2 cups water
- 3/4 lb. extra-lean (at least 90%) ground beef
- 4 oz. fresh snow pea pods, trimmed (1 cup)
- 1 (1 lb.) package Green Giant Select® Frozen Broccoli, Carrots & Cauliflower
- 1 (8 oz.) can sliced water chestnuts, drained
- 1/2 cup purchased Szechuan spicy stir fry sauce
- 3 tablespoons dry-roasted peanuts

1 Cook rice in water as directed on package.

2 Meanwhile, in 12-inch nonstick skillet or wok, brown ground beef over medium-high heat until thoroughly cooked, stirring frequently. Remove beef from skillet; drain.

3 In same skillet, combine pea pods, frozen vegetables, water chestnuts and stir fry sauce; mix well. Reduce heat to medium; cover and cook 7 to 10 minutes or until vegetables are crisp-tender, stirring occasionally.

4 Return beef to skillet; mix well. Cook 2 to 4 minutes or until thoroughly heated, stirring occasionally. Serve over rice; sprinkle with peanuts.

HIGH ALTITUDE (3500-6500 FT):
After stirring in peas pods, frozen vegetables, water chestnuts and stir fry sauce, reduce heat to medium; cover and cook 10 to 13 minutes, stirring occasionally.

NUTRITIONAL INFORMATION PER SERVING:
Calories 490 • Total Fat 10g • Saturated Fat 2g • Cholesterol 50mg • Sodium 1,910mg • Total Carbohydrate 71g • Dietary Fiber 6g • Sugars 9g • Protein 29g.
DIETARY EXCHANGES: 3-1/2 Starch • 2 Vegetable • 2 Lean Meat • 1 Fat.

balsamic sirloin and pasta sauté

READY IN: 20 MINUTES
SERVINGS: 3

1 teaspoon olive or vegetable oil

1 teaspoon butter or margarine

10 oz. boneless beef sirloin steak, cut into 2x1/2x1/4-inch strips

1/2 teaspoon dried basil leaves

3 tablespoons water

2 tablespoons balsamic vinegar

1 (1 lb.) package Green Giant® Pasta Accents® Garlic Frozen Vegetables with Pasta

1 cup diced seeded tomatoes

Fresh cilantro

1 Heat oil and butter in large nonstick skillet over medium-high heat until hot. Add beef strips and basil; cook and stir 2 to 3 minutes or until beef is browned.

2 Stir in water and vinegar. Add frozen vegetables with pasta; mix well. Bring to a boil. Reduce heat to medium; cover and simmer 4 minutes, stirring once. Add tomatoes; cover and cook 1 minute or until thoroughly heated.

3 To serve, spoon mixture onto serving platter. Garnish with cilantro or fresh basil.

NUTRITIONAL INFORMATION PER SERVING: Calories 360 • Total Fat 14g • Saturated Fat 6g • Cholesterol 65mg • Sodium 580mg • Total Carbohydrate 33g • Dietary Fiber 3g • Sugars 7g • Protein 25g.
DIETARY EXCHANGES: 2 Starch • 2 Other Carbohydrate • 1 Vegetable • 2-1/2 Lean Meat • 1 Fat.

vegetable-chicken stir fry

READY IN: 30 MINUTES
SERVINGS: 4

1 cup uncooked long-grain white rice

2 cups water

1 cup chicken broth

1 tablespoon oyster sauce

1/2 teaspoon sugar

3 teaspoons cornstarch

3/4 lb. chicken breast strips for stir frying

1/2 teaspoon ginger

1/4 teaspoon salt

1 tablespoon oil

1 cup fresh snow pea pods

1 cup fresh mushrooms, sliced

1/2 medium red bell pepper, cut into 2x1/4-inch strips

1 garlic clove, minced

1 Cook rice in water as directed on package.

2 Meanwhile, in small bowl, combine broth, oyster sauce, sugar and 2 teaspoons of the cornstarch; blend well. Set aside.

3 In medium bowl, combine chicken, ginger, salt and remaining 1 teaspoon cornstarch; mix gently to coat. Set aside.

4 Heat oil in wok or large nonstick skillet over high heat until hot. Add chicken mixture; cook and stir 3 minutes. Add pea pods, mushrooms, bell pepper and garlic; cook and stir 3 minutes or until chicken is no longer pink in center.

5 Add broth mixture; cook an additional 1 to 2 minutes or until sauce is slightly thickened and vegetables are crisp-tender. Serve over rice.

NUTRITIONAL INFORMATION PER SERVING: Calories 330 • Total Fat 5g • Saturated Fat 1g • Cholesterol 45mg • Sodium 760mg • Total Carbohydrate 44g • Dietary Fiber 1g • Sugars 3g • Protein 26g.
DIETARY EXCHANGES: 3 Starch • 3 Other Carbohydrate • 2-1/2 Very Lean Meat.

chicken puttanesca sauté

READY IN: 20 MINUTES
SERVINGS: 4

- 8 oz. uncooked angel hair pasta (capellini)
- 1 lb. chicken breast tenders
- 1/4 teaspoon salt
- 1/8 teaspoon pepper
- 1 tablespoon olive oil
- 1 (14.5 oz.) can diced tomatoes with roasted garlic, undrained
- 1/2 cup sliced green olives
- 1/8 teaspoon crushed red pepper flakes
- 1 (14.5 oz.) can cut wax beans, drained

1 Cook pasta to desired doneness as directed on package. Drain well; cover to keep warm.

2 Meanwhile, pat chicken tenders dry with paper towels; sprinkle with salt and pepper. Heat oil in large nonstick skillet over medium-high heat until hot. Add chicken tenders; cook 4 to 6 minutes or until lightly browned, turning once.

3 Add tomatoes, olives and pepper flakes; cook 4 to 6 minutes or until chicken is no longer pink in center and liquid has been reduced slightly. Add beans; cook an additional 2 to 3 minutes or until beans are thoroughly heated.

4 Place the cooked pasta in large bowl. Top with the chicken mixture.

NUTRITIONAL INFORMATION PER SERVING: Calories 450 • Total Fat 10g • Saturated Fat 2g • Cholesterol 70mg • Sodium 1,250mg • Total Carbohydrate 55g • Dietary Fiber 4g • Sugars 6g • Protein 35g.
DIETARY EXCHANGES: 3 Starch • 3 Other Carbohydrate • 2 Vegetable • 3 Very Lean Meat • 1-1/2 Fat.

orange-cumin chicken and vegetables

READY IN: 30 MINUTES
SERVINGS: 4

- 2 cups uncooked instant white rice
- 2 cups water
- 1 teaspoon coriander
- 1/4 teaspoon salt
- 1/4 teaspoon coarse ground black pepper
- 4 (4 to 6 oz.) boneless skinless chicken breast halves
- 1/4 cup Old El Paso® Thick 'n Chunky Salsa
- 1 teaspoon cornstarch
- 1/2 teaspoon cumin
- 1 tablespoon oil
- 1 medium red bell pepper, cut into thin strips
- 1 (9 oz.) package Green Giant® Frozen Sugar Snap Peas
- 3/4 cup orange juice

1 Cook rice in water as directed on package. Cover to keep warm.

2 Meanwhile, in small bowl, combine coriander, salt and pepper; mix well. Rub mixture on all sides of chicken breast halves. Discard any remaining seasoning mixture. In another small bowl, combine salsa, cornstarch and cumin; mix well.

3 Heat oil in 12-inch skillet over medium-high heat until hot. Add chicken; cook 4 minutes or until browned on both sides, turning once. Add bell pepper and sugar snap peas; cook and stir 4 minutes.

4 Reduce heat to medium-low. Add 2 tablespoons of the orange juice; cover and cook 6 minutes or until chicken is fork-tender and juices run clear, and vegetables are crisp-tender. Remove chicken from skillet; cover to keep warm.

5 Add salsa mixture and remaining orange juice to vegetables in skillet; mix well. Bring to a boil. Cook until slightly thickened, stirring occasionally.

6 To serve, cut chicken crosswise into 1/2-inch slices. Arrange chicken on individual plates. Spoon vegetable mixture over chicken. Serve with rice.

NUTRITIONAL INFORMATION PER SERVING: Calories 225 • Total Fat 7g • Saturated Fat 2g • Cholesterol 70mg • Sodium 280mg • Total Carbohydrate 12g • Dietary Fiber 2g • Sugars 9g • Protein 28g.
DIETARY EXCHANGES: 1/2 Starch • 1/2 Other Carbohydrate • 1 Vegetable • 3-1/2 Very Lean Meat • 1 Fat.

chicken fettuccine a la fuente

READY IN: 30 MINUTES
SERVINGS: 4

Kathleen Johnson
Ellensburg, WA

1 (12 oz.) package
uncooked fettuccine

1 tablespoon olive oil

4 boneless skinless chicken
breast halves (about 1 lb.),
cut into 1-inch pieces

2 cloves garlic, minced

1 (1.25 oz.) package Old El
Paso® Taco Seasoning Mix

1 cup whipping cream

1/3 cup chopped fresh
parsley

1/4 cup grated fresh
Parmesan cheese (1 oz.)

Chopped fresh parsley

Grated fresh Parmesan
cheese

1 Cook fettuccine as directed on package; drain.

2 Meanwhile, in 12-inch skillet or Dutch oven, heat oil over medium-high heat until hot. Add chicken; cook 4 to 5 minutes, stirring occasionally, until chicken turns white. Stir in garlic and taco seasoning mix. Cook 1 minute. Stir in cream. Reduce heat to low; cook 3 to 5 minutes, stirring constantly, until thoroughly heated.

3 Stir in 1/3 cup parsley and 1/4 cup cheese. Add cooked fettuccine; toss to coat. Cook 1 minute, stirring constantly, until fettuccine is thoroughly heated. Transfer mixture to large serving platter. Garnish with additional parsley and cheese if desired.

HIGH ALTITUDE (3500-6500 FT):
After heating oil in skillet, reduce heat to medium-low. Add chicken; cook 3 to 5 minutes. Continue as directed.

NUTRITIONAL INFORMATION PER SERVING:
Calories: 700 • Total Fat 31g • Saturated Fat 15g • Cholesterol 220mg • Sodium 930mg • Total Carbohydrate 64g • Dietary Fiber 3g • Sugars 6g • Protein 42g.

penne with vegetables and kielbasa

penne with vegetables and kielbasa

READY IN: 25 MINUTES
SERVINGS: 4

6 oz. uncooked penne pasta (2 cups)

1 medium red bell pepper, cut into 1-inch pieces

1 small onion, cut into thin wedges

1 (9 oz.) package Green Giant® Frozen Sugar Snap Peas

1/2 lb. smoked turkey kielbasa, sliced

1/2 cup milk

8 oz. pasteurized prepared cheese product (from 16 oz. box), cubed

1 Cook penne as directed on package. Drain; cover to keep warm.

2 Meanwhile, heat 12-inch nonstick skillet or Dutch oven over medium-high heat until hot. Add bell pepper, onion and sugar snap peas; cook 4 to 5 minutes or until vegetables are crisp-tender, stirring frequently. Drain, if necessary.

3 Reduce heat to medium. Add kielbasa, milk and cheese to vegetables. Cook over medium heat for 3 to 4 minutes or until cheese is melted and sauce is smooth, stirring constantly.

4 Add cooked penne; stir gently to coat. Cook 1 to 2 minutes or until thoroughly heated, stirring occasionally.

HIGH ALTITUDE (3500-6500 FT): Increase milk to 3/4 cup.

NUTRITIONAL INFORMATION PER SERVING: Calories 470 • Total Fat 19g • Saturated Fat 10g • Cholesterol 75mg • Sodium 1,600mg • Total Carbohydrate 48g • Dietary Fiber 4g • Sugars 13g • Protein 27g.
DIETARY EXCHANGES: 3 Starch • 1 Vegetable • 2 Medium-Fat Meat • 1-1/2 Fat.

chicken, mushrooms and sugar snap peas over rice

READY IN: 30 MINUTES
SERVINGS: 4

1-1/2 cups uncooked instant rice

1-1/2 cups water

1 tablespoon olive oil

2 garlic cloves, minced

1 (8 oz.) package whole mushrooms, quartered

1 cup chicken broth

1/2 teaspoon finely chopped fresh thyme or tarragon

4 boneless skinless chicken breast halves

1/4 teaspoon salt

1/4 teaspoon pepper

1 tablespoon cornstarch

1 tablespoon cold water

1 (9 oz.) package Green Giant® Frozen Sugar Snap Peas

1 Cook rice in 1-1/2 cups water as directed on package.

2 Meanwhile, heat oil in large skillet over medium-high heat until hot. Add garlic and mushrooms; cook about 4 minutes or until softened, stirring frequently. Add broth and thyme; bring to a boil.

3 Sprinkle chicken breast halves with salt and pepper; add to skillet. Reduce heat to medium-low; cover and cook about 10 minutes or until chicken is fork-tender and juices run clear, turning once.

4 In small bowl, blend cornstarch with 1 tablespoon cold water until smooth. Stir into chicken mixture. Increase heat to medium-high. Add sugar snap peas; cook about 5 minutes or until sauce is slightly thickened and peas are hot, stirring constantly. Serve chicken with sauce and vegetables over rice.

HIGH ALTITUDE (3500-6500 FT): Thaw the frozen sugar snap peas before use. After adding the chicken breast halves, reduce heat to medium; cover and cook the chicken about 10 minutes, turning once.

NUTRITIONAL INFORMATION PER SERVING: Calories 390 • Total Fat 8g • Saturated Fat 2g • Cholesterol 75mg • Sodium 950mg • Total Carbohydrate 44g • Dietary Fiber 2g • Sugars 3g • Protein 35g.
DIETARY EXCHANGES: 3 Starch • 3-1/2 Very Lean Meat • 1 Fat.

easy cheesy beef and bow ties

READY IN: 20 MINUTES
SERVINGS: 4

- 6 oz. uncooked bow tie pasta (2-1/2 cups)
- 1 lb. lean (at least 80%) ground beef
- 1/2 cup chopped green onions (8 medium)
- 1 (10-3/4 oz.) can condensed Cheddar cheese soup
- 1 cup Old El Paso® Thick 'n Chunky Salsa
- 1-1/2 cups shredded Cheddar and American cheese blend (6 oz.)

1 Cook pasta as directed on package. Drain.

2 Meanwhile, in 12-inch nonstick skillet, brown ground beef over medium-high heat until thoroughly cooked, stirring frequently. Drain.

3 Reserve 2 tablespoons onions for garnish; stir remaining onions, the soup and salsa into beef. Bring to a boil. Reduce heat to medium-low; cook 5 minutes.

4 Stir in cooked pasta; cook 3 to 5 minutes or until thoroughly heated, stirring occasionally. Sprinkle with cheese; cook just until melted. Sprinkle with reserved 2 tablespoons onions.

NUTRITIONAL INFORMATION PER SERVING:
Calories 645 • Total Fat 33g • Saturated Fat 16g • Cholesterol 120mg • Sodium 1,630mg • Total Carbohydrate 45g • Dietary Fiber 2g • Sugars 5g • Protein 42g.
DIETARY EXCHANGES: 3 Starch • 4 High-Fat Meat.

pepper-curry chicken

PREP TIME: 25 MINUTES
READY IN: 1 HOUR 5 MINUTES
SERVINGS: 4

- 2 tablespoons olive oil
- 1 cut-up whole chicken (3-1/2 to 4 lb.)
- 1 medium onion, finely chopped (1/2 cup)
- 1 medium green bell pepper, cut into thin bite-size strips
- 2 medium tomatoes, chopped (1-1/2 cups)
- 3 cloves garlic, minced
- 1 tablespoon curry powder
- 1/2 teaspoon dried thyme leaves
- 1/2 teaspoon salt
- 1/4 teaspoon ground red pepper (cayenne)
- 1/2 cup chicken broth
- 2 cups water
- 1-1/2 cups uncooked couscous
- 1 medium tart red apple, cut into cubes

1 In 4- to 5-quart Dutch oven, heat oil over medium heat. Add chicken pieces; cook about 5 minutes on each side or until browned (if necessary, cook chicken a few pieces at a time). Remove chicken from Dutch oven; set aside.

2 In same Dutch oven, cook onion and bell pepper 3 to 4 minutes, stirring occasionally, until onion begins to brown; drain. Stir in tomatoes, garlic, curry powder, thyme, salt, ground red pepper and broth. Return chicken pieces to Dutch oven. Reduce heat to low; cover and simmer 30 to 40 minutes or until juice of chicken is clear when thickest piece is cut to bone (180°F).

3 In 2-quart saucepan, heat water to boiling. Stir in couscous. Remove from heat; cover and let stand 5 minutes.

4 Stir apple into chicken mixture; simmer uncovered 2 minutes longer or until apple is hot. Fluff couscous lightly with fork before serving with chicken mixture.

NUTRITIONAL INFORMATION PER SERVING:
Calories 760 • Total Fat 31g • Saturated Fat 8g • Trans Fat 1g • Cholesterol 150mg • Sodium 580mg • Total Carbohydrate 64g • Dietary Fiber 6g • Sugars 8g • Protein 57g.
DIETARY EXCHANGES: 3-1/2 Starch • 1/2 Other Carbohydrate • 6-1/2 Lean Meat • 2 Fat.

chicken and broccoli cavatappi

READY IN: 30 MINUTES
SERVINGS: 6

Joni Busch
Rogers, MN

8 oz. uncooked cavatappi pasta (thin, ridged spiral macaroni)

1 tablespoon oil (from jar of sun-dried tomatoes)

1 lb. chicken tenderloins, cut in half crosswise

2 tablespoons finely chopped green onions (2 medium)

3 teaspoons dry ground mustard

2 teaspoons minced garlic

1/4 cup chopped drained oil-packed sun-dried tomatoes (from 7 oz. jar)

1 (24 oz.) bag Green Giant® Frozen Broccoli & Three Cheese Sauce

1 (6.5 oz.) package garlic-and-herb cream cheese spread

1/4 cup milk

Salt and pepper to taste

1 In 4-1/2- or 5-quart Dutch oven, cook pasta as directed on package. Drain; rinse well. Return to Dutch oven; cover to keep warm.

2 Meanwhile, in 12-inch skillet, heat oil over medium-high heat until hot. Add chicken; cook and stir 2 to 4 minutes or until chicken is beginning to brown. Stir in onions, mustard and garlic. Cook until garlic is softened. Stir in tomatoes until blended. Cook 2 to 3 minutes, stirring occasionally, until chicken is no longer pink in center. If necessary, drain off any liquid.

3 Add frozen broccoli with sauce chips; cook about 4 minutes, stirring occasionally, until sauce chips have melted. Stir in cream cheese spread. Add milk; cook about 2 minutes, stirring constantly, until well blended and thoroughly heated.

4 Gently stir broccoli mixture into cooked pasta to coat. Salt and pepper to taste if desired. Pour into serving bowl.

HIGH ALTITUDE (3500-6500 FT): If after stirring in cream cheese spread, mixture is too thick, increase milk up to 1/2 cup; cook 4 to 5 minutes, stirring constantly.

NUTRITIONAL INFORMATION PER SERVING: Calories 510 • Total Fat 25g • Saturated Fat 12g • Cholesterol 95mg • Sodium 580mg • Total Carbohydrate 39g • Dietary Fiber 4g • Sugars 6g • Protein 32g.

orzo with bacon and asparagus

READY IN: 35 MINUTES
SERVINGS: 3

6 slices bacon, cut into 1/2-inch pieces

1 (14 oz.) can fat-free chicken broth with 1/3 less sodium

6-1/2 oz. uncooked orzo or rosamarina (rice-shaped pasta) (1 cup)

8 oz. fresh asparagus spears, trimmed, cut into 1-inch pieces

1/4 cup sliced roasted red bell peppers (from a jar)

1/2 cup shredded fresh Asiago or Parmesan cheese (2 oz.)

1 Cook bacon in large non-stick skillet over medium heat until crisp. Reserve bacon and 2 tablespoons bacon drippings in skillet. Add broth; bring to a boil. Add orzo. Reduce heat to low; cover and cook 5 minutes.

2 Add asparagus and peppers; cover and cook an additional 5 to 10 minutes or until orzo and asparagus are tender, stirring occasionally. Sprinkle individual servings with cheese.

NUTRITIONAL INFORMATION PER SERVING: Calories 430 • Total Fat 14g • Saturated Fat 6g • Cholesterol 25mg • Sodium 840mg • Total Carbohydrate 52g • Dietary Fiber 2g • Sugars 3g • Protein 24g.
DIETARY EXCHANGES: 3-1/2 Starch • 3-1/2 Other Carbohydrate • 2 High-Fat Meat.

thai peanut chicken and noodles

READY IN: 30 MINUTES
SERVINGS: 5

6 oz. uncooked fine egg noodles (2-3/4 cups)

1/4 cup creamy peanut butter

1/2 teaspoon finely chopped gingerroot

1/4 teaspoon crushed red pepper flakes

1/4 cup soy sauce

1/4 cup water

1 tablespoon oil

2 cups small fresh broccoli florets

1-1/2 cups sliced fresh mushrooms (about 4 oz.)

1 cup fresh baby carrots, quartered lengthwise

1 medium red bell pepper, cut into thin bite-sized strips

1 (9 oz.) package frozen diced cooked chicken breast, thawed

1/4 cup coarsely chopped dry-roasted peanuts

Chopped fresh cilantro

1 Cook noodles as directed on package. Drain; cover to keep warm.

2 Meanwhile, in small bowl, combine peanut butter, gingerroot, pepper flakes and 2 tablespoons of the soy sauce; beat with wire whisk until blended. Gradually beat in remaining soy sauce and water until smooth. Set aside.

3 Heat oil in 12-inch nonstick skillet over medium-high heat until hot. Add broccoli, mushrooms, carrots and bell pepper; cook 4 to 6 minutes or until vegetables are crisp-tender, stirring occasionally. Add chicken; cook and stir until thoroughly heated.

4 Reduce heat to medium. Stir peanut butter mixture; stir into mixture in skillet. Add cooked noodles; toss gently to coat. Cook and stir until thoroughly heated. Sprinkle with peanuts and cilantro if desired.

NUTRITIONAL INFORMATION PER SERVING: Calories 380 • Total Fat 17g • Saturated Fat 3g • Cholesterol 75mg • Sodium 1,220mg • Total Carbohydrate 34g • Dietary Fiber 5g • Sugars 5g • Protein 28g.
DIETARY EXCHANGES: 1-1/2 Starch • 1 Vegetable • 3 Very Lean Meat • 3 Fat.

creamy chicken dijon skillet

PREP TIME: 25 MINUTES
READY IN: 35 MINUTES
SERVINGS: 4

4 boneless skinless chicken breasts

3/4 lb. fresh whole green beans

2/3 cup water

1 medium red bell pepper, cut into thin bite-size strips (1 cup)

1/4 cup creamy mustard-mayonnaise sauce

1 (10 oz.) container refrigerated Alfredo sauce

1 Heat 12-inch nonstick skillet over medium-high heat. Add chicken; cook 10 to 12 minutes, turning once, until fork-tender and juices run clear. Remove chicken from skillet; place on plate and cover loosely with foil to keep warm.

2 To same skillet, add green beans and water; heat to boiling. Cover; cook 7 to 9 minutes or until beans are tender.

3 Add remaining ingredients to skillet; stir until blended. Return chicken to skillet. Reduce heat to low; cover and simmer 3 to 5 minutes, stirring occasionally, until the bell pepper is crisp-tender.

NUTRITIONAL INFORMATION PER SERVING: Calories 340 • Total Fat 18g • Saturated Fat 9g • Trans Fat 0g • Cholesterol 110mg • Sodium 770mg • Total Carbohydrate 15g • Dietary Fiber 3g • Sugars 5g • Protein 32g.
DIETARY EXCHANGES: 1/2 Starch • 1 Vegetable • 4 Very Lean Meat • 3 Fat.

turkey kielbasa with cabbage and sweet potatoes

READY IN: 35 MINUTES
SERVINGS: 6

1 lb. cooked, smoked turkey kielbasa or Polish sausage, cut into 6 pieces

2 medium dark-orange sweet potatoes, peeled, cut into 1-inch chunks

1/2 head green cabbage, cut into 6 wedges

1/2 red bell pepper, cut into thin bite-sized strips

1/2 teaspoon dried marjoram leaves

1/4 teaspoon salt

1/4 teaspoon coarse ground black pepper

1/2 cup ready-to-serve chicken broth with 1/3 less sodium, or water

1 Place sausage pieces in 12-inch nonstick skillet or Dutch oven. Arrange sweet potatoes, cabbage and bell pepper around sausage. Sprinkle vegetables with marjoram, salt and pepper.

2 Add broth to skillet. Bring to a boil. Reduce heat to medium-low; cover and cook 15 to 20 minutes or until vegetables are tender, stirring occasionally.

NUTRITIONAL INFORMATION PER SERVING: Calories 170 • Total Fat 5g • Saturated Fat 1g • Cholesterol 50mg • Sodium 970mg • Total Carbohydrate 18g • Dietary Fiber 3g • Sugars 6g • Protein 14g.
DIETARY EXCHANGES: 1 Starch • 1 Other Carbohydrate • 1 Vegetable • 1-1/2 Very Lean Meat • 1/2 Fat.

HEALTHY HINT: Cabbage contains antioxidants which may reduce the risk of some cancers. Sweet potatoes are a great source of vitamin A, so feel free to increase these items if you'd like.

skillet beefy chili mac

READY IN: 25 MINUTES
SERVINGS: 4

6 oz. uncooked elbow macaroni (1-1/2 cups)

1 lb. lean ground beef

1 (15.5 oz.) can spicy chili beans, undrained

1 (14.5 oz.) can zesty chili-style chunky tomatoes, undrained

1/4 teaspoon salt

1/4 teaspoon pepper

1 cup shredded Cheddar cheese (4 oz.)

1 Cook macaroni as directed on package. Drain; return to saucepan. Cover to keep warm.

2 Meanwhile, brown ground beef in 12-inch nonstick skillet over medium-high heat for 5 to 7 minutes or until thoroughly cooked, stirring frequently. Drain.

3 Reduce heat to medium. Stir in cooked macaroni, beans, tomatoes, salt and pepper. Cook an additional 3 to 5 minutes or until bubbly, stirring frequently. Sprinkle with cheese.

NUTRITIONAL INFORMATION PER SERVING: Calories 595 • Total Fat 27g • Saturated Fat 13g • Cholesterol 95mg • Sodium 1,490mg • Total Carbohydrate 55g • Dietary Fiber 7g • Sugars 6g • Protein 40g.
DIETARY EXCHANGES: 3 Starch • 3 Other Carbohydrate • 4-1/2 Medium-Fat Meat • 1 Fat.

TIP: For fare that's kid-friendly, omit the shredded cheese in the chili, and use a star-shaped cutter to cut slices of American cheese into fun garnishes.

beef chow mein

READY IN: 30 MINUTES
SERVINGS: 4

1 lb. lean ground beef

1-1/2 cups sliced celery

1 (16 oz.) can bean sprouts, drained

1 (8 oz.) can sliced water chestnuts, drained

1 (4 oz.) can Green Giant® Mushroom Pieces and Stems, drained

1 (14 oz.) can beef broth

1 (2 oz.) jar diced pimientos, drained

2 tablespoons soy sauce

1/2 teaspoon ginger

2 tablespoons cornstarch

3 tablespoons water

4 cups chow mein noodles or hot cooked rice

Soy sauce

1 Brown ground beef in large skillet over medium-high heat for 5 to 7 minutes or until thoroughly cooked, stirring frequently. Drain.

2 Add celery, bean sprouts, water chestnuts, mush-rooms, broth, pimientos, soy sauce and ginger; mix well. Reduce heat; cover and simmer 15 minutes, stirring occasionally.

3 Meanwhile, in small bowl, blend cornstarch and water until smooth.

4 Stir cornstarch mixture into beef mixture. Cook until mixture is bubbly and slightly thickened. Serve over chow mein noodles. If desired, serve with additional soy sauce.

NUTRITIONAL INFORMATION PER SERVING: Calories 705 • Total Fat 38g • Saturated Fat 10g • Cholesterol 65mg • Sodium 1,460mg • Total Carbohydrate 54g • Dietary Fiber 6g • Sugars 5g • Protein 43g.
DIETARY EXCHANGES: 2-1/2 Starch • 2 Vegetable • 4-1/2 Medium-Fat Meat • 3 Fat.

chicken curry stir fry

READY IN: 25 MINUTES
SERVINGS: 6

2 cups uncooked regular long-grain white rice

4 cups water

1/4 cup olive or vegetable oil

1 medium onion, chopped (1/2 cup)

4 boneless skinless chicken breast halves, cut into 1-inch cubes

2 tablespoons water

2 teaspoons curry powder

1/4 teaspoon salt

1/8 teaspoon pepper

1/3 cup peanuts

1/3 cup chutney

2 tablespoons coconut

2 tablespoons dried currants

2 cups Green Giant® Frozen Mixed Vegetables

1 to 2 red bell peppers, cut into strips

1 Cook rice in 4 cups water as directed on package.

2 Meanwhile, heat oil in large skillet over medium-high heat until hot. Add onion; cook and stir 2 minutes. Add chicken, 2 tablespoons water, curry powder, salt and pepper; cook and stir 6 to 8 minutes or until the chicken is no longer pink in center.

3 Add peanuts if desired, chutney, coconut, currants and frozen mixed vegetables; cook and stir 7 to 8 minutes or until vegetables are crisp-tender.

4 To serve, spoon rice onto serving platter. Top with chicken mixture. Garnish with bell pepper strips.

NUTRITIONAL INFORMATION PER SERVING:
Calories 510 • Total Fat 13g • Saturated Fat 3g • Cholesterol 50mg • Sodium 900mg • Total Carbohydrate 73g • Dietary Fiber 4g • Sugars 12g • Protein 25g.
DIETARY EXCHANGES: 5 Starch • 5 Other Carbohydrate • 1-1/2 Very Lean Meat • 2-1/2 Fat.

weeknight pork and vegetable stew

READY IN: 35 MINUTES
SERVINGS: 4

1 teaspoon vegetable oil

3/4 lb. pork tenderloin, cut into 1-inch cubes

1/2 teaspoon salt

1/8 teaspoon pepper

1 cup frozen small whole onions (from 1 lb. bag)

1 tablespoon ketchup

1 teaspoon dried rosemary leaves, crushed

1/2 teaspoon chopped garlic (from 4.5 oz. jar)

1 (1 lb.) bag Green Giant Select® Frozen Broccoli, Carrots and Cauliflower

1 (12 oz.) jar pork gravy

1 In 3-quart saucepan, heat oil over medium-high heat. Add pork; sprinkle with salt and pepper. Cook 3 to 5 minutes, stirring frequently, until pork is browned.

2 Stir in all remaining ingredients. Heat to boiling. Reduce heat to low; cover and simmer 15 to 20 minutes, stirring occasionally, until vegetables are tender and pork is no longer pink in center.

NUTRITIONAL INFORMATION PER SERVING:
Calories 210 • Total Fat 7g • Saturated Fat 2g • Cholesterol 55mg • Sodium 880mg • Total Carbohydrate 14g • Dietary Fiber 4g • Sugars 4g • Protein 25g.
DIETARY EXCHANGES: 1/2 Starch • 1 Vegetable • 3 Very Lean Meat • 1 Fat.

family-style paella

READY IN: 50 MINUTES
SERVINGS: 6

- 1 tablespoon olive oil
- 1 cup coarsely chopped onions (2 medium)
- 1 cup coarsely chopped green bell pepper (1 medium)
- 1 lb. boneless skinless chicken breast halves, cut into 1-inch pieces
- 1/2 lb. smoked chorizo sausage, cut into 1/2-inch slices
- 1 cup uncooked regular long-grain white rice
- 1/2 teaspoon salt
- 1/2 teaspoon turmeric
- 2 cups chicken broth
- 1/2 lb. shelled deveined uncooked medium shrimp, tails removed
- 1 cup Green Giant Select® LeSueur® Frozen Baby Sweet Peas
- 1 (14.5 oz.) can Italian-style stewed tomatoes, undrained

1 Heat oil in 12-inch nonstick skillet or Dutch oven over medium-high heat until hot. Add onions and bell pepper; cook and stir 2 minutes. Add chicken and sausage; cook 8 to 10 minutes or until chicken and sausage are no longer pink in center, stirring frequently.

2 Add rice, salt, turmeric and broth; mix well. Bring to a boil. Reduce heat to medium-low; cover and cook 20 minutes, stirring occasionally.

3 Add shrimp, peas and tomatoes; stir gently to mix.

Cover; cook an additional 8 to 12 minutes or until shrimp turn pink and liquid is absorbed, stirring occasionally.

HIGH ALTITUDE (3500-6500 FT): After adding chicken and sausage, cook 7 to 9 minutes. When adding rice, salt, turmeric and broth, add 1/2 cup water; cover and cook 30 minutes. When adding shrimp, peas and tomatoes, add 1/4 cup water; return to a simmer. Reduce heat; cover and cook an additional 10 to 15 minutes.

NUTRITIONAL INFORMATION PER SERVING: Calories 490 • Total Fat 20g • Saturated Fat 7g • Cholesterol 135mg • Sodium 1,320mg • Total Carbohydrate 40g • Dietary Fiber 3g • Sugars 7g • Protein 38g. DIETARY EXCHANGES: 2 Starch • 1 Vegetable • 4-1/2 Lean Meat • 1 Fat.

SIMPLE SUBSTITUTION: Chorizo sausage is flavorful, coarsely ground pork sausage that contains garlic, chili powder and other spices. If it is unavailable, use Italian sausage instead.

weeknight stroganoff

READY IN: 25 MINUTES
SERVINGS: 4

- 1 medium onion, coarsely chopped (1/2 cup)
- 1 (14 oz.) can beef broth
- 1 cup water
- 8 oz. uncooked wide egg noodles (4-1/2 cups)
- 1 (4.5 oz.) jar Green Giant® Sliced Mushrooms, drained
- 1 teaspoon paprika
- 1/2 lb. cooked roast beef (from deli), cut into thin bite-sized strips
- 1 (8 oz.) container sour cream

1 Spray 12-inch skillet or Dutch oven with nonstick cooking spray. Heat over medium-high heat until hot. Add onion; cook 2 to 3 minutes or until onion is crisp-tender, stirring frequently.

2 Add broth, water, noodles, mushrooms and paprika; mix well. Bring to a boil. Reduce heat; cover and simmer 6 to 8 minutes or until noodles are of desired doneness and liquid is almost absorbed, stirring occasionally.

3 Stir in beef and sour cream. Cook an additional 1 to 2 minutes or until thoroughly heated, stirring constantly.

NUTRITIONAL INFORMATION PER SERVING: Calories 395 • Total Fat 15g • Saturated Fat 8g • Cholesterol 115mg • Sodium 1,210mg • Total Carbohydrate 44g • Dietary Fiber 3g • Sugars 5g • Protein 21g. DIETARY EXCHANGES: 3 Starch • 1-1/2 Lean Meat • 2 Fat.

weeknight stroganoff

cashew pork chow mein

READY IN: 35 MINUTES
SERVINGS: 4

1 lb. pork chow mein meat

1-1/2 cups sliced celery

1 cup thinly sliced carrots

1 medium onion, chopped (1/2 cup)

1/2 cup chopped red or green bell pepper

3/4 cup chicken broth

3/4 cup purchased stir fry sauce

2 teaspoons sugar

2 tablespoons water

2 teaspoons cornstarch

1 (5 oz.) package uncooked Chinese noodles

1/2 cup salted cashew halves

1 Spray large nonstick skillet with nonstick cooking spray. Add chow mein meat; cook over medium-high heat for 5 to 7 minutes or until browned, stirring frequently. Add celery, carrots, onion and bell pepper; cook 2 minutes, stirring occasionally.

2 Add broth, stir fry sauce and sugar; stir to mix. Cook over medium heat for 8 to 10 minutes or until vegetables are crisp-tender, stirring occasionally. In small bowl, blend water and cornstarch until smooth. Add to skillet; cook and stir until thickened.

3 Meanwhile, cook noodles to desired doneness as directed on package.

4 Serve pork mixture over noodles. Sprinkle with cashews.

NUTRITIONAL INFORMATION PER SERVING: Calories 565 • Total Fat 25g • Saturated Fat 8g • Cholesterol 70mg • Sodium 2,600mg • Total Carbohydrate 53g • Dietary Fiber 4g • Sugars 15g • Protein 32g.
DIETARY EXCHANGES: 3-1/2 Starch • 3-1/2 Other Carbohydrate • 3 Medium-Fat Meat • 2 Fat.

TIP: To streamline the recipe, use a purchased vegetable mixture for stir fry. Ramen or egg noodles or angel hair pasta can be used in place of the Chinese noodles.

turkey-cheesy fettuccine

READY IN: 15 MINUTES
SERVINGS: 4

1 (9 oz.) package refrigerated fettuccine or linguine

3/4 cup Green Giant Select® LeSueur® Frozen Baby Sweet Peas

1 (1.5 oz.) package four cheese sauce mix

1-1/2 cups milk

1 tablespoon margarine or butter

1-1/2 cups cubed cooked turkey

1/4 cup sliced roasted red bell peppers (from a jar)

1/4 cup shredded fresh Parmesan cheese (1 oz.)

1 Cook fettuccine with peas to desired doneness as directed on fettuccine package. Drain.

2 Meanwhile, prepare sauce mix with milk and margarine as directed on package. Stir in turkey and roasted peppers; cook over medium-low heat just until thoroughly heated, stirring frequently.

3 Add sauce to fettuccine and peas; toss to mix. Sprinkle individual servings with cheese.

NUTRITIONAL INFORMATION PER SERVING: Calories 345 • Total Fat 14g • Saturated Fat 6g • Cholesterol 85mg • Sodium 820mg • Total Carbohydrate 28g • Dietary Fiber 2g • Sugars 10g • Protein 27g.
DIETARY EXCHANGES: 2 Starch • 2 Other Carbohydrate • 3 Lean Meat • 1 Fat.

chicken, mushroom and asparagus stir fry

READY IN: 25 MINUTES
SERVINGS: 4

1 cup uncooked regular long-grain white rice

2 cups water

2 tablespoons oil

1 lb. chicken breast strips for stir frying

1 lb. asparagus spears, trimmed, cut into 2-inch pieces

1 medium onion, cut into 1/2-inch wedges

1 (8 oz.) package sliced fresh mushrooms (about 3 cups)

1/4 cup water

1/2 cup purchased stir fry sauce

1/4 cup oyster sauce

1 Cook rice in water as directed on package.

2 Meanwhile, heat 1 tablespoon of the oil in wok or large skillet over medium-high heat until hot. Add chicken strips; stir fry 5 to 6 minutes or until no longer pink in center. Remove chicken from wok; place on plate.

3 Add remaining tablespoon oil to wok. Add asparagus and onion; stir fry 3 minutes. Add mushrooms; stir fry an additional 3 minutes. Add water; cover and steam 2 to 3 minutes or until asparagus is tender.

4 Meanwhile, in small bowl, blend stir fry sauce and oyster sauce. Add sauce mixture and return chicken to wok; stir fry an additional minute or until thoroughly heated.

NUTRITIONAL INFORMATION PER SERVING:
Calories 460 • Total Fat 11g • Saturated Fat 2g • Cholesterol 70mg • Sodium 1,890mg • Total Carbohydrate 55g • Dietary Fiber 2g • Sugars 9g • Protein 35g.
DIETARY EXCHANGES: 3 Starch • 3 Other Carbohydrate • 1 Vegetable • 3-1/2 Very Lean Meat • 2 Fat.

chili swiss steak

PREP TIME: 25 MINUTES
READY IN: 2 HOURS 25 MINUTES
SERVINGS: 6

1-1/2 lb. boneless beef round steak, trimmed of fat, cut into serving-sized pieces

1/2 teaspoon seasoned salt

1 (14.5 oz.) can stewed tomatoes, undrained

1 (4.5 oz.) can Old El Paso® Chopped Green Chiles

1/4 cup taco sauce

1 teaspoon chili powder

1/2 teaspoon cumin

1 cup Green Giant® Niblets® Frozen Corn

1/4 cup sliced green onions

1 Spray 12-inch nonstick skillet with nonstick cooking spray. Heat over high heat until hot. Add beef; sprinkle with seasoned salt. Cook until browned on both sides.

2 Add tomatoes, chiles, taco sauce, chili powder and cumin; stir to mix. Reduce heat to low; cover and simmer 1-1/2 to 2 hours or until beef is tender, stirring and turning the beef occasionally.

3 Stir in corn and onions. Cover; cook an additional 8 to 10 minutes or until the corn is tender.

NUTRITIONAL INFORMATION PER SERVING:
Calories 190 • Total Fat 6g • Saturated Fat 2g • Cholesterol 60mg • Sodium 480mg • Total Carbohydrate 10g • Dietary Fiber 3g • Sugars 4g • Protein 24g.
DIABETIC EXCHANGES: 1/2 Starch • 1/2 Other Carbohydrate • 3 Lean Meat.

ravioli with corn and cilantro

READY IN: 20 MINUTES
SERVINGS: 3

1 (9 oz.) package refrigerated roasted chicken and garlic or cheese-filled ravioli

2 tablespoons olive oil

2 garlic cloves, minced

1 (11 oz.) can Green Giant® Mexicorn® Whole Kernel Corn, Red and Green Peppers, drained

1/4 teaspoon salt

1/4 cup chopped fresh cilantro

1 Cook ravioli to desired doneness as directed on package. Drain.

2 Meanwhile, heat oil in large skillet over medium heat until hot. Add garlic; cook and stir 2 to 3 minutes or until tender. Add the corn and salt; cook until thoroughly heated, stirring occasionally.

3 Add ravioli; toss to coat. Sprinkle with cilantro.

NUTRITIONAL INFORMATION PER SERVING:
Calories 350 • Total Fat 15g • Saturated Fat 3g • Cholesterol 75mg • Sodium 860mg • Total Carbohydrate 39g • Dietary Fiber 3g • Sugars 3g • Protein 15g.
DIETARY EXCHANGES: 2-1/2 Starch • 2-1/2 Other Carbohydrate • 1 Lean Meat • 2-1/2 Fat.

louisiana chicken and pasta

READY IN: 35 MINUTES
SERVINGS: 5

- 8 oz. uncooked gemelli (pasta twists)
- 4 slices bacon, cut into 1/2-inch pieces
- 2 boneless skinless chicken breast halves, cut into 1/2-inch pieces
- 1 cup diced green bell pepper
- 1 medium onion, finely chopped (1/2 cup)
- 1 (15 oz.) can black-eyed peas or garbanzo beans, drained
- 1/2 cup chicken broth
- 2 tablespoons Worcestershire sauce
- 1/2 teaspoon garlic-pepper blend
- 1/2 teaspoon dried thyme leaves
- 1/8 teaspoon ground red pepper (cayenne)
- 2 tablespoons chopped fresh parsley

1 Cook gemelli to desired doneness as directed on package. Drain; cover pasta to keep warm.

2 Meanwhile, cook bacon in large skillet over medium heat until crisp. Add chicken, bell pepper and onion; cook 4 to 6 minutes or until chicken is browned, stirring occasionally.

3 Add all remaining ingredients except parsley; mix well. Reduce heat to medium-low; cover and cook until chicken is no longer pink in center, stirring occasionally. Stir in gemelli; cook and stir until thoroughly heated. Sprinkle with parsley if desired.

NUTRITIONAL INFORMATION PER SERVING:
Calories 360 • Total Fat 6g • Saturated Fat 2g • Cholesterol 35mg • Sodium 620mg • Total Carbohydrate 58g • Dietary Fiber 8g • Sugars 5g • Protein 26g.
DIETARY EXCHANGES: 4 Starch • 4 Other Carbohydrate • 2 Very Lean Meat • 1 Fat.

peanut chicken with noodles

READY IN: 35 MINUTES
SERVINGS: 4

- 8 oz. uncooked spaghetti
- 2 tablespoons oil
- 1 lb. chicken breast strips for stir frying
- 1 medium carrot, cut into 2x1/4x1/4-inch strips (1 cup)
- 1 medium red bell pepper, cut into thin bite-sized strips
- 1/2 lb. fresh asparagus spears, cut into 1-inch pieces
- 3/4 cup purchased peanut sauce

1 Cook spaghetti as directed on package. Drain.

2 Meanwhile, heat 1 tablespoon of the oil in wok or 12-inch skillet over medium-high heat until hot. Add chicken; cook and stir 4 to 6 minutes or until chicken is no longer pink in center. Remove chicken from skillet; place on plate and cover to keep warm.

3 Add remaining tablespoon oil to wok. Add carrot; cook and stir 2 minutes. Add bell pepper and asparagus; cook and stir an additional 2 to 3 minutes or until vegetables are tender.

4 Add cooked spaghetti and peanut sauce. Return chicken to wok; toss to coat. Cook and stir about 2 minutes or until thoroughly heated.

NUTRITIONAL INFORMATION PER SERVING:
Calories 585 • Total Fat 23g • Saturated Fat 4g • Cholesterol 70mg • Sodium 400mg • Total Carbohydrate 55g • Dietary Fiber 4g • Sugars 7g • Protein 39g.
DIETARY EXCHANGES: 3-1/2 Starch • 4 Very Lean Meat • 4 Fat.

chicken and cabbage stir fry

READY IN: 35 MINUTES
SERVINGS: 4

2 cups uncooked instant rice

2 cups water

1 teaspoon oil

3 boneless skinless chicken breast halves, cut into bite-sized strips

1 teaspoon grated gingerroot

1 large garlic clove, minced

3 cups cabbage strips (1/2 inch wide)

1 (1 lb.) package Green Giant Select® Frozen Broccoli, Carrots and Water Chestnuts, thawed

1/3 cup purchased stir fry sauce

1/4 cup sliced green onions

Green onions

1 Cook rice in water as directed on package, omitting margarine and salt.

2 Meanwhile, heat oil in large nonstick skillet or wok over medium-high heat until hot. Add chicken, gingerroot and garlic; cook and stir 5 to 8 minutes or until chicken is no longer pink in center.

3 Stir in cabbage. Cover and cook 5 minutes, stirring occasionally.

4 Add vegetables; mix well. Reduce heat to medium; cover and cook 6 to 8 minutes or until the vegetables are crisp-tender.

5 Stir in stir fry sauce and onions. Cook 1 to 2 minutes

or until thoroughly heated. Serve over rice. If desired, garnish with green onion fans.

NUTRITIONAL INFORMATION PER SERVING: Calories 370 • Total Fat 4g • Saturated Fat 1g • Cholesterol 55mg • Sodium 800mg • Total Carbohydrate 55g • Dietary Fiber 5g • Sugars 7g • Protein 28g.
DIETARY EXCHANGES: 2-1/2 Starch • 1/2 Fruit • 3 Other Carbohydrate • 2 Vegetable • 2-1/2 Very Lean Meat.

TIP: When stir frying, heat the skillet or wok before adding the meat. This sears the surface of the meat and prevents the juices from escaping into the skillet.

creamed turkey and green beans

READY IN: 25 MINUTES
SERVINGS: 4

2 cups uncooked rotini pasta (6 oz.)

1-1/2 cups Green Giant® Frozen Whole Green Beans (from 14 oz. bag)

1/2 cup chive-and-onion cream cheese (from 8 oz. container)

1/2 cup milk

1/4 teaspoon garlic salt

2 cups diced cooked turkey

2 tablespoons cooked real bacon pieces

1 In 3-quart saucepan, cook pasta as directed on package, adding green beans during last 5 minutes of cooking. Drain in colander; cover to keep warm.

2 In same saucepan, mix cream cheese, milk and garlic salt. Cook over medium-low heat about 4 minutes, stirring frequently, until well blended and smooth.

3 Stir in cooked pasta with beans, turkey and bacon to coat. Reduce heat to low; cook 4 to 5 minutes, stirring frequently, until thoroughly heated.

HIGH ALTITUDE (3500-6500 FT): Thaw frozen whole green beans before adding to boiling water with pasta.

NUTRITIONAL INFORMATION PER SERVING: Calories 410 • Total Fat 16g • Saturated Fat 8g • Trans Fat 0g • Cholesterol 90mg • Sodium 540mg • Total Carbohydrate 38g • Dietary Fiber 4g • Sugars 4g • Protein 30g.
DIETARY EXCHANGES: 2 Starch • 1 Vegetable • 3 Lean Meat • 1-1/2 Fat.

meatball primavera

READY IN: 15 MINUTES
SERVINGS: 4

8 oz. uncooked fettuccine, broken in half

1/2 cup thin red onion wedges

2 small zucchini or yellow summer squash (or 1 of each), cut into 2x1/2-inch strips

4 Italian plum tomatoes, chopped (about 1 cup)

24 frozen cooked meatballs (about 12 oz.), thawed

1/2 cup purchased pesto

1 Cook fettuccine as directed on package. Drain.

2 Meanwhile, in 12-inch nonstick skillet, cook onion over medium heat for 2 to 3 minutes or until crisp-tender, stirring frequently. Add zucchini; cook and stir 2 minutes. Stir in tomatoes and meatballs; cook 3 to 5 minutes or until thoroughly heated, stirring occasionally.

3 Add cooked fettuccine and pesto; cook and stir just until thoroughly heated.

HIGH ALTITUDE (3500-6500 FT): After stirring in tomatoes and meatballs, cook 5 to 7 minutes, stirring occasionally.

NUTRITIONAL INFORMATION PER SERVING: Calories: 600 • Total Fat 32g • Saturated Fat 8g • Cholesterol 130mg • Sodium 870mg • Total Carbohydrate 50g • Dietary Fiber 4g • Sugars 6g • Protein 28g.
DIETARY EXCHANGES: 3 Starch • 1 Vegetable • 2-1/2 Medium-Fat Meat • 3-1/2 Fat.

lemon-basil vegetables and rice

READY IN: 35 MINUTES
SERVINGS: 4

1-1/2 cups uncooked instant brown rice

1-1/2 cups water

1 tablespoon oil

1 medium onion, chopped

1 (9 oz.) package Green Giant® Niblets® Frozen Corn, thawed

1 (8 oz.) package sliced fresh mushrooms (3 cups)

1 medium zucchini, cut in half lengthwise, sliced

1 red bell pepper, cut into small strips

1-1/2 teaspoons dried basil leaves

1/2 teaspoon grated lemon peel

1 tablespoon lemon juice

1 Cook rice in water as directed on package, omitting margarine and salt.

2 Meanwhile, heat oil in large nonstick skillet over high heat until hot. Add the onion; cook and stir 2 to 3 minutes or until tender.

3 Reduce heat to medium-high. Add corn, mushrooms, zucchini, bell pepper and basil; cook an additional 6 to 8 minutes or until the vegetables are crisp-tender, stirring occasionally.

4 Stir in the cooked rice, lemon peel, and lemon juice; mix well.

NUTRITIONAL INFORMATION PER SERVING: Calories 320 • Total Fat 6g • Saturated Fat 1g • Cholesterol 0mg • Sodium 320mg • Total Carbohydrate 58g • Dietary Fiber 6g • Sugars 6g • Protein 8g.
DIETARY EXCHANGES: 2 Starch • 1-1/2 Fruit • 3-1/2 Other Carbohydrate • 1 Vegetable • 1 Fat.

easy skillet meatballs and gravy

READY IN: 25 MINUTES
SERVINGS: 4

8 oz. uncooked linguine

1 (10.5 oz.) package frozen cooked light Italian meatballs

1 (15 oz.) can chunky Italian tomato sauce

1 (10-3/4 oz.) can condensed 98% fat-free cream of mushroom soup with 30% less sodium

1 (2.5 oz.) jar Green Giant® Sliced Mushrooms, drained

1/4 cup chopped fresh parsley

1 Cook linguine to desired doneness as directed on package. Drain; cover pasta to keep warm.

2 Meanwhile, in large skillet, combine all remaining ingredients except parsley; mix well. Bring to a boil over medium-high heat. Reduce heat to medium-low; cover and cook 8 to 10 minutes or until meatballs are thoroughly heated, stirring occasionally.

3 Serve meatballs with sauce over linguine. Sprinkle with parsley.

NUTRITIONAL INFORMATION PER SERVING:
Calories 430 • Total Fat 10g • Saturated Fat 4g • Cholesterol 30mg • Sodium 1,250mg • Total Carbohydrate 61g • Dietary Fiber 5g • Sugars 12g • Protein 25g.
DIETARY EXCHANGES: 3 Starch • 1/2 Fruit • 3-1/2 Other Carbohydrate • 1 Vegetable • 2 Medium-Fat Meat.

TIP: Meatball and Gravy Sandwiches are a snap. Just omit the pasta and serve the meatballs inside sandwich buns. Spoon the sauce over the meat.

rotini pepper steak

READY IN: 25 MINUTES
SERVINGS: 5

8 oz. uncooked rotini (spiral pasta)

1 tablespoon oil

1 lb. boneless beef sirloin steak, cut into thin bite-sized strips

1 medium onion, cut into thin wedges

1/2 teaspoon garlic-pepper blend

1 teaspoon grated gingerroot

1 medium green bell pepper, cut into 1/2-inch pieces

1 yellow bell pepper, cut into 1/2-inch pieces

3/4 cup purchased Asian or Oriental sesame salad dressing and marinade

3 to 4 Italian plum tomatoes, halved lengthwise, sliced

1 Cook rotini to desired doneness as directed on package. Drain; cover pasta to keep warm.

2 Meanwhile, heat oil in large skillet over medium-high heat until hot. Add beef and onion; sprinkle with garlic-pepper blend and gingerroot. Cook and stir 2 to 3 minutes or until beef is browned. Add bell peppers; cook and stir 2 to 3 minutes or until peppers are crisp-tender.

3 Add rotini and salad dressing; stir to coat. Stir in the tomatoes.

NUTRITIONAL INFORMATION PER SERVING:
Calories 385 • Total Fat 8g • Saturated Fat 2g • Cholesterol 50mg • Sodium 870mg • Total Carbohydrate 53g • Dietary Fiber 3g • Sugars 14g • Protein 25g.
DIETARY EXCHANGES: 3-1/2 Starch • 3-1/2 Other Carbohydrate • 2 Lean Meat • 1/2 Fat.

TIP: Look for chopped gingerroot in jars in the produce department of your grocery store. You can also use fresh gingerroot, freezing the extra, unpeeled portion in a plastic freezer bag.

weeknight beef burgundy

READY IN: 30 MINUTES
SERVINGS: 6

Susan O'Connor
Tequestas, FL

RICE
3 cups uncooked instant white rice

3 cups water

BEEF BURGUNDY
6 tablespoons butter or margarine

1-1/2 cups sliced fresh mushrooms (4 oz.)

1/2 cup chopped onion (1 medium)

1/3 cup finely chopped fresh parsley

2 (18.8 oz.) cans Progresso® Rich & Hearty Sirloin Steak & Vegetables Soup

2/3 cup dry red wine

2-1/2 tablespoons cornstarch

1/8 teaspoon pepper

1 (14.5 oz.) can sliced carrots, drained

1 Cook rice in water as directed on package.

2 Meanwhile, in 12-inch nonstick skillet, melt 6 tablespoons butter over medium-high heat. Add mushrooms, onion and parsley; cook 7 to 10 minutes, stirring frequently, until vegetables are tender.

3 Stir in soup. Reduce heat to low; cook, stirring occasionally, until thoroughly heated.

4 In small bowl, mix wine, cornstarch and pepper until smooth. Increase heat to high; stir wine mixture into vegetables, cooking and stirring until mixture boils. Reduce heat to medium; cook about 1 minute, stirring constantly, until mixture thickens slightly. Add carrots; cook 1 to 2 minutes, stirring frequently, until mixture is well blended and hot. Serve over rice.

HIGH ALTITUDE (3500-6500 FT):
Add 2 tablespoons water to wine mixture. Over high heat, stir wine mixture into vegetables, cooking and stirring until mixture boils. Reduce heat to medium; cook 2 to 3 minutes, stirring constantly, until mixture thickens slightly. Continue as directed.

NUTRITIONAL INFORMATION PER SERVING:
Calories 460 • Total Fat 16g • Saturated Fat 9g • Cholesterol 45mg • Sodium 1,530mg • Total Carbohydrate 69g • Dietary Fiber 5g • Sugars 5g • Protein 14g.

easy straw and hay

READY IN: 30 MINUTES
SERVINGS: 6

8 oz. uncooked fettuccine

8 oz. uncooked spinach fettuccine

2 cups Green Giant Select® Frozen Broccoli Florets

1 (16 oz.) jar Parmesan and mozzarella pasta sauce

6 oz. prosciutto or cooked ham, cut into thin strips

1/2 cup sliced roasted red peppers (from a jar)

1 (2.25 oz.) can sliced ripe olives, drained

1/2 cup shredded fresh Parmesan cheese (2 oz.)

1 Cook fettuccine in large saucepan to desired doneness as directed on package. (Spinach fettuccine may cook in less time; add to plain fettuccine according to times on package.) Add broccoli during last 3 to 4 minutes of cooking time. Drain in colander.

2 In same saucepan, heat sauce as directed on jar. Add fettuccine and broccoli; mix well. Stir in the ham, roasted peppers and olives. Sprinkle with the cheese.

HIGH ALTITUDE (3500-6500 FT)
Cook fettuccine following high altitude package directions, adding broccoli during last 3 to 4 minutes of the cooking time.

NUTRITIONAL INFORMATION PER SERVING:
Calories 450 • Total Fat 15g • Saturated Fat 6g • Cholesterol 120mg • Sodium 1,530mg • Total Carbohydrate 56g • Dietary Fiber 3g • Sugars 3g • Protein 23g.
DIETARY EXCHANGES: 4 Starch • 4 Other Carbohydrate • 1-1/2 Lean Meat • 2 Fat.

tasty meals for two

Thanks to the satisfying favorites found here, you can enjoy the spirit-warming goodness of piping-hot casseroles and one-dish dinners without facing leftovers for days on end. Visit this chapter for classics such as maple-flavored pork chops and macaroni and cheese, as well as new ideas including a halibut stir fry and crispy hash-brown bowls...each recipe ideal for cozy, two-person homes.

Pork Chops and
Sweet Potatoes
for Two
page 186

Hash-
Brown
Egg Cups
page 187

Beef 'n
Vegetable
Stir Fry
for Two
page 189

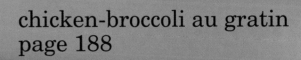

chicken-broccoli au gratin
page 188

paprika-pork and noodles

PREP TIME: 10 MINUTES
READY IN: 25 MINUTES
SERVINGS: 2

2 boneless pork loin chops (1/2- to 3/4-inch thick)

1 (12 oz.) jar pork gravy

1/2 cup chicken broth

1-1/2 teaspoons paprika

1/4 teaspoon garlic-pepper blend

1 cup uncooked medium egg noodles (2 oz.)

1/2 cup Green Giant Select® LeSueur® Frozen Baby Sweet Peas (from 1-lb. bag)

1 Heat 10-inch nonstick skillet over medium-high heat. Place pork chops in skillet; cook 3 to 5 minutes or until browned on both sides. Remove from skillet; place on plate.

2 In same skillet, mix gravy, broth, paprika and garlic-pepper blend. Heat to boiling. Stir in uncooked noodles and frozen peas. Place pork chops with pork juices over mixture.

3 Reduce heat to medium-low; cover and cook 10 to 15

minutes, stirring noodle mixture occasionally, until pork is no longer pink in center and noodles are tender.

HIGH ALTITUDE (3500-6500 FT): Increase broth to 3/4 cup. After reducing heat to medium-low, cover and cook 15 to 20 minutes longer.

NUTRITIONAL INFORMATION PER SERVING: Calories 390 • Total Fat 14g • Saturated Fat 5g • Cholesterol 95mg • Sodium 1,280mg • Total Carbohydrate 32g • Dietary Fiber 4g • Sugars 2g • Protein 36g.
DIETARY EXCHANGES: 2 Starch • 4 Lean Meat.

italian sausages marinara

READY IN: 25 MINUTES
SERVINGS: 2

- 2 uncooked Italian sausage links (4 to 5 oz. each)
- 1 cup refrigerated marinara sauce (from 15 oz. container)
- 1 medium zucchini, sliced (2 cups)
- 1/4 cup sliced ripe olives
- 1/2 medium yellow bell pepper, coarsely chopped (1/2 cup)
- 2 tablespoons shredded Parmesan cheese

1 Heat 8-inch nonstick skillet over medium heat. Add sausages; cook 3 to 5 minutes or until browned on all sides.

2 Stir in all remaining ingredients except cheese. Reduce heat to medium-low; cover and cook 10 to 15 minutes, stirring occasionally, until sausage is no longer pink in center.

3 Sprinkle with cheese; cover and cook just until cheese is melted.

NUTRITIONAL INFORMATION PER SERVING:
Calories 440 • Total Fat 28g • Saturated Fat 8g • Cholesterol 65mg • Sodium 1,530mg • Total Carbohydrate 31g • Dietary Fiber 4g • Sugars 12g • Protein 20g.
DIETARY EXCHANGES: 1/2 Starch • 1 Other Carbohydrate • 1 Vegetable • 2-1/2 High-Fat Meat • 1 1/2 Fat.

TIP: The Italian sausages are great on their own, but you can dress up the recipe by serving them over cooked pasta or in hot dog buns.

halibut and asparagus stir fry

READY IN: 25 MINUTES
SERVINGS: 2

- 1 tablespoon butter or margarine
- 1/2 lb. halibut fillet, cut into 3/4-inch pieces
- 1/2 teaspoon lemon-pepper seasoning
- 1/4 cup thin onion wedges (1/2 small onion)
- 8 oz. fresh asparagus spears, cut into 1-inch pieces (2 cups)
- 1 small red bell pepper, cut into 1/2-inch pieces (1 cup)
- 1/3 cup stir fry sauce
- 1 tablespoon lemon juice
- 1 tablespoon honey
  Hot cooked rice

1 In 10-inch nonstick skillet, melt butter over medium-high heat. Sprinkle halibut with lemon-pepper seasoning; add to skillet with onion. Cook and stir 2 to 3 minutes or until halibut is white and no longer opaque.

2 Stir in asparagus and bell pepper. Cook and stir 5 to 7 minutes or until vegetables are crisp-tender and halibut flakes easily with fork.

3 In small bowl, mix stir fry sauce, lemon juice and honey. Add to mixture in skillet; cook and gently stir until well blended and thoroughly heated. Serve over hot cooked rice if desired.

NUTRITIONAL INFORMATION PER SERVING:
Calories 290 • Total Fat 8g • Saturated Fat 4g • Cholesterol 75mg • Sodium 2,060mg • Total Carbohydrate 28g • Dietary Fiber 4g • Sugars 21g • Protein 28g.
DIETARY EXCHANGES: 1-1/2 Starch • 1 Vegetable • 3 Very Lean Meat • 1 Fat.

taco-seasoned stuffed peppers

PREP TIME: 25 MINUTES
READY IN: 40 MINUTES
SERVINGS: 2

2 medium green bell peppers, cut in half lengthwise, seeded

1/2 lb. lean ground turkey or lean (at least 80%) ground beef

2 tablespoons chopped onion

2 tablespoons Old El Paso® Taco Seasoning Mix (from 1.25 oz. package)

1 (15.5 oz.) can kidney beans, drained, rinsed

1 (8 oz.) can tomato sauce

1/4 cup sour cream

1/4 cup shredded Cheddar cheese (1 oz.)

1/4 cup chopped tomato (1/2 small)

1 Heat oven to 350°F. In 2-quart saucepan, heat 6 cups water to boiling. Add bell pepper halves; boil 5 minutes or until slightly softened. Drain and set aside.

2 Meanwhile, in 8-inch nonstick skillet, cook ground turkey and onion over medium-high heat, stirring frequently, until turkey is no longer pink; drain. Stir in taco seasoning mix, kidney beans and tomato sauce. Heat to boiling. Reduce heat to medium-low; simmer 5 minutes, stirring occasionally.

3 In ungreased 8-inch square (2-quart) glass baking dish, arrange pepper halves. Spoon turkey mixture evenly into each.

4 Bake 10 to 12 minutes or until peppers are tender. Top individual servings with sour cream, cheese and tomato.

NUTRITIONAL INFORMATION PER SERVING: Calories 640 • Total Fat 19g • Saturated Fat 8g • Cholesterol 110mg • Sodium 1,850mg • Total Carbohydrate 77g • Dietary Fiber 19g • Sugars 17g • Protein 52g.
DIETARY EXCHANGES: 2 Starch • 1 Other Carbohydrate • 2 Vegetable • 6 Very Lean Meat • 3 Fat.

pork chops and sweet potatoes for two

PREP TIME: 20 MINUTES
READY IN: 6 HOURS 20 MINUTES
SERVINGS: 2

2 tablespoons margarine or butter, melted

1 medium dark-orange sweet potato, peeled, cut into 1/2-inch thick slices (12 oz.)

2 onion slices

2 (1-inch thick) boneless pork loin chops (about 1-1/4 lb.)

6 dried apricots

1 small apple, peeled, sliced

Salt

3 tablespoons Hungry Jack® Microwave Ready Regular Syrup

1/2 teaspoon grated gingerroot

1 In 3- to 4-quart slow cooker, combine 1 tablespoon of the margarine, sweet potato and onion; mix to coat potato well. Cut slit horizontally in each pork chop, cutting to within 1/2 inch of opposite edge to form pocket.

2 Insert 3 apricots and several apple slices into each chop. (If necessary, cut apples slices in half.) Sprinkle chops with salt. Add any remaining apple slices to sweet potato mixture.

3 Heat remaining tablespoon margarine in medium skillet over medium-high heat. Add chops; cook 2 to 3 minutes or until browned, turning once.

Place chops over potato mixture in slow cooker. In same skillet, combine syrup and gingerroot; mix with pan drippings. Drizzle mixture over the chops and the potatoes.

4 Cover; cook on Low setting for 5 to 6 hours.

NUTRITIONAL INFORMATION PER SERVING: Calories 890 • Total Fat 33g • Saturated Fat 10g • Cholesterol 170mg • Sodium 580mg • Total Carbohydrate 82g • Dietary Fiber 8g • Sugars 34g • Protein 65g.
DIETARY EXCHANGES: 3 Starch • 2-1/2 Fruit • 5-1/2 Other Carbohydrate • 8 Lean Meat • 1-1/2 Fat.

roast cornish hen with vegetables

PREP TIME: 15 MINUTES
READY IN: 1 HOUR 5 MINUTES
SERVINGS: 2

1 Cornish game hen (24 oz.), thawed if frozen
1 teaspoon garlic salt
1 teaspoon chili powder
1/2 teaspoon ground ginger
1/2 teaspoon ground cumin
2 tablespoons olive or vegetable oil
1 medium dark-orange sweet potato, peeled, cut into 1-inch pieces (2 cups)
2 small red potatoes, quartered
1 small green bell pepper, cut into 1-inch pieces (1 cup)

1 Heat oven to 400°F. Spray 11x7-inch (2-quart) glass baking dish with nonstick cooking spray. Remove and discard neck and giblets from game hen. With kitchen scissors, cut hen in half; place halves, skin side up, in baking dish.

2 In medium bowl, mix garlic salt, chili powder, ginger, cumin and oil. Brush hen halves with 1 tablespoon of the oil mixture. To remaining mixture in bowl, add sweet potatoes, red potatoes and bell pepper; toss to coat. Arrange vegetables around hen halves in dish.

3 Bake 40 to 50 minutes or until hen halves are fork-tender and juices run clear, and vegetables are tender.

NUTRITIONAL INFORMATION PER SERVING:
Calories 800 • Total Fat 48g • Saturated Fat 11g • Cholesterol 240mg • Sodium 640mg • Total Carbohydrate 51g • Dietary Fiber 7g • Sugars 18g • Protein 46g.
DIETARY EXCHANGES: 3 Starch • 1/2 Vegetable • 5 Medium-Fat Meat • 4 Fat.

hash-brown egg cups

PREP TIME: 15 MINUTES
READY IN: 55 MINUTES
SERVINGS: 2

3/4 cup shredded Cheddar cheese (3 oz.)
2 cups refrigerated shredded hash-brown potatoes (from 20 oz. bag)
1/4 cup chopped green onions (4 medium)
1/2 teaspoon seasoned salt
1/8 teaspoon pepper
2 eggs
1/8 teaspoon Italian seasoning

1 Heat oven to 400°F. Spray 2 (2-cup) ovenproof bowls or ramekins with nonstick cooking spray. Reserve 2 tablespoons of the cheese for topping. In medium bowl, mix remaining cheese, the potatoes, onions, 1/4 teaspoon of the seasoned salt and the pepper. Press mixture in bottom and up side of each bowl, leaving indentation in center.

2 Bake 25 to 30 minutes or until golden brown and crisp. Remove from oven. Break egg into center of each cup. Sprinkle with remaining 1/4 teaspoon seasoned salt, the Italian seasoning and reserved 2 tablespoons cheese.

3 Return to oven; bake 8 to 12 minutes longer or until eggs are set and of desired doneness.

NUTRITIONAL INFORMATION PER SERVING:
Calories 420 • Total Fat 20g • Saturated Fat 11g • Cholesterol 255mg • Sodium 720mg • Total Carbohydrate 43g • Dietary Fiber 4g • Sugars 4g • Protein 21g.
DIETARY EXCHANGES: 3 Starch • 1-1/2 High-Fat Meat • 1 Fat.

chicken-broccoli au gratin

PREP TIME: 20 MINUTES
READY IN: 45 MINUTES
SERVINGS: 2

Kibby Jackson
Gray, GA

- 1 tablespoon olive oil
- 1 cup sliced fresh mushrooms
- 1 small onion, sliced (1/2 cup)
- 1 (10 oz.) box Green Giant® Frozen Broccoli & Zesty Cheese Sauce
- 2/3 cup ricotta cheese
- 1 cup chopped cooked chicken
- 1 (4 oz.) can Pillsbury® Refrigerated Crescent Dinner Rolls (4 rolls)

1 Heat oven to 375°F. In 10-inch skillet, heat oil over medium-high heat. Add mushrooms and onion; cook 5 to 7 minutes, stirring frequently, until tender. Meanwhile, microwave broccoli with cheese sauce as directed on box.

2 Spread 1/3 cup ricotta cheese in bottom of each of 2 ungreased 2-cup au gratin dishes or individual casseroles. Top each evenly with chicken, mushroom mixture and broccoli with cheese sauce.

3 Unroll dough; separate into 2 rectangles. Place 1 rectangle over top of each dish, tucking corners into dish as needed.

4 Place dishes on cookie sheet; bake 20 to 25 minutes or until tops are golden brown and edges are bubbly.

HIGH ALTITUDE (3500-6500 FT): In Step 1, cook mushrooms and onion 5 minutes, stirring frequently. Add chicken to mixture; cook and stir 2 minutes longer. In Step 4, bake 23 to 28 minutes.

NUTRITIONAL INFORMATION PER SERVING: Calories 560 • Total Fat 27g • Saturated Fat 7g • Trans Fat 3g • Cholesterol 70mg • Sodium 1,170mg • Total Carbohydrate 43g • Dietary Fiber 3g • Sugars 16g • Protein 38g.
DIETARY EXCHANGES: 1 Starch • 1 Other Carbohydrate • 2 Vegetable • 4-1/2 Lean Meat • 2-1/2 Fat.

crispy-top macaroni and cheese for two

PREP TIME: 10 MINUTES
READY IN: 35 MINUTES
SERVINGS: 2

- 1 lb. purchased macaroni and cheese (from deli)
- 1/4 cup real bacon pieces
- 1/4 cup sliced marinated sun-dried tomatoes
- 3 tablespoons Progresso® Italian Style Bread Crumbs
- 1 tablespoon chopped fresh chives
- 1 tablespoon margarine or butter, melted

1 Heat oven to 375°F. Spray two 12 oz. individual ovenproof casseroles or ramekins with nonstick cooking spray. In medium bowl, combine macaroni and cheese, bacon and tomatoes; stir gently to mix. Spoon evenly into the sprayed casseroles.

2 In small bowl, combine bread crumbs, chives and margarine; mix well. Sprinkle over each casserole.

3 Bake at 375°F for 20 to 25 minutes or until topping is golden brown.

NUTRITIONAL INFORMATION PER SERVING: Calories 655 • Total Fat 33g • Saturated Fat 8g • Cholesterol 30mg • Sodium 1,510mg • Total Carbohydrate 68g • Dietary Fiber 2g • Sugars 12g • Protein 22g.
DIETARY EXCHANGES: 4-1/2 Starch • 4-1/2 Other Carbohydrate • 1 High-Fat Meat • 5 Fat.

beef 'n vegetable stir fry for two

READY IN: 15 MINUTES
SERVINGS: 2

1	cup uncooked instant white rice
1	cup water
1/4	lb. extra-lean (at least 90%) ground beef
1	small onion, sliced
1-1/2	cups Green Giant Select® Frozen Broccoli Florets (from 14 oz. bag), thawed
1/2	medium red bell pepper, cut into thin bite-size strips
1/4	cup stir fry sauce
2	tablespoons water

1 Cook rice in 1 cup water as directed on package.

2 Meanwhile, in 8-inch nonstick skillet, cook the ground beef and the onion over medium heat, stirring frequently, until the beef is thoroughly cooked; drain.

3 Stir in all remaining ingredients except rice. Cover; cook 4 to 6 minutes, stirring occasionally, until vegetables are crisp-tender. Serve over rice.

NUTRITIONAL INFORMATION PER SERVING:
Calories 360 • Total Fat 5g • Saturated Fat 2g • Cholesterol 30mg • Sodium 2,060mg • Total Carbohydrate 61g • Dietary Fiber 4g • Sugars 9g • Protein 22g.
DIETARY EXCHANGES: 3-1/2 Starch • 1 Vegetable • 1 Lean Meat.

slow-cooked favorites

Fix it and forget it! That's the time-saving idea behind the dishes in this useful chapter. Peruse the following pages and you will see how an ounce of planning in the morning allows you to come home to an aromatic sensation simmering away in the slow cooker. In addition, these mouth-watering recipes offer all of the dinner-in-one convenience that today's family cooks enjoy most.

Slow-Cooked
Chop Suey
Over Rice
page 204

Winter Root
and Sausage
Casserole
page 205

Easy Italian
Meatball Stew
page 207

chicken and vegetable tortellini stew
page 213

slow-cooked pot roast and vegetables

PREP TIME: 25 MINUTES
READY IN: 10 HOURS 25 MINUTES
SERVINGS: 4

1 tablespoon Pillsbury BEST® All-Purpose Flour

1/2 teaspoon salt

1/8 teaspoon pepper

1-1/2 lb. boneless beef top round steak (1/2-inch thick), cut into 4 equal pieces

4 medium potatoes, peeled, each cut into 6 pieces

4 large carrots, cut into 1-inch pieces

1 onion, thinly sliced

1 bay leaf

1 (14 oz.) can beef broth

1 teaspoon Worcestershire sauce

2 tablespoons cornstarch

1 In shallow bowl, combine flour, salt and pepper; mix well. Add beef pieces; turn to coat both sides.

2 Spray large nonstick skillet with nonstick cooking spray. Heat over medium-high heat until hot. Add beef; cook 4 to 6 minutes or until browned, turning once. Remove beef from skillet; cover to keep warm.

3 In 3-1/2- to 4-quart slow cooker, combine potatoes, carrots and onion; mix well. Add bay leaf. Place browned beef over vegetables.

4 In small bowl, combine 1-1/2 cups of the broth (reserve and refrigerate remaining broth) and Worcestershire sauce. Pour over beef.

5 Cover; cook on Low setting for 8 to 10 hours.

6 About 5 minutes before serving, with slotted spoon, remove beef and vegetables from slow cooker; place on serving platter. Cover to keep warm.

7 Pour liquid from slow cooker into medium saucepan; remove and discard bay leaf. In small bowl, blend remaining broth and cornstarch until smooth. Add to liquid in saucepan. Bring to a boil over medium-high heat, stirring constantly. Boil 1 minute. Serve sauce with beef and vegetables. If desired, season to taste with salt and pepper.

NUTRITIONAL INFORMATION PER SERVING: Calories 370 • Total Fat 6g • Saturated Fat 2g • Cholesterol 90mg • Sodium 860mg • Total Carbohydrate 40g • Dietary Fiber 4g • Sugars 7g • Protein 39g.
DIETARY EXCHANGES: 2 Starch • 2 Other Carbohydrate • 1 Vegetable • 4-1/2 Very Lean Meat • 1 Fat.

thai chicken big bowls

PREP TIME: 25 MINUTES
READY IN: 6 HOURS 45 MINUTES
SERVINGS: 6

8 bone-in chicken thighs (about 2 lb.), skin removed

2 garlic cloves, minced

1 cup chopped onions

2 medium stalks celery, sliced

2 teaspoons grated gingerroot

1 teaspoon Chinese five-spice powder

1/2 teaspoon salt

1/2 teaspoon grated lemon peel

2 (14 oz.) cans chicken broth

2 cups uncooked regular long-grain white rice

4 cups water

6 tablespoons sliced green onions

6 teaspoons chopped fresh cilantro

1 Place chicken thighs in 3-1/2- to 4-quart slow cooker. Top with garlic, onions, celery, gingerroot, five-spice powder, salt and lemon peel. Add broth.

2 Cover; cook on Low setting for 5 to 6 hours.

3 About 30 minutes before serving, cook rice in water as directed on package. With slotted spoon, remove chicken from slow cooker; cool until able to handle. Cut chicken from bones; return chicken to slow cooker. Discard bones.

4 To serve, divide rice evenly into individual large shallow soup bowls, spreading rice up sides of bowls. Add chicken and broth. Sprinkle each with 1 tablespoon green onions and 1 teaspoon cilantro.

NUTRITIONAL INFORMATION PER SERVING: Calories 430 • Total Fat 9g • Saturated Fat 3g • Cholesterol 60mg • Sodium 860mg • Total Carbohydrate 58g • Dietary Fiber 1g • Sugars 2g • Protein 29g.
DIETARY EXCHANGES: 4 Starch • 4 Other Carbohydrate • 2-1/2 Lean Meat.

curried beef stew

PREP TIME: 15 MINUTES
READY IN: 10 HOURS 15 MINUTES
SERVINGS: 6

1 cup small whole onions, peeled

1 cup fresh baby carrots

12 small new potatoes, cut in half (about 4 cups)

2 lb. boneless beef chuck steak, cut into 1-1/2-inch pieces

1 (14.5 oz.) can diced tomatoes, undrained

1/2 cup apple juice

4 teaspoons curry powder

1/2 teaspoon salt

1/4 teaspoon pepper

1 In 3-1/2- to 4-quart slow cooker, layer onions, carrots and potatoes. Place beef over the vegetables.

2 In medium bowl, combine all remaining ingredients; mix well. Pour over beef.

3 Cover; cook on Low setting for 8 to 10 hours.

NUTRITIONAL INFORMATION PER SERVING: Calories 280 • Total Fat 7g • Saturated Fat 3g • Cholesterol 85mg • Sodium 350mg • Total Carbohydrate 25g • Dietary Fiber 4g • Sugars 6g • Protein 30g.
DIETARY EXCHANGES: 1-1/2 Starch • 1-1/2 Other Carbohydrate • 1 Vegetable • 3 Lean Meat.

slow-cooked chicken and dumplings

PREP TIME: 20 MINUTES
READY IN: 9 HOURS 50 MINUTES
SERVINGS: 5

- 1 teaspoon oil
- 1 lb. boneless skinless chicken thighs, cut into 1-inch pieces
- 1-1/2 cups sliced celery
- 1-1/2 cups fresh baby carrots
- 1 cup sliced fresh mushrooms
- 1 (1.8 oz.) package dry leek soup mix
- 4 cups water
- 1 (10.8 oz.) can Pillsbury® Grands!® Refrigerated Flaky Biscuits (5 biscuits)
- 1 tablespoon cornmeal
- 1-1/2 cups Green Giant® Frozen Sweet Peas
- 1/4 teaspoon pepper

1 Heat oil in medium skillet over medium-high heat until hot. Add chicken; cook and stir until browned.

2 In 4- to 6-quart slow cooker, combine chicken, celery, carrots, mushrooms, soup mix and water; mix well.

3 Cover; cook on Low setting for 7 to 9 hours.

4 Separate dough into 5 biscuits; cut each into 8 wedges. Sprinkle wedges with cornmeal. Stir coated biscuit pieces into hot chicken mixture.

5 Cover; cook on High setting for an additional 25 to 30 minutes or until biscuits are no longer doughy in center.

6 About 10 minutes before serving, microwave peas in covered microwave-safe dish on High for 3 to 4 minutes or until hot. Just before serving, stir peas and pepper into the chicken mixture.

NUTRITIONAL INFORMATION PER SERVING: Calories 440 • Total Fat 19g • Saturated Fat 5g • Cholesterol 60mg • Sodium 1,220mg • Total Carbohydrate 43g • Dietary Fiber 4g • Sugars 8g • Protein 24g.
DIETARY EXCHANGES: 2-1/2 Starch • 2-1/2 Other Carbohydrate • 1 Vegetable • 2 Lean Meat • 2 Fat.

meat and potato casserole

PREP TIME: 15 MINUTES
READY IN: 7 HOURS 15 MINUTES
SERVINGS: 4

- 1 lb. lean ground beef
- 1 (2.8 oz.) can french fried onions
- 1 (10-3/4 oz.) can condensed cream of mushroom soup
- 1/2 cup milk
- 1/4 teaspoon pepper
- 4 cups frozen country-style shredded hash-brown potatoes (from 32 oz. pkg.)
- 2 cups Green Giant® Frozen Cut Green Beans

1 Brown ground beef in large skillet over medium heat until thoroughly cooked, stirring frequently. Drain. Add half of the onions, soup, milk and pepper; mix well.

2 Spray 3-1/2- to 4-quart slow cooker with nonstick cooking spray. Layer potatoes and green beans in sprayed slow cooker. Top with beef mixture; spread evenly.

3 Cover; cook on Low setting for 6 to 7 hours. Top with remaining half of the onions before serving.

NUTRITIONAL INFORMATION PER SERVING: Calories 645 • Total Fat 32g • Saturated Fat 10g • Cholesterol 70mg • Sodium 820mg • Total Carbohydrate 60g • Dietary Fiber 5g • Sugars 7g • Protein 29g.
DIETARY EXCHANGES: 3-1/2 Starch • 3-1/2 Other Carbohydrate • 1 Vegetable • 2-1/2 Medium-Fat Meat • 4 Fat.

swiss steak with chipotle chile sauce

PREP TIME: 15 MINUTES
READY IN: 9 HOURS 15 MINUTES
SERVINGS: 8

1 (10-3/4 oz.) can condensed cream of mushroom soup

1 (2 lb.) boneless beef top round steak (1-1/2 inches thick)

1 tablespoon brown sugar

2 tablespoons ketchup

2 tablespoons chopped chipotle chiles in adobo sauce (from 7 or 11 oz. can)

1 garlic clove, minced

2 Italian plum tomatoes, chopped

1/2 medium green bell pepper, cut into thin bite-sized strips

1 Spoon soup into 4- to 5-quart slow cooker. Top with beef round steak, cutting into pieces if necessary to place in single layer. In small bowl, combine brown sugar, ketchup, chiles and garlic; mix well. Spread over the beef. Top with the tomatoes.

2 Cover; cook on Low setting for 8 to 9 hours.

3 About 10 minutes before serving, add bell pepper. Cover; cook an additional 10 minutes.

4 To serve, remove beef from slow cooker; place on cutting board. Cut into serving-sized pieces. Serve beef with sauce from slow cooker.

NUTRITIONAL INFORMATION PER SERVING:
Calories 180 • Total Fat 6g • Saturated Fat 2g • Cholesterol 60mg • Sodium 380mg • Total Carbohydrate 7g • Dietary Fiber 0g • Sugars 4g • Protein 24g.
DIETARY EXCHANGES: 1/2 Starch • 3 Very Lean Meat • 1 Fat.

slow-cooked pork stew

PREP TIME: 15 MINUTES
READY IN: 8 HOURS 15 MINUTES
SERVINGS: 6

1 tablespoon oil

1 (1-1/2 lb.) boneless pork shoulder roast, cut into 1-1/2-inch pieces

1/8 teaspoon salt

1/8 teaspoon pepper

8 small red potatoes, unpeeled, quartered

2 cups fresh baby carrots, cut in half lengthwise

1 (12 oz.) jar home-style pork gravy

1/4 cup ketchup

1/2 teaspoon dried rosemary leaves

1/4 teaspoon pepper

1/8 teaspoon ground sage

1-1/2 cups Green Giant® Frozen Cut Green Beans, thawed

1 Heat oil in large skillet over high heat until hot. Add pork to skillet; sprinkle with salt and 1/8 teaspoon pepper. Cook 3 to 5 minutes or until browned, stirring frequently.

2 In 4- to 6-quart slow cooker, combine pork and all remaining ingredients except the green beans.

3 Cover; cook on Low setting for 6 to 8 hours.

4 About 20 minutes before serving, stir in green beans. Increase heat setting to High; cover and cook an additional 15 to 20 minutes or until tender.

NUTRITIONAL INFORMATION PER SERVING:
Calories 380 • Total Fat 12g • Saturated Fat 3g • Cholesterol 50mg • Sodium 530mg • Total Carbohydrate 47g • Dietary Fiber 5g • Sugars 6g • Protein 20g.
DIETARY EXCHANGES: 3 Starch • 3 Other Carbohydrate • 1 Vegetable • 1-1/2 Lean Meat • 1 Fat.

ham and lentil stew

turkey and bean cassoulet

ham and lentil stew

PREP TIME: 20 MINUTES
READY IN: 9 HOURS 20 MINUTES
SERVINGS: 8

3 cups diced cooked ham

2 cups chopped celery

2 cups chopped carrot

2 cups dried lentils, rinsed

1 large onion, chopped

2 (10-1/2 oz.) cans condensed chicken broth

4 cups water

1 In 3-1/2- to 4-quart slow cooker, combine all ingredients; mix well.

2 Cover; cook on Low setting for 7 to 9 hours.

NUTRITIONAL INFORMATION PER SERVING:
Calories 290 • Total Fat 4g • Saturated Fat 1g • Cholesterol 25mg • Sodium 1,260mg • Total Carbohydrate 35g • Dietary Fiber 16g • Sugars 5g • Protein 28g.
DIETARY EXCHANGES: 2 Starch • 2 Other Carbohydrate • 1 Vegetable • 3 Very Lean Meat.

turkey and bean cassoulet

PREP TIME: 20 MINUTES
READY IN: 18 HOURS 25 MINUTES
SERVINGS: 6

1-1/2 cups dried great northern beans

1 lb. fresh turkey breast tenderloins, cut into 1-inch pieces

1 cup sliced celery

1 medium green bell pepper, chopped

1 medium onion, chopped

2 garlic cloves, minced

2 bay leaves

1/4 teaspoon pepper

1 (14-1/2 oz.) can ready-to-serve chicken broth

1-1/2 cups water

1 (14.5 oz.) can diced tomatoes, undrained

3/4 teaspoon salt

1 Place beans in medium bowl; add enough water to cover. Let beans stand overnight to soak.

2 Drain beans; discard water. Place beans and all remaining ingredients except tomatoes and salt in 3-1/2- to 4-quart slow cooker.

3 Cover; cook on Low setting for 8 to 10 hours.

4 To serve, remove bay leaves. Stir in tomatoes and salt. Cover; cook on Low setting an additional 10 minutes or until thoroughly heated.

NUTRITIONAL INFORMATION PER SERVING:
Calories 280 • Total Fat 2g • Saturated Fat 0g • Cholesterol 50mg • Sodium 640mg • Total Carbohydrate 35g • Dietary Fiber 11g • Sugars 4g • Protein 31g.
DIETARY EXCHANGES: 2 Starch • 2 Other Carbohydrate • 1 Vegetable • 3 Very Lean Meat.

TIP: Cassoulet is a classic French recipe featuring white beans and a variety of meats, poultry and sausage. This easy version calls only for turkey, but sliced smoked sausage can be added to the recipe. Serve this hearty bean and turkey stew with focaccia and a spinach salad dressed with red wine vinaigrette.

salsa swiss steak

PREP TIME: 20 MINUTES
READY IN: 10 HOURS 20 MINUTES
SERVINGS: 5

2 teaspoons oil

1-1/2 lb. boneless beef top round steak, trimmed of fat, cut into 5 pieces

1/2 teaspoon salt

1/4 teaspoon pepper

1 medium onion, halved lengthwise, sliced

1/2 medium green bell pepper, cut into bite-sized strips

1 (10-3/4 oz.) can condensed cream of mushroom soup

3/4 cup Old El Paso® Thick 'n Chunky Salsa

1 Heat oil in large skillet over medium-high heat until hot. Sprinkle steak with salt and pepper. Place steak in skillet; cook 4 to 6 minutes or until well browned, turning once.

2 Transfer steak to 4- to 6-quart slow cooker. Top with onion and bell pepper. In same skillet, combine soup and salsa; mix well. Pour over vegetables and steak.

3 Cover; cook on Low setting for 8 to 10 hours.

4 Remove steak pieces from slow cooker; place on serving platter. Stir sauce well. Serve sauce with steak.

NUTRITIONAL INFORMATION PER SERVING: Calories 260 • Total Fat 11g • Saturated Fat 3g • Cholesterol 70mg • Sodium 950mg • Total Carbohydrate 10g • Dietary Fiber 1g • Sugars 4g • Protein 30g.
DIETARY EXCHANGES: 1/2 Starch • 1/2 Other Carbohydrate • 4 Lean Meat.

moroccan lentil stew

PREP TIME: 15 MINUTES
READY IN: 10 HOURS 15 MINUTES
SERVINGS: 6

1 cup dried lentils, rinsed

1 (1 lb.) butternut squash, peeled, cut into 3/4-inch cubes

8 small new red potatoes, cut into 3/4-inch cubes

1 medium onion, chopped

1 (28 oz.) can Progresso® Crushed Tomatoes, undrained

3 teaspoons curry powder

1/2 teaspoon salt

2 cups water

1 (8 oz.) package Green Giant® Harvest Fresh® Frozen Cut Green Beans, thawed

1 In 3-1/2- to 4-quart slow cooker, combine all ingredients except green beans; stir gently to mix. Cover; cook on Low setting for 8 to 10 hours or on High setting for 5 to 6 hours or until lentils and potatoes are tender.

2 During last 15 minutes of cooking time, increase setting to High. Stir in green beans; cook an additional 10 to 15 minutes or until the beans are tender.

NUTRITIONAL INFORMATION PER SERVING: Calories 270 • Total Fat 1g • Saturated Fat 0g • Cholesterol 0mg • Sodium 530mg • Total Carbohydrate 53g • Dietary Fiber 15g • Sugars 8g • Protein 13g.
DIETARY EXCHANGES: 3 Starch • 3 Other Carbohydrate • 2 Vegetable.

TIP: Place the frozen green beans in the refrigerator to thaw while the slow cooker simmers the stew. Consider offering bowlfuls of piping hot stew with pita bread and cups of tea.

corned beef and cabbage dinner

PREP TIME: 15 MINUTES
READY IN: 12 HOURS 50 MINUTES
SERVINGS: 8

2 lb. small red potatoes

1-1/2 cups fresh baby carrots

1 medium onion, cut into 8 wedges

1 (2 to 2-1/2 lb.) corned beef brisket with seasoning packet

2 cups apple juice

Water

8 thin wedges cabbage

HORSERADISH SAUCE

1/2 cup sour cream

1/4 cup mayonnaise

2 tablespoons prepared horseradish

2 teaspoons Dijon mustard

1 Place potatoes, carrots and onion in 5- to 6-1/2-quart slow cooker. Top with corned beef brisket; sprinkle with contents of seasoning packet. Add apple juice and enough water to just cover brisket.

2 Cover; cook on Low setting for 10 to 12 hours.

3 About 40 minutes before serving, remove beef from slow cooker; place on serving platter and cover to keep warm. Add cabbage wedges to vegetables and broth in slow cooker. Increase heat setting to High; cover and cook an additional 30 to 35 minutes or until cabbage is crisp-tender.

4 Meanwhile, in small bowl, combine all horseradish sauce ingredients; mix well.

5 To serve, cut corned beef across grain into thin slices. With slotted spoon, remove vegetables from slow cooker. Serve corned beef and vegetables with sauce.

NUTRITIONAL INFORMATION PER SERVING:
Calories 410 • Total Fat 24g • Saturated Fat 8g • Cholesterol 90mg • Sodium 1,300mg • Total Carbohydrate 31g • Dietary Fiber 4g • Sugars 6g • Protein 18g.
DIETARY EXCHANGES: 1-1/2 Starch • 1-1/2 Other Carbohydrate • 1 Vegetable • 1-1/2 Medium-Fat Meat • 3-1/2 Fat.

beef ragout on polenta

PREP TIME: 20 MINUTES
READY IN: 10 HOURS 20 MINUTES
SERVINGS: 5

1 medium onion, chopped

1 green bell pepper, chopped

2 medium carrots, chopped

1 lb. beef stew meat, cut into 1-1/2-inch cubes

1/2 teaspoon coarsely ground black pepper

1 (14 oz.) jar tomato pasta sauce

1 (24 oz.) package polenta, cut into 10 slices

1 In 4- to 6-quart slow cooker, layer all ingredients in order listed, except polenta.

2 Cover; cook on Low setting for 8 to 10 hours.

3 About 10 minutes before serving, heat polenta as directed on package. Arrange 2 warm polenta slices on each individual serving plate. Top each with about 1 cup beef mixture.

NUTRITIONAL INFORMATION PER SERVING: Calories 290 • Total Fat 7g • Saturated Fat 2g • Cholesterol 60mg • Sodium 750mg • Total Carbohydrate 33g • Dietary Fiber 4g • Sugars 4g • Protein 24g.
DIETARY EXCHANGES: 2 Starch • 2 Other Carbohydrate • 1 Vegetable • 2 Lean Meat.

fisherman's wharf seafood stew

PREP TIME: 35 MINUTES
READY IN: 9 HOURS 55 MINUTES
SERVINGS: 6

2 tablespoons olive oil

1 cup sliced leek (white and light green portion)

2 garlic cloves, chopped

1 cup sliced fresh baby carrots (1/4 inch thick)

3 cups sliced quartered Italian plum tomatoes (6 large)

1/2 cup chopped green bell pepper

1/2 teaspoon fennel seed

1 bay leaf

1 cup dry white wine or water

1 (8 oz.) bottle clam juice

1 lb. cod (1 inch thick), cut into 1-inch pieces

1/2 lb. shelled deveined uncooked medium shrimp

1 teaspoon sugar

1 teaspoon dried basil leaves

1/2 teaspoon salt

1/4 teaspoon hot pepper sauce

2 tablespoons chopped fresh parsley

1 In 3-1/2- to 4-quart slow cooker, combine oil, leek and garlic; mix well. Top with carrots, tomatoes, bell pepper, fennel seed, bay leaf, wine and clam juice. Stir to combine.

2 Cover; cook on Low setting for 8 to 9 hours.

3 About 20 minutes before serving, add cod, shrimp, sugar, basil, salt and hot pepper sauce; stir gently to mix. Increase heat setting to High; cover and cook an additional 15 to 20 minutes or until fish flakes easily with fork. Remove bay leaf; stir in parsley.

NUTRITIONAL INFORMATION PER SERVING: Calories 180 • Total Fat 6g • Saturated Fat 1g • Cholesterol 95mg • Sodium 430mg • Total Carbohydrate 10g • Dietary Fiber 2g • Sugars 5g • Protein 22g.
DIETARY EXCHANGES: 1/2 Starch • 1/2 Other Carbohydrate • 1 Vegetable • 2-1/2 Lean Meat.

slow-cooked paprika chicken with mashed potatoes

PREP TIME: 25 MINUTES
READY IN: 8 HOURS 25 MINUTES
SERVINGS: 6

1-1/4 lb. boneless skinless chicken thighs, cut into 3/4-inch pieces

1-1/2 cups sliced fresh carrots

1 medium onion, halved, sliced

1 medium green bell pepper, chopped

3 teaspoons paprika

1/2 teaspoon peppered seasoned salt

1 (10-3/4 oz.) can condensed cream of chicken soup

1 cup Green Giant® Frozen Sweet Peas, thawed

1/2 cup sour cream with chives

4 cups prepared mashed potatoes

Cooked real bacon pieces

1 In 3-1/2- or 4-quart slow cooker, combine chicken, carrots, onion, bell pepper, paprika, seasoned salt and soup; mix well.

2 Cover; cook on Low setting for 6 to 8 hours.

3 About 10 minutes before serving, stir thawed peas and sour cream into chicken mixture. Cover; cook an additional 10 minutes or until thoroughly heated. Serve chicken mixture with mashed potatoes; sprinkle with bacon if desired.

NUTRITIONAL INFORMATION PER SERVING:
Calories 440 • Total Fat 22g • Saturated Fat 7g • Cholesterol 75mg • Sodium 850mg • Total Carbohydrate 39g • Dietary Fiber 5g • Sugars 7g • Protein 26g.
DIETARY EXCHANGES: 2 Starch • 2 Other Carbohydrate • 3 Lean Meat • 2-1/2 Fat.

country-style ribs and sauerkraut

PREP TIME: 10 MINUTES
READY IN: 10 HOURS 10 MINUTES
SERVINGS: 6

2 lb. boneless country-style pork loin ribs

1 medium cooking apple, sliced

1 small onion, sliced

1 (16 oz.) can sauerkraut, drained, rinsed

3 tablespoons brown sugar

1 teaspoon caraway seed

1/4 cup dry white wine or apple juice

1 Place pork ribs, apple and onion in 3-1/2- to 4-quart slow cooker. Top with sauerkraut, brown sugar and caraway seed; mix lightly. Pour wine over top.

2 Cover; cook on Low setting for 8 to 10 hours.

NUTRITIONAL INFORMATION PER SERVING:
Calories 350 • Total Fat 18g • Saturated Fat 6g • Cholesterol 95mg • Sodium 560mg • Total Carbohydrate 15g • Dietary Fiber 3g • Sugars 11g • Protein 32g.
DIETARY EXCHANGES: 1 Starch • 1 Other Carbohydrate • 4 Medium-Fat Meat.

cheesy ravioli casserole

PREP TIME: 15 MINUTES
READY IN: 6 HOURS 45 MINUTES
SERVINGS: 10

1 tablespoon olive or vegetable oil

1/2 cup chopped onion

1 large garlic clove, minced

2 (26 oz.) jars four cheese-flavored tomato pasta sauce

1 (15 oz.) can tomato sauce

1 teaspoon dried Italian seasoning

2 (25 oz.) packages frozen beef-filled ravioli

2 cups shredded mozzarella cheese (8 oz.)

1/4 cup chopped fresh parsley

1 Spray 5- to 6-quart slow cooker with nonstick cooking spray. Heat oil in Dutch oven or 12-inch skillet over medium heat until hot. Add onion and garlic; cook about 4 minutes or until onion is tender, stirring occasionally. Stir in pasta sauce, tomato sauce and Italian seasoning.

2 Place 1 cup of the sauce mixture in sprayed slow cooker. Add 1 package frozen ravioli; top with 1 cup of the cheese. Top with remaining package of ravioli and 1 cup cheese. Pour remaining sauce mixture over top.

3 Cover; cook on Low setting for 5-1/2 to 6-1/2 hours. Sprinkle with parsley before serving.

NUTRITIONAL INFORMATION PER SERVING:
Calories 500 • Total Fat 19g • Saturated Fat 8g • Cholesterol 180mg • Sodium 2,100mg • Total Carbohydrate 57g • Dietary Fiber 4g • Sugars 12g • Protein 25g.
DIETARY EXCHANGES: 4 Starch • 4 Other Carbohydrate • 2 Medium-Fat Meat • 2 Fat.

italian tortellini stew

PREP TIME: 15 MINUTES
READY IN: 8 HOURS 15 MINUTES
SERVINGS: 8

1 small onion, finely chopped

2 medium zucchini, halved, cut into 1-inch slices

2 (14-1/2 oz.) cans ready-to-serve vegetable or chicken broth

1 (28 oz.) can crushed or diced tomatoes, undrained

1 (15.5 oz.) can great northern beans, drained, rinsed

1/4 teaspoon salt

1/4 teaspoon pepper

1 tablespoon dried basil leaves

1 (8 oz.) package uncooked dry cheese-filled tortellini

1 In 4- to 6-quart slow cooker, combine all ingredients except basil and tortellini; mix well.

2 Cover; cook on Low setting for 6 to 8 hours.

3 About 20 minutes before serving, stir basil and tortellini into stew. Increase heat setting to High; cover and cook an additional 20 minutes or until tortellini are tender.

NUTRITIONAL INFORMATION PER SERVING:
Calories 170 • Total Fat 3g • Saturated Fat 1g • Cholesterol 4mg • Sodium 760mg • Total Carbohydrate 26g • Dietary Fiber 5g • Sugars 4g • Protein 9g.
DIETARY EXCHANGES: 1-1/2 Starch • 1-1/2 Other Carbohydrate • 1 Vegetable • 1/2 Medium-Fat Meat.

TIP: Ladle the stew into sturdy serving bowls, and sprinkle it with freshly grated Parmesan cheese and chopped fresh basil. At the table, pass the pepper grinder.

cheesy ravioli casserole

slow-cooked chop suey over rice

PREP TIME: 30 MINUTES
READY IN: 7 HOURS 30 MINUTES
SERVINGS: 5

1 lb. boneless pork shoulder, cut into 3/4-inch cubes

1 small onion, cut into 1/4-inch wedges

1 (5 oz.) can sliced bamboo shoots, drained

1/2 cup purchased teriyaki baste and glaze

1 teaspoon grated gingerroot

1 (1 lb.) package Green Giant Select® Frozen Broccoli, Carrots and Water Chestnuts, thawed, drained

2 cups uncooked instant white rice

2 cups water

1 In 4- to 6-quart slow cooker, combine the pork, onion, bamboo shoots, teriyaki baste and glaze, and gingerroot; mix well.

2 Cover; cook on Low setting for 5 to 7 hours.

3 About 15 minutes before serving, stir vegetables into pork. Increase heat setting to High; cover and cook an additional 10 to 15 minutes or until vegetables are tender.

4 Meanwhile, cook rice in water as directed on package. Serve pork mixture over rice.

NUTRITIONAL INFORMATION PER SERVING: Calories 430 • Total Fat 14g • Saturated Fat 5g • Cholesterol 55mg • Sodium 1,180mg • Total Carbohydrate 54g • Dietary Fiber 3g • Sugars 16g • Protein 21g.
DIETARY EXCHANGES: 2-1/2 Starch • 1 Fruit • 3-1/2 Other Carbohydrate • 1 Vegetable • 2 Lean Meat • 1 Fat.

winter root and sausage casserole

PREP TIME: 20 MINUTES
READY IN: 9 HOURS 20 MINUTES
SERVINGS: 6

1 large baking potato, cut into 1/2-inch cubes

1 large dark-orange sweet potato, peeled, cut into 1/2-inch cubes

2 medium carrots, sliced

1 medium parsnip, sliced

1 medium onion, chopped

1 lb. smoked sausage, sliced

1 (14-1/2 oz.) can ready-to-serve chicken broth

1 (14.5 oz.) can chunky tomatoes with garlic and Italian herbs, undrained

2 teaspoons sugar

1/2 teaspoon dried thyme leaves

1/4 teaspoon pepper

1/4 cup chopped fresh parsley

1 In 3-1/2- to 4-quart slow cooker, combine all ingredients except the parsley; mix well.

2 Cover; cook on Low setting for 7 to 9 hours.

3 Just before serving, stir in the parsley.

NUTRITIONAL INFORMATION PER SERVING:
Calories 430 • Total Fat 25g • Saturated Fat 9g • Cholesterol 50mg • Sodium 1,520mg • Total Carbohydrate 29g • Dietary Fiber 4g • Sugars 8g • Protein 21g.
DIETARY EXCHANGES: 2 Starch • 2 Other Carbohydrate • 2 High-Fat Meat • 1-1/2 Fat.

slow-simmered beef stew

PREP TIME: 10 MINUTES
READY IN: 10 HOURS 10 MINUTES
SERVINGS: 4

1-1/2 cups fresh baby carrots

2 medium potatoes, peeled, cut into 1-inch pieces

1 medium stalk celery, cut into 1-inch pieces

1 (1.5 oz.) package beef stew seasoning

1 lb. beef stew meat

1 cup water

1 cup Green Giant® Niblets® Frozen Corn

1 cup Green Giant® Frozen Cut Green Beans

1 In 3-1/2- to 4-quart slow cooker, layer carrots, potatoes and celery. Place stew seasoning on waxed paper or in plastic bag. Add beef; coat with seasoning. Add beef to slow cooker; sprinkle with any remaining seasoning. Add water. Layer frozen corn and green beans on top.

2 Cover; cook on Low setting for 8 to 10 hours. Stir stew before serving.

NUTRITIONAL INFORMATION PER SERVING:
Calories 360 • Total Fat 13g • Saturated Fat 5g • Cholesterol 70mg • Sodium 910mg • Total Carbohydrate 33g • Dietary Fiber 4g • Sugars 5g • Protein 28g.
DIETARY EXCHANGES: 2 Starch • 2 Other Carbohydrate • 1 Vegetable • 3 Lean Meat • 1 Fat.

gingered pork and ramen noodles

PREP TIME: 30 MINUTES
READY IN: 8 HOURS 30 MINUTES
SERVINGS: 4

2 (3 oz.) packages chicken-flavor ramen noodle soup mix

1 lb. boneless pork shoulder roast, cut into 1-inch pieces

1 teaspoon grated gingerroot

3 cups water

1 cup halved fresh snow pea pods (about 4 oz.)

1/4 cup sliced green onions

1 tablespoon soy sauce

2 teaspoons cornstarch

1 Reserve noodles from soup mixes. In 3-1/2- to 4-quart slow cooker, combine pork and contents of seasoning packets from noodle soup mixes; mix well. Add gingerroot and water; stir to mix.

2 Cover; cook on Low setting for 6 to 8 hours.

3 About 25 minutes before serving, break reserved noodles into pieces; add to pork mixture. Add pea pods and onions; mix well. Increase heat setting to High; cover and cook an additional 10 to 15 minutes or just until the vegetables are crisp-tender.

4 In small bowl, blend soy sauce and cornstarch until smooth. Stir into pork mixture. Cover; cook about 5 minutes or until sauce is slightly thickened.

NUTRITIONAL INFORMATION PER SERVING: Calories 285 • Total Fat 18g • Saturated Fat 7g • Cholesterol 80mg • Sodium 390mg • Total Carbohydrate 8g • Dietary Fiber 1g • Sugars 1g • Protein 23g.
DIETARY EXCHANGES: 1/2 Starch • 1/2 Other Carbohydrate • 3 Lean Meat • 2 Fat.

chicken and vegetable pot pies

PREP TIME: 40 MINUTES
READY IN: 7 HOURS 40 MINUTES
SERVINGS: 4

1-1/4 lb. boneless skinless chicken thighs, cut into 1-inch pieces

1 (.9 oz.) package roasted chicken gravy mix

1 cup fresh baby carrots, cut in half lengthwise

1 (4.5 oz.) jar Green Giant® Sliced Mushrooms, drained

1 cup chicken broth

1/4 cup dry white wine or water

2 cups frozen southern-style cubed hash-brown potatoes (from 32 oz. pkg.), thawed

1 cup Green Giant® Frozen Sweet Peas, thawed

1/8 teaspoon pepper

4 Pillsbury® Home Baked Classics™ Frozen Buttermilk Biscuits (from 25 oz. pkg.)

2 teaspoons milk

1/2 teaspoon dried dill weed

1 Place chicken in 3-1/2- to 4-quart slow cooker. Sprinkle with gravy mix; mix lightly to coat. Top with carrots and mushrooms. Pour broth and wine over top.

2 Cover; cook on Low setting for 5 to 7 hours.

3 About 30 minutes before serving, add potatoes, peas and pepper to chicken mixture; stir gently to mix. Increase heat setting to High; cover and cook an additional 25 to 30 minutes or until peas are tender.

4 Meanwhile, heat oven to 375°F. Place frozen biscuits on ungreased cookie sheet. Brush tops with milk; sprinkle with dill weed. Bake as directed on package.

5 To serve, spoon chicken mixture into individual serving bowls. Top each with a biscuit.

NUTRITIONAL INFORMATION PER SERVING: Calories 560 • Total Fat 22g • Saturated Fat 6g • Cholesterol 90mg • Sodium 1,480mg • Total Carbohydrate 56g • Dietary Fiber 6g • Sugars 8g • Protein 40g.
DIETARY EXCHANGES: 4 Starch • 4 Other Carbohydrate • 4 Lean Meat • 2 Fat.

easy italian meatball stew

PREP TIME: 10 MINUTES
READY IN: 8 HOURS 10 MINUTES
SERVINGS: 4

- 1 (16 oz.) package frozen cooked Italian meatballs, thawed
- 1 cup frozen pearl onions
- 1/2 teaspoon salt
- 2 (14.5 oz.) cans diced tomatoes with Italian-style herbs, undrained
- 2 tablespoons Pillsbury BEST® All-Purpose Flour
- 2 tablespoons water
- 2-1/2 cups frozen bell pepper and onion stir fry, thawed, drained
- 1/4 cup shredded fresh Parmesan cheese (1 oz.)

1 In 3-1/2- to 4-quart slow cooker, combine the meatballs, onions, salt and tomatoes; mix well.

2 Cover; cook on Low setting for 6 to 8 hours.

3 About 20 minutes before serving, in small bowl, blend flour and water until smooth. Stir flour mixture into stew. Stir in bell pepper and onion stir fry. Increase heat setting to High; cover and cook an additional 15 to 20 minutes or until stew has thickened and bell peppers are thoroughly heated. Sprinkle individual servings with cheese.

NUTRITIONAL INFORMATION PER SERVING: Calories 495 • Total Fat 25g • Saturated Fat 10g • Cholesterol 145mg • Sodium 1,480mg • Total Carbohydrate 36g • Dietary Fiber 4g • Sugars 10g • Protein 32g.
DIETARY EXCHANGES: 2 Starch • 2 Other Carbohydrate • 2 Vegetable • 3 Medium-Fat Meat • 2 Fat.

winter pork roast dinner

PREP TIME: 20 MINUTES
READY IN: 8 HOUR 20 MINUTES
SERVINGS: 6

- 1 rolled boneless pork loin roast (1-3/4 to 2 lb.)
- 1 teaspoon salt
- 1/4 teaspoon pepper
- 3 large dark-orange sweet potatoes, peeled, thinly sliced
- 1 medium onion, sliced, separated into rings
- 1-1/2 teaspoons dried thyme leaves
- 4 cups apple juice (1 quart)

1 Sprinkle pork roast with 1/2 teaspoon of the salt and the pepper; place in 4- to 5-quart slow cooker. Place sweet potatoes around and on top of roast. Top with onion; sprinkle with thyme and remaining 1/2 teaspoon salt. Pour apple juice over onion.

2 Cover; cook on Low setting for 6 to 8 hours.

3 With slotted spoon, remove vegetables from slow cooker; place on serving platter. Remove roast from slow cooker; place on cutting board. Cut roast into slices; place on platter. If desired, drizzle some of the cooking liquid from slow cooker over vegetables and roast.

NUTRITIONAL INFORMATION PER SERVING: Calories 390 • Total Fat 11g • Saturated Fat 4g • Cholesterol 85mg • Sodium 460mg • Total Carbohydrate 43g • Dietary Fiber 3g • Sugars 30g • Protein 31g.
DIETARY EXCHANGES: 1-1/2 Starch • 1/2 Fruit • 3-1/2 Very Lean Meat • 1-1/2 Fat.

short rib dinner

short rib dinner

PREP TIME: 35 MINUTES
READY IN: 10 HOURS 35 MINUTES
SERVINGS: 4

2 lb. beef short ribs, cut into individual rib sections

1/2 large onion, cut into 4 wedges

2 sun-dried tomato halves (not oil-packed), cut into thin strips

4 medium carrots, cut in half lengthwise and crosswise

8 small red potatoes (1 lb.)

1 garlic clove, minced

1/2 cup dry red wine or water

1 cup water

1 teaspoon beef-flavor instant bouillon

1/2 teaspoon salt

1/2 teaspoon dried thyme leaves

1/2 teaspoon dried basil leaves

1/4 teaspoon pepper

2 tablespoons Pillsbury BEST® All-Purpose Flour

1 Brown beef ribs in large nonstick skillet over medium-high heat until browned on all sides, turning frequently.

2 Meanwhile, in 4- to 6-quart slow cooker, layer the onion, tomato, carrots, potatoes and minced garlic.

3 Spoon browned beef into slow cooker. Drain off any fat from skillet; add wine, 1/2 cup water and bouillon to skillet. Cook over medium heat until mixture comes to a boil, stirring occasionally. Sprinkle beef with salt, thyme, basil and pepper. Pour hot wine mixture over beef.

4 Cover; cook on Low setting for 8 to 10 hours.

5 About 15 minutes before serving, with slotted spoon, remove beef and vegetables from slow cooker; place in serving bowl. Skim off fat from cooking juices in slow cooker.

6 In 4-cup glass measuring cup or medium bowl, blend remaining 1/2 cup water and flour until smooth. Pour juices from slow cooker into flour mixture; mix well. Microwave on High for 3 to 4 minutes or until mixture boils, stirring once halfway through cooking. Pour sauce over beef and vegetables.

NUTRITIONAL INFORMATION PER SERVING:
Calories 335 • Total Fat 13g • Saturated Fat 5g • Cholesterol 50mg • Sodium 700mg • Total Carbohydrate 35g • Dietary Fiber 4g • Sugars 6g • Protein 20g.
DIETARY EXCHANGES: 2 Starch • 2 Other Carbohydrate • 2 Medium-Fat Meat • 1/2 Fat.

rosemary beef and tomatoes over noodles

PREP TIME: 20 MINUTES
READY IN: 10 HOURS 20 MINUTES
SERVINGS: 4

2 tablespoons margarine or butter, melted

1 medium onion, chopped

1 teaspoon beef base

1/2 teaspoon salt

1/4 teaspoon pepper

1-1/2 lb. beef stew meat, cut into 1-1/2-inch cubes

8 oz. uncooked wide egg noodles (4-1/2 cups)

4 Italian plum tomatoes, chopped

1 tablespoon chopped fresh rosemary

1 In 4- to 6-quart slow cooker, combine margarine, onion, beef base, salt, pepper and beef; mix well.

2 Cover; cook on Low setting for 9 to 10 hours.

3 About 15 minutes before serving, cook noodles as directed on package. Meanwhile, add tomatoes and rosemary to beef mixture; mix well. Increase heat setting to High; cover and cook an additional 10 minutes. Serve beef mixture over noodles.

NUTRITIONAL INFORMATION PER SERVING:
Calories 530 • Total Fat 18g • Saturated Fat 5g • Cholesterol 170mg • Sodium 650mg • Total Carbohydrate 46g • Dietary Fiber 3g • Sugars 5g • Protein 47g.
DIETARY EXCHANGES: 3 Starch • 3 Other Carbohydrate • 5-1/2 Lean Meat.

beef roast and vegetables with horseradish gravy

PREP TIME: 25 MINUTES
READY IN: 9 HOURS 25 MINUTES
SERVINGS: 6

1 (3 lb.) boneless beef
  rump or tip roast,
  trimmed of fat

1 garlic clove, slivered

3 tablespoons creamy
  horseradish

1 (.87 oz.) package brown
  gravy mix

3 medium carrots, cut in
  half lengthwise and into
  2-inch pieces

6 to 8 small red potatoes (1
  lb.), scrubbed, quartered

1 medium stalk celery, cut
  in half lengthwise and into
  2-inch pieces

1/2 cup water

1/2 teaspoon salt

  Dash coarse ground black
  pepper

2 tablespoons cornstarch

3 tablespoons water

1 With tip of knife, make cuts
in top of beef roast; insert
garlic slivers. Spread beef with 1
tablespoon of the horseradish.
Sprinkle with 1/2 teaspoon of
the gravy mix. Place beef in
3-1/2- or 4-quart slow cooker.
Arrange carrots around beef. Top
with potatoes and celery.

2 In small bowl, combine 1/2
cup water, remaining gravy
mix, salt and pepper; mix until
well blended. Pour over the
vegetables.

3 Cover; cook on Low setting
for 8 to 9 hours.

4 Just before serving, remove
beef and vegetables from
slow cooker; place on serving
platter and cover to keep warm.
In medium saucepan, combine
cornstarch, 3 tablespoons water
and remaining 2 tablespoons

horseradish; blend well. Pour
juices from slow cooker into
cornstarch mixture; mix well.
Bring to a boil over medium-
high heat, stirring constantly.
Cut beef into slices. Serve beef
with vegetables and gravy.

NUTRITIONAL INFORMATION PER SERVING:
Calories 360 • Total Fat 8g • Saturated Fat
3g • Cholesterol 120mg • Sodium 560mg •
Total Carbohydrate 24g • Dietary Fiber 2g •
Sugars 3g • Protein 48g.
DIETARY EXCHANGES: 1-1/2 Starch • 6
Very Lean Meat • 1 Fat.

slow-cooked lasagna

PREP TIME: 20 MINUTES
READY IN: 4 HOURS 50 MINUTES
SERVINGS: 8

1 lb. lean ground beef

1 (26 to 28 oz.) jar tomato pasta sauce

1 (8 oz.) can no-salt-added tomato sauce

1/2 (9 oz.) package no-boil lasagna noodles (about 8)

1 (1 lb.) jar Alfredo pasta sauce

3 cups shredded mozzarella cheese (12 oz.)

1/4 cup grated Parmesan cheese

1 Brown ground beef in large skillet over medium-high heat until thoroughly cooked, stirring frequently. Drain.

2 Spray 4- to 5-quart slow cooker with nonstick cooking spray. Spread 3/4 cup of the tomato pasta sauce in bottom of sprayed slow cooker. Stir remaining tomato pasta sauce and tomato sauce into ground beef.

3 Layer 3 lasagna noodles over sauce in slow cooker, breaking noodles as necessary. Top with 1/3 of the Alfredo pasta sauce, spreading evenly. Sprinkle with 1 cup of the mozzarella cheese. Top with 1/3 of the ground beef mixture, spreading evenly.

4 Repeat layering twice, using 2 lasagna noodles in last layer. Sprinkle Parmesan cheese over top.

5 Cover; cook on Low setting for 3-1/2 to 4-1/2 hours. If desired, cut into wedges to serve.

NUTRITIONAL INFORMATION PER SERVING: Calories 620 • Total Fat 38g • Saturated Fat 20g • Cholesterol 115mg • Sodium 1,010mg • Total Carbohydrate 37g • Dietary Fiber 2g • Sugars 9g • Protein 32g. DIETARY EXCHANGES: 1 Starch • 1-1/2 Other Carbohydrate • 4 Medium-Fat Meat • 3-1/2 Fat.

rolled pork tenderloin and sweet potatoes for two

PREP TIME: 20 MINUTES
READY IN: 5 HOURS 20 MINUTES
SERVINGS: 2

2 tablespoons brown sugar

1/2 teaspoon Caribbean jerk seasoning

1 (3/4 lb.) pork tenderloin

1 small apple, thinly sliced

2 tablespoons sweetened dried cranberries

1 large (1 lb.) dark-orange sweet potato, peeled, cut into 1/2-inch-thick slices

2 tablespoons water

2 teaspoons Pillsbury BEST® All-Purpose Flour

1 Spray 2-1/2- to 3-1/2-quart slow cooker with nonstick cooking spray. In small bowl, combine the brown sugar and the Caribbean jerk seasoning; mix well.

2 Place pork tenderloin between 2 sheets of waxed paper or plastic wrap. Pound with rolling pin or flat side of meat mallet until 1/2 inch thick. Sprinkle pork with 1 teaspoon brown sugar mixture. Top evenly with apple slices and cranberries. Starting with one short side, roll up, tucking in fruit while rolling. Secure with kitchen string.

3 Place sweet potato slices in sprayed slow cooker. Top with pork roll. Sprinkle pork and sweet potatoes with remaining brown sugar mixture.

4 Cover; cook on Low setting for 4 to 5 hours.

5 About 5 minutes before serving, in 1-cup microwave-safe measuring cup, combine water and flour; blend well. Remove pork from slow cooker; place on cutting board. Remove sweet potatoes from slow cooker; place on serving platter. Pour juices from slow cooker into flour mixture; mix well. Microwave on High for 30 to 60 seconds or until mixture boils and thickens slightly, stirring once halfway through cooking. Cut pork into slices; place over sweet potatoes on platter. Pour sauce over top. If desired, add salt and pepper to taste.

NUTRITIONAL INFORMATION PER SERVING: Calories 505 • Total Fat 7g • Saturated Fat 2g • Cholesterol 110mg • Sodium 100mg • Total Carbohydrate 73g • Dietary Fiber 7g • Sugars 52g • Protein 42g.
DIETARY EXCHANGES: 1-1/2 Starch • 1/2 Fruit • 2-1/2 Other Carbohydrate • 5-1/2 Very Lean Meat • 1/2 Fat.

southwestern chicken and bean stew

PREP TIME: 20 MINUTES
READY IN: 20 HOURS 20 MINUTES
SERVINGS: 6

1 cup dried pinto beans

2 lb. cut-up frying chicken, skin removed

1 cup Green Giant® Niblets® Frozen Corn

1 cup Old El Paso® Salsa

1 (14-1/2 oz.) can ready-to-serve chicken broth

1 (4.5 oz.) can Old El Paso® Chopped Green Chiles

1 teaspoon cumin

2 tablespoons chopped fresh cilantro

1 Place beans in medium bowl; add enough water to cover. Let beans stand overnight to soak.

2 Drain beans; discard water. Place beans and all remaining ingredients except cilantro in 3-1/2- to 4-quart slow cooker; mix well.

3 Cover; cook on Low setting for 10 to 12 hours.

4 To serve, remove chicken from slow cooker with slotted spoon. Remove chicken from bones; discard bones. Cut chicken into pieces; return chicken to slow cooker. Add cilantro; mix well.

NUTRITIONAL INFORMATION PER SERVING: Calories 250 • Total Fat 5g • Saturated Fat 1g • Cholesterol 45mg • Sodium 650mg • Total Carbohydrate 29g • Dietary Fiber 9g • Sugars 3g • Protein 23g.
DIETARY EXCHANGES: 2 Starch • 2 Other Carbohydrate • 2-1/2 Very Lean Meat.

chicken and vegetable tortellini stew

PREP TIME: 35 MINUTES
READY IN: 8 HOURS 35 MINUTES
SERVINGS: 6

2 medium carrots, sliced (about 3/4 cup)

2 garlic cloves, minced

1 lb. boneless skinless chicken thighs, cut into 3/4-inch pieces

1 medium fennel bulb, chopped

1 (19 oz.) can cannellini beans, drained, rinsed

1/2 teaspoon salt

1/4 teaspoon pepper

1 (14 oz.) can chicken broth

2 cups water

1 (9 oz.) package refrigerated cheese-filled tortellini

1 cup firmly packed fresh baby spinach leaves

2 green onions, sliced

1 teaspoon dried basil leaves

2 tablespoons shredded fresh Parmesan cheese

1 In 3-1/2- to 4-quart slow cooker, layer carrots, garlic, chicken, fennel and beans. Sprinkle with salt and pepper. Pour broth and water over top. Stir to combine.

2 Cover; cook on Low setting for 6 to 8 hours.

3 About 20 minutes before serving, stir tortellini, spinach, onions and basil into chicken mixture. Increase heat setting to High; cover and cook 15 to 20 minutes or until tortellini are tender. Sprinkle individual servings with Parmesan cheese.

NUTRITIONAL INFORMATION PER SERVING: Calories 325 • Total Fat 11g • Saturated Fat 4g • Cholesterol 85mg • Sodium 850mg • Total Carbohydrate 34g • Dietary Fiber 8g • Sugars 3g • Protein 30g.
DIETARY EXCHANGES: 2 Starch • 2 Other Carbohydrate • 3-1/2 Lean Meat.

cheesy ham au gratin

PREP TIME: 10 MINUTES
READY IN: 8 HOURS 10 MINUTES
SERVINGS: 10

3 cups milk

1 (10-3/4 oz.) can condensed Cheddar cheese soup

2 (5 oz.) packages cheesy scalloped potatoes with skin-on potatoes

2 cups diced cooked ham

2 (11 oz.) cans Green Giant® Mexicorn® Whole Kernel Corn, Red and Green Peppers, drained

2 cups boiling water

1 Spray 3-1/2- to 4-quart slow cooker with nonstick cooking spray. In large bowl, combine milk, soup and contents of seasoning packets from potatoes; blend well. Add potatoes, ham and corn; mix well. Pour mixture into sprayed slow cooker. Pour boiling water over potato mixture; stir to mix.

2 Cover; cook on Low setting for 7 to 8 hours.

NUTRITIONAL INFORMATION PER SERVING: Calories 270 • Total Fat 8g • Saturated Fat 3g • Cholesterol 25mg • Sodium 1,350mg • Total Carbohydrate 36g • Dietary Fiber 2g • Sugars 6g • Protein 13g.
DIETARY EXCHANGES: 2-1/2 Starch • 2-1/2 Other Carbohydrate • 1 Lean Meat • 1 Fat.

beef and barley stew

PREP TIME: 15 MINUTES
READY IN: 12 HOURS 15 MINUTES
SERVINGS: 5

1 lb. boneless beef round steak (1/2 inch thick), trimmed of fat, cut into 3/4-inch pieces

2 cups Green Giant® Frozen Cut Green Beans

1 cup shredded carrots (1 to 2 medium)

1/2 cup uncooked regular pearl barley

1 (4.5 oz.) jar Green Giant® Sliced Mushrooms, drained

1 (12 oz.) jar mushroom gravy

2-1/2 cups water

2 teaspoons beef-flavor instant bouillon

1/2 teaspoon dried thyme leaves

1/4 teaspoon pepper

1 In 3-1/2- or 4-quart slow cooker, combine all ingredients; mix well.

2 Cover; cook on Low setting for 10 to 12 hours.

NUTRITIONAL INFORMATION PER SERVING: Calories 290 • Total Fat 12g • Saturated Fat 4g • Cholesterol 55mg • Sodium 1,110mg • Total Carbohydrate 27g • Dietary Fiber 5g • Sugars 4g • Protein 24g.
DIETARY EXCHANGES: 1 Starch • 1 Vegetable • 3 Lean Meat • 1/2 Fat.

SIMPLE SUBSTITUTION: Don't have the round steak this recipe calls for? Looking to beat the kitchen clock on a busy weeknight? Try using 1 pound of cubed beef stew meat instead. You can also replace some of the vegetables with any leftovers you might have sitting in the refrigerator.

turkey and stuffing with onion glaze

PREP TIME: 15 MINUTES
READY IN: 6 HOURS 15 MINUTES
SERVINGS: 5

1 tablespoon margarine or butter

1/2 cup chopped onion

1 tablespoon apple jelly

1 (6 oz.) package turkey-flavor one-step stuffing mix

3/4 cup water

1 (2 to 2-1/2 lb.) boneless skinless turkey breast half

Salt

Pepper

1 Melt margarine in medium skillet over medium heat. Add onion; cook 4 to 5 minutes or until tender and lightly browned, stirring occasionally. Stir jelly into onion mixture. Cook an additional 1 to 2 minutes or until golden brown, stirring occasionally.

2 Meanwhile, spray 4- to 6-quart slow cooker with nonstick cooking spray. Place stuffing mix in sprayed slow cooker. Drizzle with water; mix gently. Sprinkle turkey breast half with salt and pepper. Place over the stuffing mix. Spoon onion mixture over turkey; spread evenly.

3 Cover; cook on Low setting for 5 to 6 hours.

4 Cut turkey into slices. Serve stuffing topped with the turkey slices.

NUTRITIONAL INFORMATION PER SERVING: Calories 400 • Total Fat 7g • Saturated Fat 1g • Cholesterol 150mg • Sodium 790mg • Total Carbohydrate 27g • Dietary Fiber 2g • Sugars 5g • Protein 58g.
DIETARY EXCHANGES: 2 Starch • 2 Other Carbohydrate • 7-1/2 Very Lean Meat.

beef and barley stew

layered enchilada dinner

PREP TIME: 30 MINUTES
READY IN: 6 HOURS
SERVINGS: 6

1 lb. lean ground beef

1 small onion, chopped (about 1/3 cup)

1 garlic clove, minced

1 (10-3/4 oz.) can condensed cream of mushroom soup

1 (4.5 oz.) can Old El Paso® Chopped Green Chiles

1 (10 oz.) can Old El Paso® Enchilada Sauce

10 (6-inch) corn tortillas

3 cups shredded Monterey Jack cheese (12 oz.)

Paprika

Chopped fresh cilantro

1 In large skillet, cook ground beef, onion and minced garlic over medium-high heat until browned and thoroughly cooked, stirring frequently. Drain. Stir in soup and chiles.

2 Spray 3-1/2- or 4-quart slow cooker with nonstick cooking spray. Spread about 1/4 cup of the enchilada sauce in bottom of slow cooker. Place 4 corn tortillas over sauce, overlapping and breaking in half as necessary to make an even layer. Top with 1/3 of beef mixture, spreading evenly. Drizzle with about 1/4 cup enchilada sauce. Sprinkle with 1 cup of the cheese.

3 Repeat layering twice, using 3 corn tortillas and half of remaining beef mixture, enchilada sauce and cheese in each layer. Sprinkle paprika over top.

4 Cover; cook on Low setting for 4-1/2 to 5-1/2 hours.

5 Let stand about 5 minutes before serving. Sprinkle individual servings with cilantro.

NUTRITIONAL INFORMATION PER SERVING:
Calories 530 • Total Fat 32g • Saturated Fat 16g • Cholesterol 95mg • Sodium 1,050mg • Total Carbohydrate 29g • Dietary Fiber 3g • Sugars 4g • Protein 32g.
DIETARY EXCHANGES: 2 Starch • 3-1/2 Medium-Fat Meat • 2-1/2 Fat.

chicken and vegetables with pineapple

PREP TIME: 20 MINUTES
READY IN: 5 HOURS 45 MINUTES
SERVINGS: 6

1-1/4 lb. boneless skinless chicken thighs, cut into 1/2-inch strips

2 tablespoons soy sauce

2 medium carrots, sliced (about 3/4 cup)

1 (8 oz.) can sliced water chestnuts, drained

1 (8 oz.) can pineapple chunks in unsweetened juice, drained, reserving juice

2 cups uncooked regular long-grain white rice

4 cups water

1/2 cup purchased sweet-and-sour sauce

2 teaspoons cornstarch

1 teaspoon grated gingerroot

1-1/2 cups fresh snow pea pods (about 6 oz.)

3 green onions, cut into 1-inch pieces, if desired

1 In 3-1/2- to 4-quart slow cooker, combine chicken and soy sauce; mix to coat evenly. Add carrots, water chestnuts and reserved pineapple juice. Stir to combine.

2 Cover; cook on Low setting for 4 to 5 hours.

3 About 30 minutes before serving, cook rice in water as directed on package.

4 Meanwhile, in small bowl, combine sweet-and-sour sauce, cornstarch and gingerroot; stir until well blended. Stir into chicken mixture. Add pea pods, onions if desired and pineapple chunks; stir gently to mix. Increase heat setting to High; cover and cook an additional 20 to 25 minutes or until pea pods are crisp-tender. Serve chicken mixture over rice.

NUTRITIONAL INFORMATION PER SERVING: Calories 490 • Total Fat 9g • Saturated Fat 3g • Cholesterol 60mg • Sodium 450mg • Total Carbohydrate 75g • Dietary Fiber 3g • Sugars 12g • Protein 27g.
DIETARY EXCHANGES: 5 Starch • 5 Other Carbohydrate • 1-1/2 Lean Meat • 1 Fat.

TIP: Grate peeled gingerroot on the smallest holes of the grater. Freeze remaining (unpeeled and tightly wrapped) gingerroot in an airtight container for up to 6 months. Grate frozen gingerroot without thawing or peeling it.

seafood stew

PREP TIME: 20 MINUTES
READY IN: 5 HOURS 5 MINUTES
SERVINGS: 8

- 2 cups chopped onions
- 2 medium stalks celery, finely chopped (1 cup)
- 5 garlic cloves, minced
- 1 (28 oz.) can diced tomatoes, undrained
- 1 (8 oz.) bottle clam juice
- 1 (6 oz.) can tomato paste
- 1/2 cup dry white wine or water
- 1 tablespoon red wine vinegar
- 1 tablespoon olive or vegetable oil
- 2-1/2 teaspoons dried Italian seasoning
- 1/4 teaspoon sugar
- 1/4 teaspoon crushed red pepper flakes
- 1 bay leaf
- 1 lb. firm-fleshed white fish, cut into 1-inch pieces
- 3/4 lb. shelled deveined uncooked medium shrimp, tails removed
- 1 (6-1/2 oz.) can chopped clams with juice, undrained
- 1 (6 oz.) can crabmeat, drained
- 1/4 cup chopped fresh parsley

1 In 5- to 6-quart slow cooker, combine onions, celery, garlic, tomatoes, clam juice, tomato paste, wine, vinegar, oil, Italian seasoning, sugar, pepper flakes and bay leaf; mix well.

2 Cover; cook on High setting for 4 hours.

3 Stir fish, shrimp, clams with juice and crabmeat into stew. Reduce heat setting to Low; cover and cook an additional 30 to 45 minutes or until fish flakes easily with fork.

4 Just before serving, remove and discard the bay leaf. Stir in parsley.

NUTRITIONAL INFORMATION PER SERVING:
Calories 215 • Total Fat 4g • Saturated Fat 1g • Cholesterol 125mg • Sodium 610mg • Total Carbohydrate 15g • Dietary Fiber 3g • Sugars 5g • Protein 30g.
DIETARY EXCHANGES: 1/2 Other Carbohydrate • 1 Vegetable • 4 Very Lean Meat • 1/2 Fat.

TIP: Ladle out large bowls of steaming-hot stew with flat bread, crusty French bread or crackers. Cantaloupe wedges alongside vanilla ice cream make an easy, weeknight dessert.

slow-cooked chicken cacciatore

PREP TIME: 35 MINUTES
READY IN: 8 HOURS 35 MINUTES
SERVINGS: 4

- 4 bone-in chicken thighs, skin removed
- 4 chicken drumsticks, skin removed
- 1 (15 oz.) can Italian-style tomato sauce
- 1 (4.5 oz.) jar Green Giant® Whole Mushrooms, drained
- 1 teaspoon dried oregano leaves
- 1 small onion, sliced
- 1 small green bell pepper, cut into 1-inch pieces
- 2 garlic cloves, minced
- 1/4 cup water
- 2 tablespoons Pillsbury BEST® All-Purpose Flour

1 In 3-1/2- to 4-quart slow cooker, combine all ingredients except water and flour; stir gently to mix.

2 Cover; cook on Low setting for 6 to 8 hours.

3 About 15 minutes before serving, with slotted spoon, remove chicken and vegetables; place in serving bowl. Cover to keep warm.

4 In small bowl, blend water and flour until smooth. Stir into liquid in slow cooker. Increase heat setting to High; cover and cook an additional 5 to 10 minutes or until thickened. Stir well; spoon mixture over chicken and vegetables. If desired, serve with hot cooked pasta or rice.

NUTRITIONAL INFORMATION PER SERVING: Calories 250 • Total Fat 8g • Saturated Fat 2g • Cholesterol 90mg • Sodium 850mg • Total Carbohydrate 15g • Dietary Fiber 3g • Sugars 6g • Protein 30g.
DIETARY EXCHANGES: 1/2 Starch • 1/2 Other Carbohydrate • 1 Vegetable • 3-1/2 Lean Meat.

cajun pot roast with corn and tomatoes

PREP TIME: 10 MINUTES
READY IN: 10 HOURS 10 MINUTES
SERVINGS: 6

- 1 (2 to 2-1/2 lb.) boneless beef chuck roast
- 1 tablespoon dried Cajun seasoning
- 1 (9 oz.) package Green Giant® Niblets® Frozen Corn
- 1/2 cup chopped onion
- 1/2 cup chopped green bell pepper
- 1 (14.5 oz.) can diced tomatoes, undrained
- 1/8 teaspoon pepper
- 1/2 teaspoon hot pepper sauce

1 Rub entire surface of beef roast with Cajun seasoning. Place roast in 4- to 6-quart slow cooker. Top with corn, onion and bell pepper.

2 In small bowl, combine tomatoes, pepper and hot pepper sauce; mix well. Pour over vegetables and roast.

3 Cover; cook on Low setting for 8 to 10 hours.

4 To serve, cut roast into slices. Serve corn mixture with slotted spoon.

NUTRITIONAL INFORMATION PER SERVING: Calories 270 • Total Fat 9g • Saturated Fat 3g • Cholesterol 105mg • Sodium 580mg • Total Carbohydrate 12g • Dietary Fiber 2g • Sugars 4g • Protein 36g.
DIETARY EXCHANGES: 1 Starch • 1 Other Carbohydrate • 4 Very Lean Meat • 1 Fat.

slow-and-easy chicken alfredo

slow-and-easy chicken alfredo

PREP TIME: 25 MINUTES
READY IN: 6 HOURS 25 MINUTES
SERVINGS: 5

1-1/4 lb. boneless skinless chicken thighs, cut into 3/4-inch pieces

1 (4.5 oz.) jar Green Giant® Sliced Mushrooms, drained

1/2 cup roasted red bell pepper strips (from a jar)

2 tablespoons dry sherry

1 (16 oz.) jar Alfredo sauce

3 cups Green Giant® Frozen Broccoli Cuts

10 oz. uncooked fettuccine

2 tablespoons shredded fresh Parmesan cheese

1 In 3-1/2- to 4-quart slow cooker, layer chicken, mushrooms and roasted pepper strips. Drizzle with sherry if desired. Evenly pour Alfredo sauce on top.

2 Cover; cook on Low setting for 5 to 6 hours.

3 About 25 minutes before serving, rinse broccoli with warm water to thaw; drain well. Add broccoli to chicken mixture. Increase heat setting to High; cover and cook an additional 20 minutes. Meanwhile, cook fettuccine to desired doneness as directed on package. Drain.

4 Just before serving, stir cooked fettuccine into chicken mixture. Sprinkle with Parmesan cheese.

NUTRITIONAL INFORMATION PER SERVING: Calories 745 • Total Fat 43g • Saturated Fat 23g • Cholesterol 215mg • Sodium 660mg • Total Carbohydrate 51g • Dietary Fiber 5g • Sugars 4g • Protein 44g.
DIETARY EXCHANGES: 3 Starch • 3 Other Carbohydrate • 1 Vegetable • 4-1/2 Lean Meat • 6 Fat.

slow-cooked jambalaya-style red beans and rice

PREP TIME: 30 MINUTES
READY IN: 8 HOURS 30 MINUTES
SERVINGS: 8

1 medium onion, chopped

3/4 lb. boneless skinless chicken thighs, quartered

1 garlic clove, finely chopped

1 green bell pepper, chopped

2 bay leaves

1 (15.5 oz.) can red beans, drained, rinsed

1 (6 oz.) can tomato paste

1 (14.5 oz.) can diced tomatoes, undrained

1/2 teaspoon salt

1 (12 oz.) package frozen shelled deveined cooked small shrimp, thawed

1/2 lb. precooked kielbasa or Polish sausage, halved lengthwise, cut into 1-inch slices

4 cups uncooked instant white rice

4 cups water

1 In 4- to 6-quart slow cooker, layer all ingredients in order listed, except shrimp, sausage, rice and water.

2 Cover; cook on Low setting for 6 to 8 hours.

3 About 10 minutes before serving, gently stir shrimp and sausage into chicken mixture. Remove and discard bay leaves. Increase heat setting to High; cover and cook an additional 5 to 10 minutes or until shrimp and sausage are hot.

4 Meanwhile, cook rice in water as directed on package. Serve meat mixture over rice. If desired, serve with hot pepper sauce.

NUTRITIONAL INFORMATION PER SERVING: Calories 440 • Total Fat 12g • Saturated Fat 4g • Cholesterol 130mg • Sodium 900mg • Total Carbohydrate 56g • Dietary Fiber 5g • Sugars 4g • Protein 28g.
DIETARY EXCHANGES: 3-1/2 Starch • 3-1/2 Other Carbohydrate • 2-1/2 Lean Meat • 1/2 Fat.

make-ahead casseroles

Family-pleasing comfort awaits when you assemble a one-dish meal the night before. No matter how busy your schedule becomes, the following recipes deliver homespun flavor with time-saving convenience and stick-to-your-ribs results. Dig into creamy standbys including turkey tetrazzini, or surprise your loved ones with something new such as satisfying Make-Ahead Cheeseburger Lasagna.

Easy Cheese
Tortellini Alfredo
page 226

Pork Chops
with Apple-
Sage Stuffing
page 228

Artichoke and
Bacon Potato
Bake
page 230

overnight meatball and pasta casserole
page 227

shrimp and spinach strata

PREP TIME: 25 MINUTES
READY IN: 9 HOURS 40 MINUTES
SERVINGS: 8

10 to 12 (1/2-inch-thick) slices French bread

1/2 cup purchased pesto

2 cups shredded Gouda cheese (8 oz.)

1 lb. shelled deveined uncooked medium shrimp, tails removed

1 (1 lb.) package Green Giant® Frozen Cut Leaf Spinach, thawed, squeezed to drain well

1 (1 lb.) package frozen bell pepper and onion stir fry, thawed, drained

8 eggs

2 cups milk

1/2 teaspoon seasoned salt

1 Spray 13x9-inch (3-quart) glass baking dish with nonstick cooking spray. Arrange bread slices in bottom of sprayed baking dish. Cut cubes from bread to fill in empty spaces.

2 Spread pesto over bread. Sprinkle with 1 cup of the cheese. Layer shrimp, spinach, and bell pepper and onion stir fry, and remaining 1 cup cheese over bread.

3 In large bowl, beat eggs, milk and seasoned salt until well blended. Pour over mixture in baking dish. Cover with foil; refrigerate at least 8 hours or overnight.

4 Heat oven to 350°F. Uncover baking dish; bake 40 to 50 minutes or until set and knife inserted in center comes out clean. Let stand 15 minutes before serving.

HIGH ALTITUDE (3500-6500 FT):
Bake uncovered at 375°F for 40 to 50 minutes.

NUTRITIONAL INFORMATION PER SERVING:
Calories 420 • Total Fat 24g • Saturated Fat 9g • Cholesterol 330mg • Sodium 790mg • Total Carbohydrate 22g • Dietary Fiber 2g • Sugars 6g • Protein 29g.
DIETARY EXCHANGES: 1 Starch • 2 Vegetable • 3 Lean Meat • 3 Fat.

overnight mexican tortilla lasagna

PREP TIME: 25 MINUTES
READY IN: 9 HOURS 5 MINUTES
SERVINGS: 6

1/2 lb. extra-lean ground beef

1 cup chopped Italian plum tomatoes (3 medium)

1 cup julienne-cut zucchini (2x1/4x1/4-inch)

1/2 cup finely chopped green onions

1 (15 oz.) can black beans, drained, rinsed

1 (10 oz.) can Old El Paso® Enchilada Sauce

1 (8 oz.) container nonfat sour cream

1 teaspoon Old El Paso® 40% Less Sodium Taco Seasoning Mix (from 1.25 oz. pkg.)

8 (6-inch) corn tortillas, halved

1-1/2 cups shredded reduced-fat Cheddar cheese (6 oz.)

1/3 cup chopped fresh cilantro

1 Spray 13x9-inch (3-quart) glass baking dish with nonstick cooking spray. Brown ground beef in medium nonstick skillet over medium-high heat for 5 to 7 minutes or until thoroughly cooked, stirring frequently. Drain.

2 In medium bowl, combine tomatoes, zucchini, onions and beans; mix well. Stir in cooked ground beef. Reserve 1/3 cup enchilada sauce; set aside. In another medium bowl, combine remaining enchilada sauce, sour cream and taco seasoning mix.

3 Spoon 2 tablespoons enchilada sauce mixture in bottom of sprayed baking dish. Arrange 8 tortilla halves over sauce, overlapping as necessary. Spoon half of vegetable-bean mixture over tortillas. Sprinkle with 1/2 cup of the cheese. Spoon half of remaining sauce mixture over cheese. Repeat layers, reserving 1/2 cup cheese for top. Top with reserved 1/3 cup enchilada sauce. Cover with foil; refrigerate at least 8 hours or overnight.

4 Heat oven to 375°F. Bake casserole for 30 to 35 minutes or until thoroughly heated. Uncover; sprinkle with reserved 1/2 cup cheese. Bake uncovered an additional 5 minutes or until cheese is melted. Let stand 5 minutes before serving. Sprinkle with the cilantro.

HIGH ALTITUDE (3500-6500 FT): Increase first bake time to 35 to 40 minutes.

NUTRITIONAL INFORMATION PER SERVING: Calories 335 • Total Fat 8g • Saturated Fat 3g • Cholesterol 30mg • Sodium 780mg • Total Carbohydrate 47g • Dietary Fiber 7g • Sugars 9g • Protein 26g.
DIETARY EXCHANGES: 2-1/2 Starch • 2-1/2 Other Carbohydrate • 2-1/2 Lean Meat.

meatball and ravioli casserole

PREP TIME: 5 MINUTES
READY IN: 9 HOURS
SERVINGS: 4

1 (14.5 oz.) can diced tomatoes with Italian-style herbs, undrained

1 (12 oz.) jar beef gravy

1 teaspoon sugar

12 oz. frozen small round cheese-filled ravioli (about 22 ravioli)

18 frozen cooked Italian meatballs (about 8 oz.)

1-1/2 cups Green Giant® Frozen Mixed Vegetables

1 cup shredded mozzarella cheese (4 oz.)

1 Spray 12x9-inch sheet of foil with nonstick cooking spray. In large bowl, combine tomatoes, gravy and sugar; mix well. Add frozen ravioli, frozen meatballs and mixed vegetables; mix well. Spoon into ungreased 11x8-inch (2-quart) glass baking dish. Cover with foil, sprayed side down; refrigerate at least 8 hours or overnight.

2 Heat oven to 350°F. Bake covered for 40 minutes.

3 Uncover baking dish; sprinkle cheese evenly over top. Bake uncovered an additional 10 to 15 minutes or until bubbly and thoroughly heated.

HIGH ALTITUDE (3500-6500 FT): Bake covered at 350°F for 55 to 60 minutes. Continue as directed.

NUTRITIONAL INFORMATION PER SERVING: Calories 690 • Total Fat 36g • Saturated Fat 16g • Cholesterol 240mg • Sodium 2,230mg • Total Carbohydrate 47g • Dietary Fiber 5g • Sugars 10g • Protein 49g.
DIETARY EXCHANGES: 3 Starch • 5-1/2 Medium-Fat Meat • 1-1/2 Fat.

make-ahead cheeseburger lasagna

PREP TIME: 40 MINUTES
READY IN: 10 HOURS 10 MINUTES
SERVINGS: 8

1-1/2 lb. lean ground beef

3 tablespoons dried minced onion

1 (15 oz.) can tomato sauce

1-1/2 cups water

1/2 cup ketchup

1 tablespoon prepared mustard

1 egg

1 (15 oz.) container ricotta cheese

2 cups shredded Cheddar and American cheese blend (8 oz.)

12 uncooked lasagna noodles

1 cup shredded Cheddar cheese (4 oz.)

1 cup shredded lettuce

1 medium tomato, sliced

Dill pickle slices

1 Spray 13x9-inch (3-quart) glass baking dish and large nonstick skillet with nonstick cooking spray. In sprayed skillet, cook ground beef and onion over medium-high heat for 5 to 7 minutes or until beef is thoroughly cooked, stirring frequently. Add tomato sauce, water, ketchup and mustard; mix well. Simmer 5 minutes, stirring occasionally.

2 Meanwhile, beat egg in medium bowl. Add ricotta cheese and 2 cups of the cheese blend; mix well.

3 Spread 1 cup beef mixture in bottom of sprayed baking dish. Arrange 4 uncooked noodles over sauce. Spoon and spread half of ricotta cheese mixture over noodles; top with 1-1/2 cups beef mixture. Repeat layers once. Top with remaining 4 noodles, beef mixture and the 1 cup Cheddar cheese. Cover

with foil; refrigerate at least 8 hours or overnight.

4 When ready to bake, heat oven to 350°F. Bake lasagna covered for 45 minutes.

5 Uncover baking dish; bake an additional 25 to 35 minutes or until bubbly. Remove from the oven. Cover with foil; let stand 5 to 10 minutes before serving.

6 Just before serving, top with lettuce, tomato and pickle slices. If desired, serve with additional ketchup.

HIGH ALTITUDE (3500-6500 FT):
Increase water to 1-3/4 cups.

NUTRITIONAL INFORMATION PER SERVING:
Calories 585 • Total Fat 31g • Saturated Fat 16g • Cholesterol 135mg • Sodium 1,220mg • Total Carbohydrate 38g • Dietary Fiber 2g • Sugars 10g • Protein 38g.
DIETARY EXCHANGES: 2-1/2 Starch • 2-1/2 Other Carbohydrate • 4-1/2 Medium-Fat Meat • 1-1/2 Fat.

easy cheese tortellini alfredo

PREP TIME: 5 MINUTES
READY IN: 9 HOURS 10 MINUTES
SERVINGS: 6

1 (16 oz.) jar Alfredo pasta sauce

1-1/4 cups water

1/2 teaspoon dried basil leaves

1/4 teaspoon pepper

2 (9 oz.) packages refrigerated cheese-filled tortellini

1 (14 oz.) package Green Giant Select® Frozen Broccoli Florets

1 cup Parmesan croutons, slightly crushed

1 In large bowl, combine Alfredo pasta sauce, water, basil and pepper; mix well with wire whisk. Stir in tortellini and broccoli. Spoon into ungreased 11x7-inch (2-quart) glass baking dish. Cover with foil; refrigerate at least 8 hours or overnight.

2 Heat oven to 350°F. Bake covered for 45 minutes.

3 Uncover baking dish; stir well. Sprinkle croutons evenly over top. Cover; bake an additional 15 to 20 minutes or until bubbly and thoroughly heated.

NUTRITIONAL INFORMATION PER SERVING:
Calories 465 • Total Fat 32g • Saturated Fat 18g • Cholesterol 145mg • Sodium 510mg • Total Carbohydrate 29g • Dietary Fiber 2g • Sugars 3g • Protein 15g.
DIETARY EXCHANGES: 2 Starch • 1 High-Fat Meat • 4-1/2 Fat.

overnight meatball and pasta casserole

PREP TIME: 25 MINUTES
READY IN: 9 HOURS 10 MINUTES
SERVINGS: 6

1 (14 or 15 oz.) jar tomato pasta sauce

1 (10-3/4 oz.) can condensed Cheddar cheese soup

1 cup water

6-1/2 oz. uncooked mini lasagna noodles (3 cups)

1 cup frozen bell pepper and onion stir fry, larger pieces cut up

1 (18 oz.) package frozen cooked Italian meatballs

1-1/2 cups shredded mozzarella cheese (6 oz.)

2 tablespoons chopped fresh parsley

1 In ungreased 13x9-inch (3-quart) glass baking dish, combine pasta sauce, soup and water; mix well. Stir in uncooked noodles, and bell pepper and onion stir fry. Add meatballs; turn to coat with sauce. (Noodles should be completely covered with sauce.) Cover tightly with foil; refrigerate at least 8 hours or overnight.

2 When ready to bake, heat oven to 350°F. Bake casserole covered for 45 minutes.

3 Uncover baking dish; sprinkle with cheese and parsley. Bake uncovered an additional 5 to 10 minutes or until casserole is bubbly and cheese is melted.

NUTRITIONAL INFORMATION PER SERVING:
Calories 340 • Total Fat 12g • Saturated Fat 5g • Cholesterol 25mg • Sodium 940mg • Total Carbohydrate 43g • Dietary Fiber 2g • Sugars 7g • Protein 15g.
DIETARY EXCHANGES: 3 Starch • 3 Other Carbohydrate • 1 High-Fat Meat • 1 Fat.

spinach and beef lasagna

PREP TIME: 20 MINUTES
READY IN: 5 HOURS 35 MINUTES
SERVINGS: 8

1-1/2 lb. lean (at least 80%) ground beef

1 (15 oz.) can Italian-style tomato sauce

1 (1 lb.) package frozen bell pepper and onion stir fry, thawed, drained

1 (15 oz.) container ricotta cheese

1 (16 oz.) jar Alfredo pasta sauce

8 uncooked lasagna noodles

1 (1 lb.) package Green Giant® Frozen Cut Leaf Spinach, thawed, squeezed to drain

1 cup shredded mozzarella cheese (4 oz.)

1 Spray 13x9-inch (3-quart) glass baking dish with nonstick cooking spray. In 12-inch nonstick skillet, brown ground beef over medium-high heat until thoroughly cooked, stirring frequently. Drain. Stir in tomato sauce. Reduce heat to medium; cook 5 minutes, stirring occasionally.

2 Meanwhile, in medium bowl, combine bell pepper and onion stir fry, and ricotta cheese; mix well. Spoon 1/2 cup of the Alfredo sauce in bottom of sprayed baking dish. Arrange 4 uncooked lasagna noodles over the sauce.

3 Top with half each of the ricotta mixture, spinach, beef mixture and mozzarella cheese. Repeat with remaining noodles, ricotta mixture, spinach and beef mixture. Spoon remaining Alfredo sauce over top; sprinkle with remaining mozzarella cheese. Spray sheet of foil with nonstick cooking spray; place sprayed side down on baking dish and seal tightly. Refrigerate at least 4 hours or overnight.

4 Heat oven to 350°F. Bake covered for 45 minutes. Uncover; bake an additional 20 to 25 minutes or until bubbly and thoroughly heated. Let stand 5 to 10 minutes before serving.

NUTRITIONAL INFORMATION PER SERVING:
Calories 595 • Total Fat 35g • Saturated Fat 19g • Cholesterol 130mg • Sodium 780mg • Total Carbohydrate 33g • Dietary Fiber 3g • Sugars 5g • Protein 37g.
DIETARY EXCHANGES: 1-1/2 Starch • 2 Vegetable • 4 Medium-Fat Meat • 3 Fat.

pork chops with apple-sage stuffing

taco fiesta chicken lasagna

PREP TIME: 30 MINUTES
READY IN: 9 HOURS 30 MINUTES
SERVINGS: 8

2 (14-1/2 oz.) cans diced tomatoes with zesty mild green chiles, undrained

1/4 cup taco sauce

3 cups cubed cooked chicken

1 (16 oz.) can Old El Paso® Refried Beans

1/2 cup sour cream

12 uncooked lasagna noodles

3 cups shredded Colby-Monterey Jack cheese (12 oz.)

1/2 cup chopped green onions

1/4 cup sliced ripe olives

2 tablespoons chopped fresh cilantro

1 Spray 15x12-inch sheet of foil and 13x9-inch (3-quart) glass baking dish with nonstick cooking spray. In large bowl, combine tomatoes and taco sauce; mix well. Stir in chicken. In medium bowl, combine refried beans and sour cream; mix well.

2 Spread about 1 cup chicken mixture in bottom of sprayed baking dish. Top with 4 uncooked noodles, breaking to fit if necessary. Spread with half of bean mixture and 1-1/2 cups chicken mixture. Sprinkle with 1 cup of the cheese, half of the onions and half of the olives.

3 Layer 4 more noodles, remaining bean mixture, 1-1/2 cups chicken mixture and 1 cup cheese. Top with remaining 4 noodles, chicken mixture, onions, olives and cheese. (Be sure top noodles are covered.) Cover with foil, sprayed side down. Refrigerate at least 8 hours or overnight.

4 Heat oven to 350°F. Bake covered lasagna for 50 minutes. Uncover baking dish; bake an additional 18 to 22 minutes or until bubbly and thoroughly heated. Let stand 10 minutes before serving. Sprinkle with cilantro. If desired, garnish each serving with dollop of sour cream, chopped tomato and shredded lettuce.

HIGH ALTITUDE (3500-6500 FT): Add 1/4 cup water with tomatoes and taco sauce. Bake covered lasagna at 350°F for 55 minutes. Uncover baking dish; bake an additional 25 to 30 minutes.

NUTRITIONAL INFORMATION PER SERVING: Calories 470 • Total Fat 22g • Saturated Fat 12g • Cholesterol 100mg • Sodium 750mg • Total Carbohydrate 39g • Dietary Fiber 5g • Sugars 5g • Protein 34g.
DIETARY EXCHANGES: 2-1/2 Starch • 4 Lean Meat • 1 Fat.

pork chops with apple-sage stuffing

PREP TIME: 15 MINUTES
READY IN: 9 HOURS 5 MINUTES
SERVINGS: 4

1 tablespoon butter

1/2 cup chopped onion (1 medium)

1/2 cup thinly sliced celery

1 cup chopped apple

1/2 cup raisins

1 cup apple juice

1 (6 oz.) package sage and onion-seasoned one-step stuffing mix

4 (4 oz.) boneless smoked pork chops

2 tablespoons apple jelly

1 Spray 8-inch square (2-quart) glass baking dish with nonstick cooking spray. Melt butter in large skillet over medium heat. Add onion and celery; cook 3 to 4 minutes or until crisp-tender, stirring occasionally.

2 Add apple, raisins and apple juice; cook 2 to 3 minutes or until mixture comes to a boil. Remove from heat; stir in stuffing mix. Spread mixture in sprayed baking dish. Top with pork chops. Cover with foil; refrigerate at least 8 hours or overnight.

3 Heat oven to 350°F. Bake covered for 30 minutes.

4 Uncover baking dish; brush pork chops with jelly. Bake uncovered an additional 15 to 20 minutes or until pork chops are thoroughly heated.

HIGH ALTITUDE (3500-6500 FT): Bake covered at 375°F for 45 minutes. Continue as directed.

NUTRITIONAL INFORMATION PER SERVING: Calories 510 • Total Fat 14g • Saturated Fat 5g • Cholesterol 65mg • Sodium 2,210mg • Total Carbohydrate 68g • Dietary Fiber 3g • Sugars 30g • Protein 28g.
DIETARY EXCHANGES: 3 Starch • 1 1/2 Fruit • 2-1/2 Lean Meat • 1 Fat.

make-ahead turkey tetrazzini

PREP TIME: 30 MINUTES
READY IN: 9 HOURS 25 MINUTES
SERVINGS: 8

8 oz. uncooked spaghetti

1/4 cup margarine or butter

2 cups sliced fresh mushrooms

3 tablespoons Pillsbury BEST® All-Purpose Flour

2 cups chicken broth

3/4 cup half-and-half

1 to 3 tablespoons dry sherry

1/4 cup chopped fresh parsley

1 teaspoon salt

1/8 teaspoon nutmeg

Dash pepper

3 cups cubed cooked turkey

1/2 cup grated Parmesan cheese

Chopped fresh parsley

1 Cook spaghetti as directed on package. Drain.

2 Meanwhile, melt margarine in Dutch oven over medium heat. Add mushrooms; cook 5 minutes or until tender, stirring frequently. Reduce heat to medium-low. Add flour; cook and stir until bubbly. Gradually add broth, stirring constantly, until mixture boils and thickens. Remove from heat; stir in half-and-half, sherry if desired, 1/4 cup parsley, salt, nutmeg and pepper.

3 Add cooked spaghetti and turkey to mushroom mixture; stir gently to mix. Spoon mixture into ungreased 13x9-inch (3-quart) glass baking dish. Cover with foil; refrigerate at least 8 hours or overnight.

4 Heat oven to 350°F. Uncover baking dish; sprinkle Parmesan cheese over top. Cover; bake for 45 to 55 minutes or until thoroughly heated, removing foil during last 10 minutes of baking time. Sprinkle with parsley if desired.

HIGH ALTITUDE (3500-6500 FT): Increase chicken broth to 2-1/2 cups. Bake at 350°F for 50 to 60 minutes, removing foil during last 10 minutes of baking time.

NUTRITIONAL INFORMATION PER SERVING: Calories 340 • Total Fat 15g • Saturated Fat 5g • Cholesterol 60mg • Sodium 900mg • Total Carbohydrate 27g • Dietary Fiber 1g • Sugars 2g • Protein 24g. DIETARY EXCHANGES: 2 Starch • 2-1/2 Lean Meat • 1-1/2 Fat.

artichoke and bacon potato bake

PREP TIME: 30 MINUTES
READY IN: 9 HOURS 35 MINUTES
SERVINGS: 6

8 slices bacon, cut into 1/2-inch pieces

4 cups frozen potatoes O'Brien with onions and peppers (from 28 oz. pkg.)

1-1/2 cups shredded sharp Cheddar cheese (6 oz.)

1 (14 oz.) can quartered artichokes, drained

4 eggs

3/4 cup milk

1/2 teaspoon garlic-pepper blend

1/4 teaspoon salt

1 medium Italian plum tomato, thinly sliced

1 Spray 8-inch square (2-quart) glass baking dish with nonstick cooking spray. Cook bacon in large skillet over medium-high heat until crisp. Remove bacon from skillet; drain on paper towel.

2 In large bowl, combine cooked bacon, potatoes and 1 cup of the cheese; toss to mix. Spread half of potato mixture in sprayed baking dish. Top with artichokes and the remaining potato mixture.

3 In same large bowl, beat eggs, milk, garlic-pepper blend and salt until well blended. Pour over potato mixture. Sprinkle with

remaining 1/2 cup cheese. Cover with foil; refrigerate at least 8 hours or overnight.

4 Heat oven to 350°F. Bake covered for 45 minutes.

5 Uncover baking dish; arrange tomato slices over top. Bake uncovered an additional 15 to 20 minutes or until knife inserted in center comes out clean. Let stand 10 minutes before serving.

NUTRITIONAL INFORMATION PER SERVING: Calories 365 • Total Fat 18g • Saturated Fat 9g • Cholesterol 180mg • Sodium 690mg • Total Carbohydrate 37g • Dietary Fiber 6g • Sugars 5g • Protein 20g. DIETARY EXCHANGES: 2 Starch • 2 High-Fat Meat • 1/2 Fat.

havarti ham and egg lasagna

PREP TIME: 1 HOUR
READY IN: 10 HOURS
SERVINGS: 8

4 eggs
1 (16 oz.) jar Alfredo pasta sauce
1 (14 to 16 oz.) package frozen asparagus cuts (3 cups)
1/2 cup drained sliced roasted red bell peppers (from a jar)
1/2 cup water
9 uncooked lasagna noodles
2 cups diced cooked ham
3 cups shredded Havarti cheese (12 oz.)
1/2 cup Progresso® Parmesan Bread Crumbs
2 tablespoons butter, melted

1 Place eggs in single layer in small saucepan. Add enough water to cover eggs by 1 inch. Bring to a boil. Immediately remove from heat; cover and let stand 15 minutes. Drain; rinse with cold water. Place eggs in bowl of ice water; let stand 10 minutes.

2 Meanwhile, spray 13x9-inch (3-quart) glass baking dish with nonstick cooking spray. In large bowl, combine Alfredo pasta sauce, asparagus, roasted peppers and water; mix well.

3 Drain eggs. Peel; coarsely chop eggs. Arrange 3 uncooked noodles in bottom of sprayed baking dish. Top with 2/3 cup of the ham, 1/3 of the eggs and 1 cup cheese. Spread with 1-1/2 cups Alfredo sauce mixture. Repeat layers 2 more times ending with sauce. (Be sure top noodles are covered with sauce.) Cover; refrigerate at least 8 hours or overnight.

4 Heat oven to 350°F. Bake covered for 30 minutes.

5 In small bowl, mix bread crumbs and butter. Uncover baking dish; sprinkle crumb mixture evenly over top of lasagna. Bake uncovered an additional 30 minutes or until thoroughly heated and topping is golden brown. Let stand 10 minutes before serving.

HIGH ALTITUDE (3500-6500 FT): When preparing hard-cooked eggs, after bringing eggs to a boil, boil 5 minutes. Immediately remove from heat; cover and let stand 15 minutes. Continue as directed. For recipe preparation and baking, increase water to 1 cup; increase oven temperature to 375°F. Continue as directed.

NUTRITIONAL INFORMATION PER SERVING: Calories 625 • Total Fat 43g • Saturated Fat 25g • Cholesterol 235mg • Sodium 1,170mg • Total Carbohydrate 30g • Dietary Fiber 1g • Sugars 4g • Protein 29g. DIETARY EXCHANGES: 2 Starch • 3 High-Fat Meat • 4 Fat.

alphabetical index

general recipe index

GENERAL RECIPE INDEX **239**